THE HALF-WORLD
OF AMERICAN CULTURE

The Half-World
of American Culture

A MISCELLANY

CARL BODE

PREFACE BY C. P. Snow

Southern Illinois University Press · *Carbondale*

FOREWORD

THE term "American culture" can still bring a slight smile to the face of the European or Asian intellectual. The Latin American too has been known to condescend to the civilization north of him. Some of this condescension is deserved, on counts too familiar to need rehearsing. Some of it is not, however, and comes from seeing only the advertised elements in American life. There is still much to be known, good as well as bad, complex as well as simple—and some of it is unexpected. In this book I have brought together my essays and notes on several things in American culture which seem to me worth talking about.

I have talked most about American writing. The writing I discuss includes both the great and the purely popular, *Walden* and *Magnificent Obsession,* works of what in the jargon of the trade is called mass culture as well as works of what is called high culture. To me both cultures are worth looking into, though not always for the same reasons. In the area of high culture I find the books of Henry David Thoreau especially interesting. I have written more about him than about any other writer. In the area of mass culture I have written especially about bestsellers and most often about those innocent of literary merit. The threads that tie together my investigations of high culture and mass culture—that give this book such unity as it has—are my interest in the social surroundings of a printed work and in the possible motivations of both the writer and the reader. I have often asked the question Why? Some of my answers about motivation have been guesses and shaky ones at that. What I have written here are, in fact, *essais* in Montaigne's old sense. But I hope through the very raising of my questions, and despite the tentativeness of the answers, to make American culture a little easier to understand. And I hope to share a little further the pleasure I had in preparing these pieces.

Eight of them appeared first in Great Britain, fourteen in America. Each of these has been somewhat revised. The remaining two have not been published before. I have called this book *The Half-World of American Culture* because its investigations often fall into two fields which still seem to the academic mind slightly irregular. For these essays are as a rule either on works of popular culture, which are, by definition, of lower literary quality than works of high culture; or on works of high culture in which I attempt to go beneath the surface and find out something about the unconscious element.

C. B.

University of Maryland
April 1964

PREFACE

CARL BODE made a great impression on the English literary world during his nearly three years' term as Cultural Attaché at the U.S. Embassy in London. He found his way through our local jungle—which is a peculiarly intricate one—with a sure-footedness that won admiration from all factions. I doubt if any official emissary has ever known us more intimately. I have often wished that he would write at length on the contemporary English literary scene, but he also had to perform another function which, to those of us who are fond of America and know it a little, was at least as important. That is, he had to give to Englishmen, some of whom are not all that well disposed, some physical embodiment of the American culture of today. In this delicate act of presentation he was outstandingly successful, mainly by being integrally himself. English writers and painters found that he was wise, tolerant, and, in the best sense, very American. Long before this term of office was over, people found him a friend who was like a rock in times of trouble. It is not usual for a Cultural Attaché to be called upon to solve people's personal difficulties: but Carl Bode took those on, along with his other duties, and when he left London he left a gap in our lives.

This volume of essays reveals many of the qualities which made him such a personal success. First of all, he is abnormally well-informed in an unobtrusive sort of way, and in particular very well-informed about topics on which most Englishmen are ignorant. Nineteenth-century America is still a mysterious country to most Englishmen. An essay like *The Sound of American Literature a Century Ago,* unpretentious, enterprising, utterly sensible, explains to us a lot that we simply did not know before. And the tone of the explanation, like the tone of his private explanations, is one that is specially well adapted for English ears. We are a little tired of apocalyptic incantations. Some of our academic critics, like their American colleagues, have been producing these. My wife keeps a file here under the title of "Codwallop," for the weekly pieces of esoteric nonsense. But we shrug them off. In the very long run, sense has a knack of prevailing over its opposite.

The lucid last essay in this collection, *The American Imagination,* would not be improved if it were made incomprehensible.

Yet, in his writing, just as in his influence on London literary life, Carl Bode remains quintessentially American. It used to surprise us that a man so temperate should invoke Freudian interpretations almost like first nature. Very few Englishmen could do that, and very few Europeans either. A predilection for Freudian analysis has become as much an American preserve as high-school basketball or Thanksgiving dinner. I have often wondered why this should be. Anyway, Bode has his full share of this national enthusiasm, as one can see from his work on Thoreau. As a matter of fact, Thoreau, like D. H. Lawrence, in many respects an English equivalent, probably is a suitable subject for Freudian questions. But I think a European critic, analyzing either, would want to ask a good many social questions too.

Bode is not easily frightened. He thinks it right—and this is very valuable—that popular literature should be examined, as well as fashionable academic topics. I have never read anything about Lloyd Douglas before, and very little about Erskine Caldwell. And yet, if we are going to understand our society, we are obliged to understand why certain books are read by millions. Quite unsnobbish, Bode applies himself as an open-minded student of our culture to matters which most of us are too genteel to touch. We all ought to wish that there were more like him.

C. P. Snow

20 April 1965

CONTENTS

THOREAU AND
ASSORTED OTHERS

The Hidden Thoreau

AS I SEE IT there are three lives of Henry David Thoreau. The first is the conventional one. It inhabits the encyclopedias, the polite biographies, and the world of American literary folklore. The second is marked by some dispute and doubt; its two great areas of argument concern Thoreau's relationship with Emerson's wife and the timing of Thoreau's growth and decline as a literary artist. The third is so controversial that it has only been hinted at in print; it is Thoreau's unconscious life. Now, a century after his death, he is one of the world figures in American literature and it would seem that whatever furthers our understanding of him and his work ought to be brought out.

Emerson, the man who knew Thoreau best, once spoke of his "simple and hidden life." Simple it was, in the sense of being Spartan, and hidden too in ways no biographer has published. This is not to say that there was scandal in Thoreau's life; it is that his subconscious side has largely gone unstudied. The insights and valuable hypotheses of Freudian psychology have been ignored in the various biog-

3

raphies. Time has modified some of Sigmund Freud's constructions; fresh research has upset some of his analogies. But there is little doubt that we can comprehend Thoreau better if we take his unconscious into account. The finicky critic is put off, even today, by the Freudian emphasis on sexuality. The Freudian stress on childhood experience may seem unwarranted; and the very fact that there is a Freudian jargon can prejudice the reader. Yet the life of Thoreau remains full of riddles and the writing of Thoreau abounds in nuances that still need to be understood. The only Freudian study of any length is an unpublished doctoral dissertation done in 1957 by Raymond Gozzi. Most of its deductions come from an analysis of the imagery in Thoreau's writing, the rest from an interpretation of certain biographical data. Building on Gozzi's remarkable findings we can put Thoreau into another perspective, look at him from one more point of view. It is not at all impossible that we shall see things we may not wish to see. For our conclusion will be that Thoreau was not a normal man — though his writing was the richer for it.

To the Freudian, abnormality is mainly a matter of degree. Other children suffer the shocks that Thoreau doubtless did; other youths and men endure the same frustrations. Yet few others react as vehemently. It is normal for a boy to replay the Oedipus myth, to wish to marry his mother and obliterate his father, and then to be maimed by his unconscious feeling of guilt. It is not normal to have the effects linger throughout manhood and maturity. Much can be explained in Thoreau by assuming that they did, however.

A highly aware observer of his own psyche, he sensed what had happened to him and projected it on others. "How many men," he once exclaimed, "meet with some blast in the moist growing days of their youth, and what should have been a sweet and palatable fruit in them becomes a mere puff and excrescence!" He realized that he had been warped. Under the rubric of "Chastity and Sensuality" he collected many of his thoughts and enclosed them in a letter to his disciple

H. G. O. Blake. "I send you the thoughts," Thoreau wrote, "with diffidence and shame, not knowing how far . . . I betray my peculiar defects." The salient defect, to the Freudian, was that Thoreau never outgrew his mother-fixation. It was ambivalent, with some hate supporting the love, in the typical way of the unconscious. Savoring her strength, his mother, Cynthia Thoreau, dominated her husband and children, outliving them all, incidentally, except for one daughter. When Henry before leaving college asked her what profession he should choose, she answered him promptly, "You can buckle on your knapsack, and roam abroad to seek your fortune"; and tears came to his eyes. It was she who commanded his regard.

With the notable exception of a girl named Ellen Sewall, young women failed to interest him even when he was a young man. He could see the reason for looking at pretty girls but not for trying to talk with them. That was his point of view. From their point of view, the matter was summed up when Elizabeth Hoar remarked that, as for taking Henry's arm, she would as soon think of taking the arm of an elm tree.

With an older woman Thoreau could be more responsive. There was above all Lidian, Ralph Waldo Emerson's severely beautiful wife; and she was nearly fifteen years his senior. He once wrote to her, "You must know that you represent to me woman." She remained, if by default, the principal love of his life. Yet it is worth remembering that another older woman preceded her. It was Lidian's own sister. To Mrs. Lucy Jackson Brown, three years older than Lidian, he sent his best youthful effort, the poem "Sic Vita," along with a bunch of violets. Mrs. Brown joined the Thoreau family at intervals over a period of several years. She and Henry found no dearth of things to say when they met, and when distance separated them they corresponded. The correspondence included a good deal of platonizing though not quite enough for Henry's taste. "Dear Friend," he suggested in one letter, "We always seem to be living just on the brink of a pure and lofty intercourse." He meant not only himself and Lucy Brown but the world. With Lidian the brink was passed more than once. Thoreau continued to be attracted to older women rather than younger ones; and up to the end he kept his devotion to his mother.

Because nothing in his culture could countenance a mother-fixation, Thoreau sought to shift its psychic energies to other ends. One was the attachment to older women. The other, with bountiful creative results, was his writing. There he adapted and extended the idea of Mother Nature until it became one of his chief conceptions. Kind, lovely, she let him immerse his loneliness and tension in her. Yet in her kindness and love she could be strict as a mother is strict. "In her most genial moment her laws are . . . steadfastly and relentlessly fulfilled." In Freudian terms this is Nature as the superego, the conscience. This is Cynthia Thoreau demanding obedience. Out of a loving, strict Nature Henry's needs were met, or so he maintained. The attitude he took is exemplified in a telling image: "I make it my business to extract from Nature whatever nutriment she can furnish me. . . . I milk the sky and the earth."

Alma Natura appeared in his ideas, his descriptions, and his tropes. The amount of female matter in Thoreau's nature writing is remarkable. Perhaps the most illuminating thing is his love for swamps. He enjoys being in them, enjoys writing about them. His friend Ellery Channing, who walked with him as often as anyone, noted the interest in swamps and bogs. It proved to be long-lived. As early as 1840 Thoreau could rhapsodize, "Would it not be a luxury to stand up to one's chin in some retired swamp for a whole summer's day?" And as late as 1857 he could still write with relish, "Methinks every swamp tends to have or suggests . . . an interior tender spot. The sphagnous crust that surrounds the pool is pliant and quaking, like the skin or muscles of the abdomen." Sometimes the subject or the imagery was masculine. The male too could find analogue and metaphor in Thoreau's writing. Throughout the pages on nature there are many references, masculine and feminine, overt and covert, which have a Freudian significance. The towering pine, the shrub oak, the snake in the stream, the unclimbable mountain: these are among them. At its apex Thoreau's sexual energy emerges as a desire for mystic union with nature. This is clearest perhaps in his poem "The Thaw":

> Fain would I stretch me by the highway-side,
> To thaw and trickle with the melting snow,
> That mingled soul and body with the tide,
> I too may through the pores of nature flow.

Beyond the domain of nature and nature's sexual images, Thoreau's energy was channeled into ideas about friendship and into their figurative expression. The ideas at the conscious level were austere, for at that level Thoreau set a superhumanly high standard. He prescribed a stony perfection for his friend. At the unconscious level it can be guessed that they were marked by an incipient homosexuality. The same mother-fixation that barred a normal sexual partnership with a woman also prejudiced a normal friendship with a man by charging it with undue emphasis and tension. Such a friendship Thoreau never enjoyed. We can recall the judgment Emerson pronounced: "No equal companion stood in affectionate relations with one so pure and guileless."

To make up for his deficiency Thoreau consistently showed far more than the usual amount of aggressiveness and independence. It is indeed in a combination of the two that the world has come to recognize the stance typical of him. The literary results have been brilliant, *Walden* and "Civil Disobedience" most notably; but there are four or five other pieces, such as "Life without Principle" and "Slavery in Massachusetts," which also radiate those qualities. His very writing was an act of defiance. For a man to dedicate his life to authorship was an affront to the commercial culture which surrounded him. Much more than most people he had to live to himself, set his own standards, reject those of others. Yet he was not inhuman. He stiffened partly to resist a world which in its own heavy fashion resisted him. But only partly. Most of the time he stood alone by choice. The others he reached out to were few.

The roots of his attitude can be traced back to his earliest years. We may remember that he was a grave, withdrawn child. As a boy he was called "The Judge." Some friends of his family thought he resembled an Indian in his iron demeanor. Before college he belonged to a debating society where he often showed himself cross-grained. In his college days he was known to unbend at times but he customarily kept to himself. And so he did during the rest of his life. One reason for the attitude lies, in all probability, in the Oedipal conflict; his reserved demeanor, I believe, resulted mostly from the strength of his repressions. From the outset his unconscious urge to displace his father and enjoy his mother must have been unusually keen. And yet his developing superego, his implanted conscience, certainly asserted that this was sinful. Here we see the typical Freudian ambivalence, which would flourish in Thoreau. Here is hate for the father, but also love for him and shame for wanting to displace him. Here is the ancestor of the more general love-hate which became a staple of Thoreau's life and works. The two emotions are aspects of one, as Thoreau himself testified.

Because of inadequacies in both his father and himself he felt compelled to search for a father-substitute. His father, John Thoreau, Sr., was a mechanic and a bumbling businessman. He relished the crowded company of his fellows. No introverted scholar, he was still not quite strong enough to make Henry want to identify with him through fear. The search for the father took several forms during Thoreau's life but was always tinged — except at the end when John Brown satisfied Thoreau's deepest requirements — with hostility and even hate. No satisfactory God as Father could be found in Thoreau's religion. No satisfactory father could be found among his relatives or teachers. There was not even one among Thoreau's older friends and this in spite of the fact that the number included Emerson. But Emerson clearly came the closest.

When Thoreau at twenty returned to Concord to live, Emerson was thirty-four. The enormous influence he had on Thoreau was not only mental but physical. Understandably, the first impact was the greatest. James Russell Lowell, for instance, a classmate of Thoreau's at Harvard, wrote dryly in 1838, the year after Thoreau and Emerson became acquainted: "I met Thoreau last night, and it is exquisitely amusing to see how he imitates Emerson's tone and manner. With my eyes shut, I shouldn't know them apart." Yet when he was nearly forty Thoreau could still wear his collar turned over like Emerson's. Although Emerson's influence would diminish and Thoreau would certainly become his own man, it is easy to see why he was originally impressed. Emerson was by all accounts an American saint. Bronson Alcott, most captious of the Transcendentalists, testified that his friendship with Emerson was "the greatest prize and privilege" he enjoyed aside from his family life. That was praise from somebody who knew him intimately, but even his lecture audiences recognized that they were listening to a most impressive man. In view of the widespread admiration Emerson commanded, it is the more revealing to see Thoreau gradually reject him. The love for him as father in Thoreau's heart is more and more offset by hate. Or if hate is too strong a word, then by a growing and carping hostility; or, to put it at its mildest as Thoreau tried to, by a "certain bitter-sweet sentiment." However, I think we could stand by the word "hate," for with the passing of time Thoreau added the classic Freudian incentive to hate when he fell in love with Lidian, with the wife of his father-substitute. The Oedipal drama played itself out, leaving him to fight a painful sense of shame.

So far in our examination of Thoreau's unconscious we have been saying that its main characteristic was a marked Oedipus complex which aborted his emotional life but richly informed his writing. It made him look for a mother in older women instead of a mate and look for a father in Emerson (and later John Brown). It allowed him to compensate, however, by developing an extraordinary aggressiveness and independence; and it allowed him to sublimate through literary creation.

Now we have three more propositions to advance. One is that Thoreau's hatred for the state was an extension of his Oedipal hatred for his father and of his occasional dislike (the other side of the coin of love) of his dominating mother. Another is that he finally found his father-substitute in John Brown, as the fanatical leader who detested the state and defied it to the death. The last is that Thoreau, with a history of conversion maladies, found his burden of guilt so great when his father and Brown died, both within the same year, that he became convinced he too must die in expiation. Each of these three can be supported from Freudian psychology, although certain evidence is lacking and the likelihood of the propositions must be based partly on the previous constructions.

We can safely conclude that Thoreau resented parental authority. To understand his resentment of his father we need to look again at the character of John Thoreau, Sr. There is ground for stressing that he was not merely the mild man married to Cynthia Thoreau. Professor Gozzi suggests in his dissertation that the older Thoreau was capable of violent speech if not violent action, that he had an air of some firmness and determination, and that he was well respected outside his house. Though he was more of a man outside his house than inside, even there he gradually proved able to get his son to play Apollo to his own King Admetus. He managed, that is, to involve the reluctant Henry in the family business from time to time and when his father died Henry was forced to succeed him in charge of it. Accordingly, he had qualities that could increase his son's unconscious resentment. He stood, in essence, for the talky, noisy world of trade which Thoreau despised. Much as Thoreau loved his mother he could also be irked by her authority. More than one passage in his journal suggests an animosity towards her. And he had hard things as well as kind ones to say about parents in general. It is probable that he suppressed many of the criticisms of his father and mother. Yet there are at least a few times when he could not restrain his bitterness. Surely he was looking at his own household as well as others when he cried, "The fathers and the mothers of the town . . . don't want to have any prophets born into their families — damn them!"

For Thoreau it was only a step from resentment of the authority of the parent to resentment of the authority of the state. The first recorded conflict came when the state, according to Thoreau, "commanded me to pay a certain sum toward the support of a clergyman." He declined, although another man saw fit to pay it for him. He had made his point, however, and was never dunned for the church tax again. At the request of the state's nearest representatives, the selectmen of Concord, Thoreau prepared a declaration for their files: "Know all men by these presents, that I, Henry Thoreau, do not wish to be regarded as a member of any incorporated society which I have not joined." This sweeping affirmation represented another victory but not a permanent one. For Thoreau after declining for six years to pay a second tax, his poll tax, was put in jail on this account. A little of the edge was taken off that battle too, it must be admitted, because someone else, once again, paid the tax. But not before Thoreau had the opportunity to pass his memorable night in jail. When he wrote about it later he tinged his words with amusement and contempt for authority. However, his jailer reported that Thoreau was "mad as the devil" when released. Fighting audaciously against the state, he had been punished like a stubborn child, by being shut up. His imprisonment helped to embitter and harden Thoreau. It was one — though only one — of the factors that in the next decade persuaded him that he could approve of armed rebellion, of war itself. And that, as

the fifties neared their finish, was what John Brown determined to wage against the United States of America.

He waged it on rocklike principle, to Thoreau's absolute
satisfaction. He had already met Brown, we know, and been
impressed by him two years before the attack on Harpers
Ferry. But the chain of events beginning with the assault
and ending with Brown's hanging on December 2, 1859
stirred Thoreau profoundly. Ellery Channing reported that
Thoreau's "hands involuntarily clenched together at the
mention of Captain Brown." There can be little doubt that
the strongest aggressions in him found an outlet through
Brown. He identified himself with Brown and fought by
empathy at his side. So strong did the empathy prove that,
after briefly considering that Brown was dead before his
trial, Thoreau refused to accept the idea that Brown was
dead at all. He was not speaking rhetorically when he said,
"I heard, to be sure, that he was hung, but I did not know
what that meant." When he wrote and spoke passionately
for Brown he was also justifying himself. And justification
was needed, it may be assumed, for Thoreau could realize
that Brown's hanging was the greatest punishment the state
could inflict. In his stormy ambivalence Thoreau no doubt
felt that Brown was completely right but also that the punishment he suffered was a judgment. It was a mistaken one
to Thoreau but a judgment nonetheless. In one sense as
Brown had failed so had he. In a feverish resolution of the
problem he likened Brown to a Christ crucified by the state
for the slaveholder.

We come now to the last and most controversial of the
three propositions: that Thoreau died because he felt he
should — and died content. I agree with the past biographers
that on the conscious level he died of tuberculosis; and so
I have said elsewhere. But I agree with Professor Gozzi that
at the unconscious level Thoreau ended his life of his own
accord. He was convinced that he had to die chiefly because
his father and John Brown had died. He had to expiate his
intolerably increasing load of guilt. Christian contrition

was not for him but leaving life represented ample expiation.

If this seems unbelievable to admirers of Thoreau, we can look back into his life to find out if anything there has a bearing on the matter. By first noting that his family had a history of lingering illness — typically the Thoreaus were said to die from consumption — we can isolate a physical factor which would make it easier for the psychic ones to operate. On the psychic side we can start, suggestively enough, with the child who got sick at thunder storms. About Thoreau's health during his boyhood we cannot be sure but we know that he was sick in college and had to drop out for a while. When he was nineteen he wrote a Harvard classmate that his health was so much improved that he would return next term; the letter was written in August 1836. In February 1841 he had another siege of illness, probably having to do with his lungs. During the next year he experienced a case of illness through empathy which is a classic. For when his brother John died in January 1842 after bitter suffering, Henry suffered too. Shortly after John's death Emerson wrote that Thoreau "was ill and threatened with *lockjaw!* his brother's disease. It is strange — unaccountable — yet the symptoms seem precise and on the increase." Though the disease left after a while, its marks on Thoreau's psyche remained for a long time. According to one source it was years before he could speak of John's death without perceptible pain. In 1843 he became ill at least twice. Once it was apparently pulmonary weakness but in the other case it was probably because he had abandoned his beloved Concord for a term on Staten Island as a tutor. He himself called that illness unaccountable. Then came some years of better health. However, by the spring of 1855 he had contracted a lingering disorder from which he failed to recover until the summer of 1857. This siege too looks psychosomatic. Sometime after it started he wrote to H. G. O. Blake saying that he had been on his back for two or three months. He added, "I should feel a little less ashamed if I could give any name to my disorder, but I cannot, and our doctor cannot help me to it."

By the late 1850's he was alternating periods of health with growing periods of sickness. The most damaging blow to him before Brown's death was the death of John Thoreau, Sr., in February 1859. With his father dead Henry's Oedipal foe was gone. The son had triumphed, the mother was his. He had become head of the house and was responsible for conducting the family business as well. His feeling of guilt, though, at replacing his father must have been severe. His psyche now had suffered serious damage. His state of mind grew more and more depressed. He found some surcease in his writing and in the abolitionist movement but drew none from the family business and little from his friends. Brown's crusade jolted him out of himself for a time, giving him a cause to which he could dedicate his diminishing energies. There is an important if oblique statement to that effect in the journal for October 22, 1859: "How many a man who was lately contemplating suicide has now something to live for!" But then came the crushing end to the crusade, Brown's execution. As Ellery Channing recalled, "At the time of the John Brown tragedy, Thoreau was driven sick." Actually, it must have been the final blow to his spirit.

His end would not, however, come swiftly nor would his decline be steady. He would live for two years and some months more. Though I think that he soon realized he had no other recourse but death, I am sure that the will to die was not consistent. It waxed and waned. Thoreau could still write and talk even if the writing grew sluggish and the talk torpid. He could still show himself capable of indignation especially about the South and slavery. Yet gradually his fists unclenched. Returning to Concord in July 1861 after a futile trip to Minnesota for his health, he tried to go on his accustomed rounds. It was no use. By November he had written the last of the manifold pages of his journal; by December he had taken to his bed. Nearing death he told Ellery Channing that he had no wish to live except for his mother and sister. "Some things must end," he observed significantly to Channing. But perhaps the most significant comment was made by a visitor to his bedside, Sam Staples. Sam, who was Thoreau's friend as well as his onetime jailer, spoke to Emerson about the visit. "Never spent an hour with more satisfaction," he said. "Never saw a man dying with so much pleasure and peace."

By the time he died he had already published his two best books, *A Week* and *Walden*. His most provocative essay, "Civil Disobedience," had reached print and so had the passionate polemics for John Brown. So had most of his poetry. After his death the finest of his nature essays appeared, essays better than anyone else could write, then or now. "Walking," "Autumnal Tints," "Wild Apples": each is an artist's and a naturalist's delight. Last came the travel books, edited for the most part by his surviving sister and Ellery Channing, *The Maine Woods, Cape Cod, A Yankee in Canada*. As public interest in Thoreau grew, much of his private writing was published, particularly the extensive journal. In our time bits and pieces continue to appear, new leaves of the journal for instance, some college essays, and a few other fugitive pages. There is more to be read yet but the best has been in print long enough to establish Thoreau as a writer whom the world would ignore only to its loss. And it is to understand Thoreau as a writer that we have speculated about his unconscious, theorized about his psychological problems. If our speculation seems forced, perhaps we can go back to the gentle, moderate way he himself once put it: "The poet cherishes his chagrins and sets his sighs to music."

Columbia's Carnal Bed

IN THE WINTER of 1961–62 I appeared as a witness for the defense in two cases brought against Henry Miller's novel, *Tropic of Cancer*. By that time the book had been in print for more than a quarter of a century, though it had just been published in the United States, and I wondered after the trials whether *Tropic* represented any kind of American tradition. I was the more interested because one of the judges had picturesquely pronounced it foreign filth. In particular, I wondered whether *Tropic's* concentration on sex, usually expressed in the bluntest terms, had any historical antecedents. Were there early twentieth-century *Tropics;* were there nineteenth-century ones? I decided to do some exploration beginning with the nineteenth century and to take up twentieth-century materials at a later time.

The problems were not small. The first was the long-established taboo on the study of sex. Many an American scholar still feels hesitant about discussing sex; many a reader still greets an exposition of it with an automatic sneer. The second problem derived from the first: it was the paucity of previous scholarship. There was almost nothing in print dealing with sex in explicit physical terms. There was a good deal of scholarly writing on nineteenth-century sentimental love; this research reported that hearts and violets were scattered everywhere. Yet I could see how scholars might have found only sentimental love to write about, for the books on sex or with much sex in them would ordinarily be driven underground. They would belong to the half-world of American culture. Few would be copyrighted, fewer would come from a major publishing house. Whether scientific or sensual in approach, they would be apt to be printed either privately or by a minor publisher. When they appeared they would be circulated surreptitiously. At the end of their career they would usually have been read to tatters or dropped in a trash can.

Even if they survived, the scholar seldom saw them. Sometimes they drifted into private collections, to be seen only by the collector's best friends and to be dispersed, no doubt, on the collector's death by his embarrassed widow. More often they fell into public hands, which held them gingerly. The typical public library had, and still has, a few rows of erotica locked up in a glass case. Even our national library, the Library of Congress, does little better. It continues to segregate works on sex in its "Delta" collection, which is opened fully only to the serious student — if he ever appears. I know of at least one trustee of the Kinsey Institute who has told me he was turned down. The best collection is housed at the Kinsey Institute itself, or more properly the Institute for Sex Research. It has its gaps and weaknesses but its potentialities are unequaled. Its facilities, moreover, are designed to be used.

In spite of the handicaps facing the scholar, a certain amount of information on sex in the nineteenth century can be gleaned. Some of it deals with birth control, which was a prime concern to the social reformer. The specter of an over-populated and starving world, conjured up by Malthus' writings, made a considerable impression. The response of several nineteenth-century social thinkers was to turn to the idea of voluntary birth control as the answer. The earliest response of any importance to the American scene was that of Robert Dale Owen, a Scottish-born sociologist who was later elected to Congress from Indiana. His *Moral Physiology* was published in London and New York in 1831. Eager for the new utopia, he described the social and economic advantages of birth control as he saw them. His basic premise in the book is that the instinct for reproduction is "a master principle" and all social planning must take it into account. He agrees with Malthus about the dangers of over-population but rejects his doctrine of "moral restraint" as unrealistic, even inhuman. Contraception, not continence, is Owen's answer.

He tries to clear the ground of the arguments he hears against a knowledge of birth control. It will not make a woman a prostitute. It will not degrade a decent girl, who is surely "no whit the better for believing, until her marriage night, that children are found among the cabbage leaves in the garden." For married men and women he says emphatically, "In no case can it be mischievous." Instead, as a matter of fact, it will be a demonstrable good. It will bring into the world only the children of loving, willing parents. Owen is equally positive about the merit of birth control for the unmarried person. Premarital chastity is no problem, for Owen follows Benjamin Franklin in defining it as "temperate satisfaction . . . of those desires which are natural to all healthy adult beings." And he follows his father, Robert Owen, in defining it also as "sexual intercourse *with* affection" (prostitution being sexual intercourse without it). Taking this generous view, Owen commends sexual intercourse as something close to a panacea. Not the least of its advantages is that it will reduce what the nineteenth century usually referred to as "onanism," or masturbation.

In spite of their tendentious nature Owen's views are theoretical rather than practical. There is no particular method of birth control that he describes or endorses warmly. He rejects the method of abstinence and ends up by giving qualified approval to coitus interruptus. But if he is vague about contraception, this is by no means true of his most controversial follower, Dr. Charles Knowlton.

Knowlton, who was born in 1800 and died in 1850, took his medical degree at Dartmouth College in 1824. In 1831 the subject of birth control was suggested to him by his reading of *Moral Physiology*. The book persuaded him of the value to mankind of some good check on conception but he failed to find it in Owen. As a result, he investigated and discovered that there was none described anywhere. He set his mind to the problem and finally arrived at a method that satisfied him. This he proceeded to embody in a little book prepared during the summer of 1831 and published anonymously the next year under the urbane title of *Fruits of Philosophy*. It created a minor riot. Other editions, his own and pirated, appeared in the United States and England both. Attacks were made on the book and on Knowlton as well. Not long after it reached public notice he was fined in court at Taunton, Massachusetts, and then jailed for three months in Cambridge. According to Professor Norman Himes, who in 1937 edited the only modern reprinting of *Fruits*, there were several other prosecutions which resulted in hung juries. In England the book apparently escaped the attention of the prosecutor until the term of 1877–78. Then in a widely heralded case, Regina *v.* Charles Bradlaugh and Annie Besant, the Crown was defeated and the sales of the book multiplied.

The announced aim of this incendiary publication is "to recommend . . . a simple, cheap, and harmless method of preventing conception." In the first of his five short chapters Knowlton attacks what he takes to be the two main arguments against providing information for birth control. One is that it leads to illegal intercourse. He denies that chastity can be weakened by a mere method. The other is that it is contrary to nature. In rebuttal he points out that all civilization is "against nature." When we set up a lightning rod we go against nature. And so on. Turning from rebuttal to positive arguments for birth control, he asserts that it will combat prostitution by expediting marriage for the young. It will cut down on poverty, ignorance, and crime. It will prevent the spread of inherited disease. Used selectively it will improve the human stock. It will reduce abortion and infanticide. And it will be a godsend to the sickly mother.

Knowlton's second chapter is largely given to a detailed description of the male and female sex organs. It also includes some speculations on how generation takes place. The fourth chapter, to skip the third for a moment, discusses the signs of pregnancy. It is factual in the main and includes information on the growth of the foetus. The fifth chapter has opinion as well as information. In it Knowlton inveighs against intemperate intercourse and also against onanism. He concludes with some remarks on sterility and impotence.

It was the third chapter which excited the bitterest public hostility. The very title could raise the public's hackles: "Of Preventing Conception without Sacrifice of Enjoyment." Here Knowlton unveils his method of control and gives detailed directions for using it. What he proposes is douching with a syringe and he even prescribes the ingredients, alum and vinegar among them, for an effective solution. He notes the pitfalls which human nature puts in the way of any kind of contraception and argues that his method avoids them all except for the woman's having to get out of bed to douche.

Knowlton's little work is in its way definitive; at any rate I have found nothing that transcends it in the rest of the nineteenth century. I suspect that its title alone caused it finally to drop out of sight. It had little competition. Birth control aside, however, there were a few other works which described the physiology of sex. Probably the most popular was one alleged to be by Aristotle. It came down to the nineteenth century from the eighteenth century and before. A representative edition is the one printed in 1831 in "New England." It is a 247-page duodecimo, *The Works of Aristotle . . . Containing . . . his Complete Master-Piece.* It first anatomizes the male and female sex organs and then discusses generation and pregnancy. Following the

"Master-Piece" itself are three other essays of which the most important is the "Experienced Midwife."

The *Aristotle*, the *Fruits of Philosophy*, and *Moral Physiology* all are distinguished by a kind of scientific tone. The opposition they generated came from the subject: they treated sex with an explicitness the times refused to tolerate. They are in their way books of fact. There were also occasional books which mixed fiction with the fact. They apparently appeared more often after the Civil War than before.

Typical of this sort is *Satan in Society*, written by Nicholas F. Cooke under the pseudonym of "A Physician." It was entered for copyright in 1870 with the imprint of Edward Hovey of New York. The title gives the book away though its avowed purpose is propriety itself. The book is said to be designed to train the young and counsel the mature. There is a whole chapter on male masturbation, complete with a livid picture of the typical male masturbator; there is another on female masturbation, with a corresponding picture of the typical female. There are uplifting chapters on wholesome marriage and on woman's role in the world. There is a chapter condemning prostitution. At the end there is a motley collection of "Conjugal Aphorisms."

Cooke's technique is one of attack and sensationalism. He is against a good many things. He is against co-education ("the wrongful commingling of sexes in the Public Schools") because of the sexual opportunities it affords; against abortion ("it is . . . criminal"); against wicked physicians ("pimps of Satan") who advise on sex; and against sex for the elderly. Finally, he is against any birth control except abstinence and perhaps the rhythm system. His writing is exclamatory; his tone smug. In various passages he colors his prose to excite his reader. His is the kind of book which has an underlying prurience absent from Knowlton's and Owen's work and absent from the *Aristotle*. It is the kind of book which can be bought today, in lurid covers, at drugstores and magazine stands.

Another physician, Alice Stockham, published two books

which are a blend not of sex and sensation but of sex and oriental mysticism. She bestowed esoteric titles upon both. The first was *Tokology;* that was apparently (I have not seen it) a manual which, in the author's own words, taught "possible painless pregnancy and parturition" and also dealt with other matters affecting female health. The second was *Karezza: Ethics of Marriage,* "Karezza" meaning "to express affection in both words and actions." Dr. Stockham published it herself, as she had the first book, in 1896. The thesis of *Karezza* is that "sexual science . . . teaches that there are deeper purposes and meanings to the reproductive faculties and functions than are understood and taught by most people." In applying the thesis Dr. Stockham drew on East as well as West; oriental overtones can be heard throughout *Karezza.* As the result of being in India, she had acquired an unusual awareness of the difference between an Eastern and a Western civilization, and she felt that the disciplined passivity of the East had much to recommend it. She speaks respectfully of karma and makes other references to Eastern religious ideas. The most significant of these for the thesis of the book is that we can learn to control any physical function of ours and any organ.

This idea is the basis for her conviction that sexual intercourse can be controlled while going on. "Karezza," she asserts, "consummates marriage in such a manner that through the power of will, and loving thoughts, the final crisis is not reached, but a complete control by both husband and wife is maintained throughout the entire relation." Dr. Stockham does not fail to be specific. The immediate object of Karezza is "the complete but quiet union of the male and female organs." The consequence of attempting such a union is that "in the course of an hour the physical tension subsides, the spiritual exaltation increases, and not uncommonly visions of a transcendent life are seen and consciousness of new powers experienced." At the highest a mystic, mutual trance is achieved.

Still another physician published the pamphlet *The*

Psychical Correlation of Religious Emotion and Sexual Desire in 1897. However, while Dr. Stockham turned to Asia for her inspiration, Dr. James Weir, Jr., turned to Europe. There, since the nineteenth century was drawing to its end, he found an already mature scholarship on his subject. His writing shows the marks of his research into anthropology and psychology; he refers to numerous European authorities, among them Krafft-Ebing. Weir uses such terms as "libido" and impresses the reader with his sophistication. His thesis was extremely controversial but he presented it without being defensive. He argues, as the title of his book indicates, that a close relation exists between sexual and religious feeling. They spring from the same source; they have the same effect. Furthermore, one is often convertible into the other. To Dr. Weir man's primary interest is in sex, however, not in religion. When man is too young or too old for sex, religion is ready to take its place. It is the adolescent who usually experiences "salvation," or the old man or old woman. Just as there are differences according to age, there are differences according to gender. In our culture, woman generally turns to religion for compensation more than does man. This is because woman has fewer sexual opportunities. The marked cases of religious ecstasy have mostly been observed in woman. In evidence Dr. Weir culls many cases from the lives of female saints. They clearly show, he suggests, that the love of God and the love of man look very much alike.

Some of the works I have discussed have more weight than others. All have certain limitations. All are surpassed by a book not yet mentioned, *The Truth about Love*. To the best of my knowledge it has no peers in nineteenth-century culture. Its author was David Goodman Croly and the book is distinguished by his candor of mind and honesty of approach. Born in 1829, Croly became a journalist and newspaper editor. In the world of ideas he showed himself to be as daring as Dr. Knowlton. He invented the word "miscegenation" and publicly endorsed the idea, saying that what the American needed to bring him to the peak of perfection was a strain of Negro blood. He founded a magazine which he called *The Modern Thinker* and gave it views to match. While he was managing editor of the New York *World* he composed his most notable work. *The Truth about Love* found a publisher in David Wesley & Co. of New York. The first edition came out in 1872; the second, with the language softened in spots, was issued later in the same year. The book, which runs to 285 pages, is an extended dialogue between the author and over two dozen others. These include a Philosopher, a Religious Moralist, a Strong-Minded Woman, a Sentimentalist, a Physician, a Wanton, a Positivist, a Catamite, and a Platonist. Addressing themselves to the author they give him the opportunity to make replies of unparalleled frankness.

Croly announces at the outset, "I propose to discuss fairly and without any reserve the relation of the sexes and the passion of love." He hopes in doing this, he adds, to serve humanity. He strikes the notes of candor and calmness from the very first pages. When one of his early questioners, a Young Man, exclaims, "Teach me how to solve this terrible riddle of passion and principle," Croly reassures him: "Calm these agitations." He goes on to give some comforting advice based on his belief in the goodness of human nature and of the universe. Yet it is not an unqualified belief, for Croly sees much that has been stunted or blighted. He looks at the America of his time, so grossly rich and self-indulgent. "If there is no check put upon the career of wealth in this country," he warns, "the year 2000 will see the inhabitants of the larger cities . . . launched upon a career of debauchery such as the world has never before witnessed."

As Croly surveys the contemporary scene he assesses the helps and hindrances to sexual expression. To him the problem of sex is universal; it plagues the young, the middle-aged, and the old. The manifestations of it are many but a general relief for them all can be found. He thinks that relief lies in "a new religious faith founded upon the facts of nature." In other words, he wants a religion of sane sexuality. In the face of American puritanism he maintains that the sex act is itself good. It is not only health-giving, it is "speaking physically, a moral act."

Young unmarried persons should have all possible sexual "opportunities suited to their state of life and physical power." (On hearing this the Reformer cries out "Heavens! what a notion!") Croly boldly denies one of the main tenets of the American sexual creed in the course of talking with the Physician. "There is no honor in being a virgin; it is a burden to most young girls; it is the one thing of which they are most anxious to be rid." But denying the tenet point-blank will not destroy it; if anything it will cause the multitude of readers to reaffirm its validity. Croly is ready, in consequence, to settle for what he regards as the next best thing. If our culture still demands virginity from the bride, he suggests that we welcome all means to make it merely nominal. Accordingly, any gratification which stops short of intercourse ought to be encouraged. He wants the parents of the young to "permit kissing, embracing, waltzing, and even novel-reading." If society will allow such liberties to young persons, then it can preserve its musty custom of virginity and also help them to escape both the perils of pregnancy and the evils of onanism.

Croly has not much less startling things to say about married love. For the married man or woman he does not advocate adultery; he thinks the marriage bond should be kept intact. But he concedes that it may become irksome. Remarkably enough for a nineteenth-century man, he spends as much time on the problems of the mature female as he does on those of the male. This is partly because he believes that hers are more pressing. In spite of the fact that "women are more conscious of sex than men are," their sexual adjustment is rarely satisfactory. "I believe," Croly says, "if the facts were known, that five women out of six do not experi-

ence physical pleasure when they have relations." Among
the causes a frequent one is fear of pregnancy. To cut
down the chances of a woman's having unwanted children,
Croly strongly advocates birth control. The best device for
it he thinks is the syringe.

If youth and maturity have their difficulties, so does old
age. Croly feels sorry for the elderly person. Sex is a "peren-
nial fire in the veins": it still troubles many a venerable man,
many a gray-haired woman. Now, however, sexual satisfaction is far harder for them to come by than when they were
younger. This is one reason why they should have taken
advantage of all the sexual opportunities of their youth.
When in the dialogue the Old Maid says, "Have I not done
well to preserve my virginity?" the author answers bluntly,
"No, you have not done well."

In this society without enough outlets for sex, what should
the people do? Croly has some suggestions. The most electri-
fying is that prostitution should be regarded as a proper
vocation for a woman, just as legitimate as shopwork or
hat-making. If not more legitimate; for Croly asserts that the
prostitute has greater value for society than the parson. "If
every church in the city of New York was shut up for the
next six months, very little harm would result"; on the other
hand, if the brothels were closed we would see "the most
frightful outrages." His other suggestions, like the one about
prostitution, are based on his belief in the maximum of
sexual activity. But it must be normal, heterosexual activity.
He rejects onanism. And he has nothing but detestation for
homosexuality. When the Catamite speaks up and asks plain-
tively, "But why not say a word for me?" the prompt answer
is "Out of my sight — you horror!"

In his determination to speak the truth as he saw it, nobody went beyond Croly. Yet the other writers I have described, with the exception perhaps of the author of *Satan in
Society*, strove to speak frankly and truly too. If we agree that
writing is generally designed either for pleasure or for instruction, those writers patently tried to instruct. They

wanted to teach us something. What, however, about the writers whose purpose was to entertain? Were there any writers of works with a warmer tone, works designed to titillate rather than to teach? Was there literary erotica available to Americans?

There was a trickle of it from overseas in the seventeenth century which broadened slightly in the eighteenth century. In the nineteenth century, and especially after the Civil War, more of the foreign classics of sex were imported. The works of Ovid, Boccaccio, and John Cleland are variegated examples. Yet there were still not many, apparently. Nor does there seem to have been much other prose and poetry of an erotic nature. In poetry we can find only at intervals a work like *Cupid's Own Book of Amorous Poetry,* which was compiled by an anonymous editor and issued in 1850 in New York by one Elton, Publisher. It draws mainly from the lustier of British love lyrics. Dryden's "Pains of Love," for instance, Rochester's "The Inconstant," and some sprightly verses by Herrick are among those reprinted. Here is a typical selection:

TO CORINNA

> I only begg'd to kiss your hand,
> You said your lips I might command;
> Should I now ask those lips to kiss
> Would you not grant a greater bliss?

Any verse more daring was a rarity, whether classical or not, whether foreign or American. Professor Robert Walker, when examining over six thousand volumes of native nineteenth-century verse for social content, saw only a single volume of erotic poetry. It was *Psalms of the Race Roots* by John William Lloyd, who specialized in portraying sexual union in ornate metaphorical terms.

Erotic American prose was somewhat less scarce. In his slapdash *An Unhurried View of Erotica* (1958) Ralph Ginzburg can cite a handful of prose titles. These include *Sodom in Union Square,* allegedly by an ex-police captain from New York, and *The Secret Services and Duties of Major Lovitt.* Here and there we can find a hint of more. Lists of obviously erotic works are advertised in a gamy weekly called the *New York Clipper.* The Institute for Sex Research owns one number, for March 22, 1856; it advertises little books, priced at a quarter, written by someone styled Charles Paul de Kock. Among them are *The Mysteries of Venus, The Bar Maid at the Old Point House,* and *The Adventures of a French Bedstead.*

The only striking example of mid-nineteenth-century pornography in prose at the Institute is an anonymous novel, *The Libertine Enchantress,* published in New Orleans in 1863. On it Dr. Kinsey has penciled the notation that it is very rare. The stuff of the story is erotic episodes; the treatment is purposefully prurient. There are two variations from the pornographic norm, however. One is that the heroine, Lucinda, sees the sexual transactions instead of taking part in them. Led into voyeurism as a little girl, she engages in it till maturity. Throughout the book keyholes and knotholes appear regularly for her to peek through. She remains physically a virgin until her marriage, in the final pages, to her Frederick. The other variation is the tone of benediction at the end. Lucinda concludes her sensational observations with: "We led a happy life. We had a number of fine children. Now that we are old, Frederick and I love each other as well as we ever did in our lives."

Some marginal instances are to be found in the Gothic romances of George Lippard, led by *The Quaker City* (1844). In their day these books were a sensation but there are only patches of prurient material in them. His heroines, and bold anti-heroines, are shown to have bosoms (milk-white) and limbs (marble); there are episodes leading up to seduction and attempted rape; there is a hectic flush to some of the writing. And yet both the general aim and general effect are less than pornographic. Even near the end of the century, when printing and publishing boomed, relatively little pornography seems to have appeared. By that time there should have been, for example, many a feverish story of Negro slave-girls whipped and violated. All I have found of that sort at the Kinsey Institute, and I have not found anything elsewhere, is a novel dated 1892 and centering on the experiences of a male slave rather than a female. The author is anonymous.

Paul, the hero of *The Story of a Slave,* is a handsome, modest mulatto. Looking back on his youth before the Civil War, he tells how he and the beautiful Miss Virginia, daughter of his owner, became lovers. His account is moderately erotic. There are some filmy garments and heaving breasts. There is some bold action, particularly Virginia's seizing the initiative while Paul shies away. At the climax of the story she exclaims, "Take me, take me," and Paul does. There are also some midnight bedroom scenes. Much of the erotic effect is blunted for the reader by the clumsy writing. The dialogue, with Paul at times speaking like a law book, is stilted indeed. For instance: Virginia, afraid she is pregnant, tells Paul, who hints at abortion. When she says that this would be close to murder, he replies in the most wooden of accents, "No physiological conditions are present as yet which could possibly admit a shadow of justice in such a charge." Incidentally, she is not pregnant and near the conclusion of the novel marries a callow planter. She still has Paul make love to her; she says in fact that she would rather be Paul's mistress than the planter's wife. As the book ends, she bears the planter's child, however, and leaves the plantation.

Although *The Story of a Slave* came out in 1892, its atmosphere and style are both old-fashioned. A generation and more separate it from the *Maidenhead Stories* printed in Chicago only two years later. These are hardcore pornography. The scene is a supper given by a set of lusty young fellows who are members of a secret fraternity at "Smith College." The book starts with the seduction of the one remaining virgin in the group, Frank Eaton. Then, in the

tradition of the *Decameron* and *Heptameron,* each member
of the fraternity tells a salacious story. There are fifteen
stories in all, all concerned with sexual gymnastics, among
them a few perversions. The tone is sly; the style is studded
with such coy circumlocutions as "quivering instrument"
and "mossy dales."

The *Maidenhead Stories* are as lubricious as American
pornography of the time apparently could become. Yet they
have an amateurish turn to them, reminiscent of stag-night
monologues. They pale beside the professional scandalous-
ness of the worst foreign importations. They must have
found it hard to compete with, for instance, *The Bagnio
Miscellany,* which was published in London in 1892 and
reached America by devious means.

The miscellany, attributed to "Miss Lais Lovecock," runs
to a hundred pages and contains three items. The first is
Lais' own story; the second is a set of "Dialogues between
a Jew and a Christian," the Jew being an old villain and the
Christian a young bawd; and the third is "The Force of Instinct," a story about the sexual adventures of a Miss Wharton under the tutelage of her resourceful maid, Betty. The
first is technically the best.

The tale told by Miss Lais is purest pornography. Her
mounting sexual experience is described from the time she
enters a girls' school until she reaches what can only be
called the fullest maturity. She goes from one encounter to
another and relates them with relish. She lingers lovingly
over each detail. Her introduction to life begins at school
with flagellation and girlish lesbianism and then goes on to
other perversions and practices including experimentation
by one, two or three persons. The multiple exercises are extremely imaginative. However, Lais does not neglect the
simple sexual act of coupling; many an episode of that is
described. As a matter of fact, she does not go as far in her
perversity as she might. In her story bestiality and sodomy
are absent and there is no male homosexuality whatever.

The point of view is female, if not feminine, and this adds

to the lubricious effect. Yet in a curious way the story seems almost pastoral. Its world of sex is so simple, basically, as to be primitive. The weather is always summer; intercourse can go on within doors or without. Disease, discovery, disgrace: these when they exist at all are negligible details, to be dismissed in a sentence. Any discomfiture, indeed, in this amoral atmosphere is minor. The lives of both sexes are untroubled, the appetites wonderfully hearty. When Lais and the other wantons make love they are in transports. The men give them an ineffable experience; the girls show, flutteringly, that they appreciate it to the full. When the pleasure of love reaches a climax they faint with ecstasy. Then they recover to faint again.

Lais' adventures are set forth in a neat, graphic style. The vocabulary is unmistakably clear. The author's aim is plainly to be as explicit and salacious as possible, and he succeeds. The set of dialogues which follow are considerably less effective. And the concluding story, "The Force of Instinct," is not as full of spirit as the first; perhaps the author's invention flagged. Yet the account of Miss Wharton's instruction in debauchery has its memorable moments. For the reader of erotica, "The Force of Instinct" has another virtue: it includes an informal guide to further reading. Toward the end of this story the heroine's maid tells her about some of the classics of pornography. She names with praise *Fanny Hill, The Spirit of Flagellation, The Memoirs of a French Lady of Pleasure,* and other real or imagined epics of the bed. The maid adds that they are all illustrated.

No doubt there has always been pornography, to a larger or smaller extent. If we can judge by what remains, however, little appeared in nineteenth-century America. It is certainly appropriate for us to ask why, but we can only speculate about the answer. For here we touch on a major problem of human behavior: the relation of sex to its supposed stimulants. Did Americans fail to produce much pornography in those days because they were so well satisfied sexually that they felt no need for titillation? Or were they so busy conquering a continent that they had little time for reading about sex? Did sexual license have to wait for an era of luxury? This, incidentally, was David Croly's impression. Looking back at Rome and Byzantium and then contemplating America of the Gilded Age, he decided that the older and richer a country grew, the more its moral fiber slackened. Or was the hand of New England puritanism still heavy on America, repressing sexual activity and weighting sex with sin?

We can see that in the nineteenth century serious books about sex were almost as rare as pornography. Today the scientific book is seldom interdicted; the serious literary work remains open to attack. For we still do not know what pornography is and we still quarrel about its effects. The courts themselves are confused about it. Does *Tropic of Cancer* arouse lustful desires and perhaps lead to lustful acts? Currently some judges and juries are saying yes; more are saying no. But the issue is far from being decided, and the notes offered in this essay are only notes.

Foreign Ports and Exotic Places:
1840-1860

THE SPRINGTIME of American travel literature came in
the two decades before the Civil War. Yet we had found it
a congenial kind of writing ever since colonial days; it had
in fact been our first species of popular literature. Such
pioneering works as Captain John Smith's *True Relation*
and Alexander Whitaker's *Good News from Virginia* described the new-found lands invitingly and generously spiced
fact with fancy. Throughout the seventeenth and eighteenth centuries travel writers, foreign and domestic, continued to write and to find a certain American public for
their works. In the early nineteenth century Washington
Irving raised travel writing to the level of an art. But it was
not till the twenty years before the war that, through a
combination of social circumstances, our travel literature
really began to flourish. Then its spirit, richness, and youthful abundance made it so attractive that it is surprising that
it has been little studied since.

Take a weak-eyed Harvard boy and have him ship as a
common seaman on a voyage round the Horn, thereby

toughening his body, sharpening his sight, and bringing out the basic strength of his character. This was the recipe for the most popular of marine travel books of the time. Richard Henry Dana, Jr., had barely reached twenty-five when he published *Two Years Before the Mast.* Harper & Brothers issued it after giving him only $250 for the copyright. Since they seemed far more interested in pirating English authors than in paying American ones, they allowed Dana's book to try to sell itself — and it did. With several reprintings and editions in its first two years, it quickly became a success. Later on, sales dropped for a time but then a completely unexpected occurrence, the gold rush, drove them up again. Dana had devoted the whole middle section of the book to his adventures in California, the farthest point of his voyage. When the gold fields opened there in 1848, his proved to be the only easily available book on the region. Copies promptly disappeared from bookstores and Harpers' book-bins. On returning to California a generation later, Dana said with pleasure that he found that almost every American in California had read him.

Even if we discount an author's optimism, little doubt exists about the popularity of *Two Years.* At the beginning the acclaim it earned in England exceeded the acclaim it received over here, but by the 1850's its high quality was universally acknowledged. Yet it was only one of many such books. Works on travel dot the pages of antebellum bibliographies; lectures on travel became one of the staples of the lyceum system; and novels and short stories with a faraway setting grew in number.

The origins of this interest in travel books lay in a noteworthy complex of American characteristics. Restlessness was perhaps the main element, betraying itself in countless ways. "Men are in constant motion," Tocqueville observed in *Democracy in America.* Our population demonstrated what the demographer would call a high degree of mobility. That meant that a family had relatively few qualms about picking up and moving away to improve its situation. The American seldom felt a compulsion to endure misery

when he could alleviate it by settling somewhere else, prefer-
ably in the West. If times grew bad in New England and
rocks seemed to multiply in the field, the Yankee farmer
heeded Ohio's call or Iowa's.

But travel did not have to be purely a means of reaching
richer land. It was also, as other foreign observers remarked,
a recreation. Going somewhere for the sake of going. This
had not yet become the land of the summer-vacation trip
but notwithstanding, the riverboats and packets were
crowded, the trains were full, and even the jolting stages
and carriages kept their share of business.

Visitors to this country noted still another, more personal, aspect of American restlessness. That was the habit
we had of walking fast, of being unable to sit still, of
erupting into all sorts of brisk motions from drumming our
fingers to tapping our feet. And deeper than all this lay the
psychological restlessness of a people without the security
and fixity of class status, the restlessness created by a break
from the European tradition without a new tradition to
replace it.

Restlessness, in its various manifestations, was the main
but not the only thing that favored the circulation of travel
books. Allied to it was a thirst for new experience and
knowledge. The desire to explore deserves to be called an
American trait too. If this desire could not be satisfied in
real life — and of course circumstances often barred even a
mobile American's way — it might be satisfied secondhand
through travel literature. And that is what happened. It
found such varied fare to feed on as the trappers' tales of
the great West, the South Sea idyls, and the sagas of the
frozen North.

These travel books furnished at least two, considerably
different, kinds of vicarious experience. The first is a glory-
ing in physical hardship, in the surmounting of rugged ob-
stacles. In literature even more than in life, one can climb
the Rockies and cross the ocean, treating Nature as an opponent to be tricked and then beaten down. As athletic Bayard
Taylor wrote at twenty, "Sometimes I almost desire that dif-

ficulties should be thrown in my way, for the sake of the additional strength gained in surmounting them." Anglo-Saxon poetry often displays a similar relish for the trials and ordeals of seafaring life, based on the conviction that they can be endured.

The other kind of experience is a sybaritic, sensual escape, an escape from the cramping confines of a prim Victorian existence to a land of sinuous dancing girls. Rich in its appeal to the somewhat starved senses of the mid-century American, it brought him — and her, through identification — the release that motion pictures and television provide today. Satisfactions that would be unthinkable in the United States could be savored vicariously if the scene were a Turkish harem or a South Sea isle.

The classic example of hardship endured and conquered is Dana's book. It appeared in 1840 but similar volumes came out all during the years before the war. Elisha Kent Kane's account of his Arctic explorations dominated the new books of the 'fifties by selling a remarkable 130,000 copies before the decade ended. The pioneer in the field of South Sea idyls was Herman Melville's *Typee* (1846), but the full flowering of the sybaritic species did not come until the publication of Bayard Taylor's lush *Lands of the Saracen* in 1854.

In form if not content, *Two Years Before the Mast* is actually a far better book than young Dana knew how to write. The strenuous experience was all his — no one has ever maintained (as we now do for *Typee*) that the author mingled fiction with his fact — but even the minor incidents fall into an artful order. The basic plot is almost certain to satisfy the reader: the green young fellow overcomes the hazards set up by circumstance and grows into a man. Furthermore, the plot is defined and limited in a perfectly natural way: the brig *Pilgrim* sails from Boston Harbor, makes its long voyage, and returns.

For this voyage, in other words, reality itself supplied an Aristotelian beginning, middle, and end. The beginning is the time the brig is outward bound, a time of increasing misery for all the crew, a misery temporarily accentuated by the cold of the Antarctic and crescendoed, when the California coast is reached, by the captain's flogging of two crew members. The middle is the extended period, full of descriptions of California life, when the *Pilgrim* sails back and forth along the coast exchanging her cargo of Boston wares for bullocks' hides. Dana helps to collect and stow the hides on board ship. In addition, he picks up a knowledge of Spanish which facilitates his frequent meetings with the Spanish inhabitants when he travels on shore. The end is the journey home. Once the Horn is rounded, even the physical rigors disappear. The brutal captain has already been transferred to another vessel. Morale rises. The winds are good, so is the weather, and the whole ship seems quickened by the wish to reach port. The *Pilgrim* sails into Boston Harbor with the now robust Dana keyed up in excitement at coming home.

The tone of the book is an outgrowth of the man. It is never exclamatory or shrill. Even its few formal passages of description are modulated. One of the finest examples is Dana's picture, given at the end of a lazy, sparkling Sunday on the return trip, of the *Pilgrim* at full sail. Dana had clambered and crawled to the end of the flying-jib boom and, on turning back, was struck with the beauty of the sight below him. "There rose up from the water, supported only by the small black hull, a pyramid of canvas, spreading out far beyond the hull, and towering up almost, as it seemed in the indistinct night air, to the clouds." Then in ascending order he enumerates the sails from the lowest ones to the skysail at the very apex of the pyramid. The cumulative effect is almost grand. He continues: "So quiet, too, was the sea, and so steady the breeze, that if these sails had been sculptured marble they could not have been more motionless." But now he needs something to round off his description. He finds it in the remark of an old sailor who had climbed up with him but whose presence has not been mentioned till now. This seaman gazes down too before he speaks. At this point the risk of emotionalizing the scene is considerable, but Dana avoids it perfectly by letting him say of the full, still sails only, "How quietly they do their work!"

The style is in keeping. Harvard's Professor E. T. Channing, Thoreau's former teacher, described it in the *North American Review* shortly after the book came out. He thought the writing "plain, straightforward, and manly, never swollen for effect, or kept down from apprehension. There is no appearance of seeking for words; but those that will best answer the purpose come and fall into their proper places of their own will; so that, whatever the transitions may be, the composition flows on. . . . This we suppose is the perfection of style."

One more thing, which has already been noted but needs to be stressed, is important in appraising the story. It is the fact that *Two Years Before the Mast* was a democratic book. It took the side of the crew, not the captain. Probably no nation disliked absolute power as much as nineteenth-century America. In the Jacksonian era just closing when the book appeared, even the rich often concealed their strength behind a democratic manner, and tyranny was hateful. When Captain Thompson ordered two seamen spread-eagled and then flogged them in a frenzy with his rope, Dana, "disgusted, sick, . . . turned away, and leaned over the rail, and looked down into the water." Other instances of cruelty in the book, less dramatic, were nevertheless many. In every case the reader's sympathies lay with the miserable sailors.

Herman Melville, like Dana, was a young seaman when he went through the experiences embodied in his first travel book. But Melville was, unlike Dana, a great writer, though proper appreciation of his stature has come slowly. He displayed even as a young man the intuitive understanding of human needs which Freud so admired in the writer of genius. If we agree with Freud on these needs, we take the position that we — and man in general — can extract only a meager satisfaction from actual everyday life. Surrounded by circumstances which force us to control our drives of sex and aggression, confined by conditions which make us lead only one life and that by no means what we dreamed of, we have ample reason for surrendering ourselves to fantasies. They may be either daydreams or the fantasies of art, particularly the fantasies found in literature. But we must not surrender ourselves completely to them or else we lose touch with life. We must feel in our reading the repression as well as the expression, the check as well as the surge, the pain as well as the pleasure. It is when a writer consciously or unconsciously composes a story with a balanced mixture of fact and fantasy and with the fantasy itself nicely adjusted to his readers' desires that we have a book of extraordinary popular appeal. Such a book is *Typee, or Life on the Marquesas Islands. Moby-Dick* and the other works of Melville's maturity are now world-renowned but it is undeniably true that in his own day they were overshadowed by *Typee.* Even late in life he was still known as "Marquesas" Melville, the author of travel books.

Young Melville strikes the right note on the very first page of *Typee.* He has been aboard ship for a long time. Weary of the starveling life at sea, he learns with delight that his ship will now sail for the Marquesas. "The Marquesas!" he marvels. "Naked houris — cannibal banquets — groves of cocoa-nut — coral reefs — tattooed chiefs — and bamboo temples; sunny valleys planted with breadfruit trees — carved canoes dancing on the flashing blue waters — savage woodlands guarded by horrible idols — *heathenish rites and human sacrifices.*"

While the ship is making for the Marquesas, Melville gives the reader some notion of the past of the islands. He will give us fact and then fancy, in anticipation of the Freudian doctrine of mingling the two. At the outset, consequently, we have a page or two of history. Then he modulates the history into two linked anecdotes, one contrasting with the other but both sexual in nature. This is important because the most pressing need for the American of Melville's time was not relief for the drive of aggression — a growing, crowing country offered exceptional opportunities for that — but relief for sex. And *Typee* will provide the sexual surcease with such happy effect that it will become the prototype for a kind of South-Sea island romance still applauded, with the musical play *South Pacific* as today's most popular example. The two anecdotes are nicely set off. The first is about the young and beautiful wife of a missionary. The Marquesan natives were over-awed on first seeing her in her voluminous attire but when they dared to investigate they discovered that under all her clothing she was merely a female. "To the horror of her affectionate spouse," Melville remarks, "she was stripped of her garments, and given to understand that she could no longer carry on her deceits with impunity." She and her husband fled the Marquesas for a safer place. The contrasting anecdote is about the shapely wife of the King of Nukuheva. Invited with her husband to inspect a French ship, she was enchanted by the tattooing on one old sailor and enthusiastically lifted her skirts to show him her own tattoos. The French, says Melville, were shocked. In both cases his tone invites the reader to smile with the innocent savages at the expense of the civilized whites.

To prepare us for his world of sexual fantasy Melville makes use of one other preliminary. Freud, again, has noted that for a reader to appreciate a fantasy he must not be tense but as relaxed as possible. Melville puts the reader in a receptive mood by describing the state of the ship and its seamen as it sailed slowly toward the Marquesas. "What a delightful, lazy, languid time we had whilst we were thus gliding along." It was almost as if everyone were "under the influence of some narcotic."

When the ship reaches Nukuheva Bay she is boarded by a lovely group of native nymphs. Their charms, their naked innocence appeal to all. "Who would think of tumbling those artless creatures overboard," Melville asks, "when they had swum miles to welcome us." He describes how they looked to the sailors: "Their extreme youth, the light clear brown of their complexions, their delicate features, and inexpressibly graceful figures, their softly molded limbs, and free unstudied action, seemed as strange as beautiful." In the evening they danced for the sailors on the deck but it was with an "abandoned voluptuousness" which Melville says he dare not describe. And rightly so. For here is the point where he could easily have antagonized his reader; here the hackles of our puritanism might well have been raised. To hold the reader Melville must maintain a balance; the story must mirror the conflict between the forces of expression and repression. So Melville follows this part of his account with a general comment on the orgy that ensues and then concludes the chapter by moralizing on how the trusting natives have been debauched by the decadent European.

Thereafter Melville's personal adventures begin. He deserts his ship, makes his way across the island with all sorts of difficulty including sickness, and falls into the hands of the cannibal Typee tribe. In spite of his initial fears the Typee warriors treat him well and Typee girls are a delight. He lives an enviable life throughout much of the book. Slowly, however, he realizes that there is evil in Eden. Kind as they appear, his captors refuse to let him go; moreover, he finds out that they can be cannibals indeed. He feels a mounting need to escape. The book concludes with his flight back to "European civilization" and shipboard life.

The plot is enriched, the appeal greatly intensified, by the sexual fantasies. They center around the lovely Fayaway, who lives in the household which the Typee chief assigns to Melville. With her gentle, loving ways and her "free pliant figure" she is the model for all future charmers who will adorn the South-Sea romances just mentioned. Her complexion is "a rich and mantling olive," her face "a round oval" with each feature perfect. Her hair, "parted irregularly in the middle, flowed in natural ringlets over her shoulders, and whenever she chanced to stoop, fell over and hid from view her lovely bosom." Customarily she clings to the "garb of Eden," though she sometimes puts on a tunic of tapa cloth reaching from her slim waist to her knees. Her only aim is to make Melville happy. She takes care of him; she frolics with him. She is the child-mistress of male fantasy. Is she Melville's mistress? Melville again stops at the edge of explicit impropriety and lets the situation speak for itself.

Fayaway is the center but by no means the sum total of the sensual appeal of *Typee*. Melville puts himself into a paradise where every girl is shapely and half-clothed. In addition to this he builds up the sexuality in other ways. The setting is compact with suggestive imagery. Granted the danger in pushing Freudianism too far, the main scene itself, the "Happy Valley," is a symbol of the female. The undergrowth and foliage are lush too, and female in their suggestions. So are the caves and other parts of the sur- roundings described. Male symbols also abound; they are principally phallic. At times they are combined with the female and then the effect is striking. The most notable ex- amples of the combining are two in number. In one Fay- away while canoeing with Melville turns herself into a mast. On impulse she strips off her tapa cloth, stands nude in the bow of the boat, and holds the cloth as a sail high over her head. "A prettier little mast than Fayaway was never shipped aboard of any craft" is Melville's verdict. In the other instance he describes how the girls in his household, their bright eyes beaming with kindness, anoint his whole body each evening with palm oil. He greets the "daily occurrence of this luxurious operation" with delight.

Effective as much of this symbolism is, it remains basically a supplement to the girls themselves. Melville enjoys them at all times but especially in the water. As he blandly re- marks, "Bathing in company with troops of girls formed one of my chief amusements." Most of the episodes involving the girls would have held the reader's attention then even more than today. No episodes would have had a more searching psychological claim, probably, than the Eden-like bathing parties with Fayaway and her friends. To the hard-working American male of a century ago, as well as his womenfolk, such parties doubtless represented the pagan peak of dalliance. To a generation used to being muffled in heavy clothes, the idea of bathing naked was a shocking, tantalizing thing. Swimming itself constituted more of an innovation than one might expect. It would not be until years after *Typee* that American men and women would often begin to enjoy their oceans, lakes, and rivers. When they did it would be with three-quarters of their bodies covered with woolen bathing suits. Then too, the genial waters of the South Pacific were a perfect fertility symbol, regardless of whether the nineteenth-century readers of *Typee* recognized it or not. With Melville, eyes alight, they watched the girls in the water, "springing buoyantly into the air, and revealing their naked forms to the waist, with their long tresses dancing about their shoulders, . . . and their gay laughter pealing forth at every frolicsome incident."

This is the picture of a sexual idyl. Yet it is one-sided, and any analysis of *Typee* would be incomplete if it did not consider the other side — the appeal to the powerful puritanical impulses of the reader. The role of conscience, the superego in Freudian terms, cannot be ignored; for the reader will feel the deepest satisfaction only when it is taken into account. Melville can have Fayaway but he must also be punished for having her. So we see in *Typee* an idyl but one with a dark current of anxiety running through it. At times the current is strong, during Melville's flight across the island, for instance, when he worries greatly about whether cannibals will catch him. At times it is weak, especially in the middle section of the book when he is much occupied with Fayaway and native festivals. Toward the end of the book the current of anxiety grows greater than ever before. Throughout *Typee* it is personified by the male savages. Generally they treat him well if arbitrarily, but he always realizes that he is in the hands of savages and he gradually realizes that they may do him serious harm. While they turn their best side toward him they are also eating their enemies. Generous to Melville as a male, they surround their women with harsh taboos. Melville enjoys the privileges he gets by being a man, but he dislikes the taboos and even succeeds in seeing one set aside for Fayaway, the taboo that prohibits a woman from touching a canoe. He likes the men's club (also taboo to women); he likes the male feasts and learns to twirl a finger in their savory poi-poi. Yet the atmosphere of male menace deepens, and at the end Melville is profoundly relieved to escape even to the poor life aboard ship.

I have yet to mention the most important symbol of the puritan conscience. It is Melville's diseased leg. Shortly after he deserts his ship at the beginning of the book, he finds that one leg has become swollen and painful. We are never told why. Melville as a matter of fact calls it his "unaccountable malady." He suffers throughout the course of the book. At times, when life is most attractive, the pain is nearly gone; at times it is so great that he cannot even limp and must be carried. This is a sexual paradise but a paradise never devoid of pain; the diseased leg is doubtless a phallic symbol. As the end of the book nears, the reader is constantly reminded of Melville's disability. To get to the ship which will take him away, he must be carried down to the shore. At the shore itself he forces himself to limp the final steps to the water with a spear.

When he is being rowed to his new ship, away from his once pleasant and peaceful life on the island, his last memories will be of pursuit by a savage swimming after him in rage, ready to kill him and stopped only by Melville's striking him in the throat with a boathook. In this way conscience will have its due; but the reader can better remember the bewitching Fayaway standing in the pleasant shallows of the island's little lake.

Along with its potent fantasy *Typee* has other appeals. We must have fact to mix with the fantasy, and *Typee* is full of it. There are many pages given to graphic accounts of the ceremonies of the islanders, to descriptions of their exotic life, to incidents of plot, and to a gallery of minor characters headed by Melville's former shipmate Toby, though he disappears midway through the book, and Melville's faithful retainer Kory-Kory. The book has an attractive thesis as well. Melville does his best to persuade us that man in a state of nature is man at his best. Although he salts the thesis with many exceptions, he clearly believes in the Noble Savage. His targets are the ruthless colonizer and the missionary. His caustic comments on soul-saving in the South Seas are many; they much offended American piety when *Typee* appeared. Life on Melville's island, given freedom from white interference, is as near Utopia as we can get. There are occasional forays and bloodshed but never any disputes within the tribe. "During my whole year on the island," Melville asserts, "I never witnessed a single quarrel." No one works hard, since all the needs for food, clothing, and shelter are modest. Everyone plays or relaxes. Perhaps the most dramatic contrast between the islanders and the fretting Americans is in the attitude toward sleep. The Typees, Melville notes agreeably, "pass a large portion of their time in the arms of Somnus." On this island it is always a summer afternoon.

Most Americans associated Dana with only one book; they associated Melville with only two. Having attracted widespread attention with *Typee,* he followed it with an almost equally popular sequel, *Omoo.* But his succeeding works received less and less applause. To the public even as late as the Civil War he remained "Marquesas" Melville. From Bayard Taylor, on the other hand, readers gratefully received travel book after travel book. A man of fewer literary gifts by far than Melville or even Dana, he established himself as the prince of professional travelers. He went everywhere, and then talked and wrote about it. His books spanned the last two-thirds of our period. *Views A-Foot, or Europe Seen with Knapsack and Staff* (1846) was his first one; *Travels in Greece and Russia, with an Excursion to Crete* (1859) was the last before the Civil War began. And there were five in between.

Before Fort Sumter was fired on, over a dozen editions (totaling 30,000 copies) of *Views A-Foot* had been exhausted. A brisk, breezy account of a grand tour of Britain and the Continent, it captivated its audience the more because it was the tour of a personable but poor young man. Taylor had only $140 with him when he started out, yet he managed to stay in Europe for nearly two years. They proved to be memorable ones, crammed with every kind of interesting incident. He went to Abbotsford and gazed reverently at Sir Walter Scott's study. He wandered through Westminster Abbey. He remained in Germany for months, learning in particular to love the ancient university town of Heidelberg. He went to Vienna and sat in a beer garden listening to Strauss play his own waltzes. He crossed the Alps to Italy, meeting Hiram Powers in Florence and praising the statue *Eve*, which the sculptor had recently completed. Then he turned to France, where he spent the last pennies of his little hoard, swung back to England — and then home.

Horace Greeley had said bluntly, when he and Taylor talked about writing up his tour in letter form for the *Tribune*, that he wanted "no descriptive nonsense. Of that I am damned sick." If Taylor found that he could not, and would not, obey Greeley's dictum entirely, he nevertheless kept it in mind. Accordingly, the descriptive passages in *Views A-Foot* are held within bounds. The narrative does not stop while the author indulges his love for picturesque composition. As a matter of fact, Taylor's ability to combine description with anecdote accounted for a good deal of the book's popularity.

Furthermore, since this was the book of a poor young man, stately prose would have been off key. Taylor sees all the sights but sees them from below. His status and his nationality come out in other ways. Early in the book, for instance, just before the visit to Abbotsford, he writes about journeying to Ayr for the Burns festival. He becomes sarcastic about the fact that admission costs him fifteen shillings, a sum that once would have barred Burns himself from such a function. Shortly afterward, while passing through Newcastle, he happens to see a group of striking miners who sing a plaintive ballad on their wrongs. "It made my blood boil," says Taylor, "to hear those tones, wrung from the heart of poverty by the hand of tyranny."

American readers responded warmly to Taylor's book as they would never have to that of, say, a well-to-do Philadelphia banker. They responded to his basic democracy, as manifested most by his interest in the underdog but also revealed in many a humanitarian aside during his tour. They responded, further, to the evident contrast between his young American uprightness and the decadence of the Old World. When he noticed that Burns' homestead had become a sordid tavern, his readers waxed indignant with him. When he knitted his brows at European vice, they too grew disturbed and shocked. And — most important in Taylor's own judgment — they responded to what he himself later characterized as "that spirit of boyish confidence and enthusiasm, to which alone I must attribute the success of the work."

Besides these factors in the book's success, one more, of a different kind, can be detected. It was the implied challenge to the reader to see Europe on as little money as possible. When Taylor opened a chapter on Germany with "I have lately been computing how much my travels have cost me up to the present time, and how long I can remain abroad to continue the pilgrimage," many a Yankee reader probably leaned forward to figure it out with him. In this way *Views A-Foot* proved to be a how-to-do-it book, for it demonstrated how to see Europe cheaply. Taylor soon saw the value of this function of the book; a year after its initial publication he tacked on a chapter of advice to impecunious would-be tourists.

A decade separated the handsome lad who tramped through Europe from the bearded celebrity who took ship for the Near East to gather material for *The Lands of the Saracen*. By this time Taylor had come to love native costume, and we have several pictures of him in Arab dress. In one of them he looks away from the reader, his heavy-lidded eyes brooding under his turban, his nostrils arched, his dashing beard and mustachioes a-curl. His hand lies on his scimitar, ready to draw if need be. This is the Bayard Taylor who made ladies swoon when he lectured. This is, in fact, a kind of matinee idol though without any repellent glossiness or prettiness.

The tour that *The Lands of the Saracen* was based on covered Syria, Palestine, Lebanon, Turkey, Malta, Sicily, and Spain. Though the chapters on Turkey turned out to be the richest and best, the whole book when compared with *Views A-Foot* shows both a substantial change and a great advance. It is an older, surer, sophisticated traveler writing now. With maturity has come a genuine skill in the management of scene as well as the ability to relish the spicy appeals to sense. The humanitarian young Victorian has been submerged in the worldly artist. The boyish enthusiasm has been transmuted into a taste for exotic experience.

Evidences of increased deftness in writing can be found everywhere in the pages of the book. The descriptive pieces continue to move instead of standing still — perhaps Taylor remembered Greeley's advice — but move with added grace. There are many other good points too. The sentences, though inclined to be long, are reasonably well knit. If Taylor's grasp of English syntax is not that of Thoreau, it has nevertheless improved. The verbs are often powerful and vivid. The vocabulary is frequently rich but seldom heavy.

Here, for instance, is Taylor painting a nighttime scene.

He is watching for the arrival by boat of the Turkish Sultan, who intends to pray ceremonially at a mosque across the water from where Taylor stands:

A long barge, propelled by sixteen oars, glides around the dark corner of Tophaneh, and shoots into the clear, brilliant space in front of the mosque. It is not lighted, and passes with great swiftness towards the brilliant landing-place. There are several persons seated under a canopy in the stern, and we are trying to decide which is the Sultan, when a second boat, driven by twenty-four oarsmen, comes into sight. The men rise up at each stroke, and the long, sharp craft flies over the surface of the water, rather than forces its way through it. A gilded crown surmounts the long, curved prow, and a light though superb canopy covers the stern. Under this, we catch a glimpse of the Sultan and Grand Vizier, as they appear for an instant like black silhouettes against the burst of light on shore.

This paragraph moves in swift surges, driven by its active, immediate verbs. The phrases, often separated by commas, are short. The vocabulary is not ornate, yet it contributes to the Eastern atmosphere. The management of light and shade — the chiaroscuro, the visual imagery — reveals the hand of a conscious artist. Equally important, the scene is well contrived dramatically. When the first boat scuds out, we expect the Sultan to be in it. But before we can identify him, another and more magnificent boat has skimmed into view; and this is the one he occupies. Much as we want to see him, we glimpse him only for a moment. Then he vanishes, into the mosque. The paragraph rises swiftly to its climax and then drops.

The adroitness of Taylor's writing contributed of course to its popularity. It is a safe guess, however, that the average reader felt rather than comprehended Taylor's art; he was far more interested in what Taylor was saying than in how he managed to say it so effectively.

For what he was offering the reader of *The Lands of the Saracen* was an abundance of escape. True, this volume did not have the dancing girls in person to symbolize the fact.

So far as Taylor's work was concerned they had already appeared, it happened, with their bodies curving "like a snake from the hips to the shoulders," in his preceding book, *A Journey to Central Africa,* along with a section entitled "A Sensuous Life Defended." But *The Lands of the Saracen* had no need of them. It contained the two most remarkable set pieces of their sensory kind in all Taylor's travel books.

One is the chapter "The Visions of Hasheesh." The other is "A Dissertation on Bathing and Bodies." Taylor purposely put them next to each other at the end of the first quarter of the book.

He had already taken hasheesh once and described his sensations in *A Journey to Central Africa.* Yet this had been a superficial experience. His insatiable curiosity (he confessed it frankly) impelled him to take it again, this time in a much heavier dose. Because he had eaten supper first, it was slow in affecting him. But then it began.

"The walls of my frame were burst outward and tumbled into ruin. . . . I felt that I existed throughout a vast extent of space. . . . Within the concave that held my brain were the fathomless deeps of blue; clouds floated there, and the winds of heaven rolled them together, and there shone the orb of the sun."

The exultation increased.

Before me — for a thousand leagues, as it seemed — stretched a vista of rainbows, whose colors gleamed with the splendor of gems — arches of living amethyst, sapphire, emerald, topaz, and ruby. By thousands and tens of thousands, they flew past me, as my dazzling barge sped down the magnificent arcade; yet the vista still stretched as far as ever before me. I reveled in a sensuous elysium, which was perfect, because no sense was left ungratified. But beyond all, my mind was filled with a boundless feeling of triumph. My journey was that of a conqueror — not of a conqueror who subdues his race, either by Love or by Will, for I forgot that Man existed — but one victorious over the grandest as well as the subtlest forces of Nature. The spirits of Light, Color, Odor, Sound, and Motion were my slaves; and, having these, I was master of the universe.

That was the climax of the ecstasy. Then the drug started to stimulate him too much. He became "a mass of transparent jelly, and a confectioner poured me into a twisted mold. I threw my chair aside, and writhed and tortured myself for some time to force my loose substance into the mold." The torment grew till he could bear it no longer. "I threw myself on my bed, with the excited blood still roaring wildly in my ears, my heart throbbing with a force that seemed to be rapidly wearing away my life, my throat dry as a potsherd, and my stiffened tongue cleaving to the roof of my mouth — resisting no longer, but awaiting my fate with the apathy of despair."

In a stupor for several days and nights, he finally recovered consciousness enough to go to a nearby bath. It restored some of his alertness. A brown Syrian polished his limbs; another attendant gave him a glass of tingling sherbet; and he started to feel like himself again.

Thus the chapter ended. But the note of the bath had been introduced and in the next chapter it was amply developed. The two chapters are as different as the proverbial day and night. In contrast to the violent, aching, almost insane sensations of "The Visions of Hasheesh," those of the "Dissertation" lave the traveler in seas of mellowness, flowing through his almost etherealized body and giving it a sense of perfect well-being.

There is nothing that approaches the "Dissertation" in American writing of the forties and fifties. As a poet Taylor created little but commonplace rhymes. As an essayist, as a man of letters, he seldom rose above mediocrity. But the chapter on bathing and bodies, though marred for Americans in one or two places by poor taste, is a tour de force, a minor triumph. It exalts the body, and particularly the male body, as did nothing else of the time.

"Come with me," he proposes, "and I will show you the mysteries of the perfect bath." From the bright bazaar we go into the elaborate building that houses the public baths of Damascus. Taylor describes the first rites of the ceremony; and then the attendant — only a dark shape in the mist —

leads us into an inner hall, with a steaming tank in the center. Here he slips us off the brink, and we collapse over head and ears in the fiery fluid. Once — twice — we dip into the delicious heat, and then are led into a marble alcove, and seated flat upon the floor. The attendant stands behind us, and now we perceive that his hands are encased in dark hair-gloves. He pounces upon an arm, which he rubs until, like a serpent, we slough the worn-out skin, and resume our infantile smoothness and fairness. No man can be called clean until he has bathed in the East. Let him walk directly from his accustomed bath and self-friction with towels, to the Hammam el-Khyateën, and the attendant will exclaim, as he shakes out his hair-gloves, "O Frank! it is a long time since you have bathed."

Next come the successive basins of hot and cold water, and after that the soaping. The attendant brings in a wooden bowl, a piece of soap, and a bunch of palm fibers.

He squats down beside the bowl, and speedily creates a mass of snowy lather, which grows up to a pyramid and topples over the edge. Seizing us by the crown-tuft of hair upon our shaven head, he plants the foamy bunch of fibers full in our face. The world vanishes; sight, hearing, smell, taste (unless we open our mouth), and breathing are cut off; we have become nebulous. Although our eyes are shut, we seem to see a blank whiteness; and, feeling nothing but a soft fleeciness, we doubt whether we be not the Olympian cloud which visited Io. But the cloud clears away before strangulation begins, and the velvety mass descends upon the body. Twice we are thus "slushed" from head to foot, and made more slippery than the anointed wrestlers of the Greek games.

Then the basins again, and the bath nears its end. One more hot plunge, one more rest, and then "the course of passive gymnastics, which excites so much alarm and resistance in the ignorant Franks." "Give yourself with a blind submission into the arms of the brown Fate," Taylor advises, "and he will lead you to new chambers of delight." We enter those chambers, it turns out, by allowing the boy to crack all our joints. But that is only part. After various other gymnastics are over, "the slight languor left from the bath is gone, and an airy, delicate exhilaration, befitting the winged Mercury, takes its place."

Afterward we lie in transcendent repose, having drunk a *"finfan* of foamy coffee, followed by a glass of sherbet cooled with the snows of Lebanon." We puff lazily on a narghileh, drowse a bit in "a bed of rosy clouds, flooded with the radiance of some unseen sun," and awake reborn, to return into the sunny streets of Damascus. "But as we go homewards, we involuntarily look down to see whether we are really treading upon the earth, wondering, perhaps, that we should be content to do so, when it would be so easy to soar above the house-tops."

Granted, this is not a prose of mandarin elegance or of classical refinement. But in its epicurean tasting of physical sensation, in its yielding utterly to physical delight, the "Dissertation" is matchless. Doubtless many an American male gazed in the distance after reading it and drew on his cigar with a certain discontent. Many an American female too probably closed the chapter with a slight blush, and thereafter looked at her husband a bit more speculatively than before.

At any rate, the travel books of Taylor, of Melville, of Dana and their fellows satisfied an American need, or, more strictly, a complex of needs. The number of travel books multiplied throughout the twenty years preceding the war. A few of the bestsellers of the period would even stay in print after the new century began. There would be twentieth-century editions of *Two Years Before the Mast, Views A-Foot,* and *The Lands of the Saracen.* And *Typee* and *Omoo,* riding on the billows of Melville's modern vogue, would ultimately come out in full scholarly as well as popular form.

Thoreau the Actor

WHEN Henry David Thoreau, at the height of his powers in the winter of 1852, made his first personal appearance before a Boston audience, it was to lecture on his sojourn at Walden Pond. With him went his friend Bronson Alcott, one of the sanest eccentrics of his time. They walked to the place in Tremont Row where Thoreau was scheduled to speak. A snowstorm had helped to cut down attendance and there were not a dozen listeners who came in. It was, however, a reading room of some sort, and a number of young clerks and apprentices were looking at newspapers at the far end of the room. Alcott tried to get them up to hear Thoreau, saying, "This is his book which he is reading; this is his life. We ought all to be interested in a man's life, ought we not?" But, so the story goes, "they generally clung to their evening's paper."

Today the company of persons interested in Thoreau is both large and international. One year, 1955, saw three separate editions of *Walden* published in England alone; more have followed and most are still in print. "Civil Disobedience" and several of the nature essays are widely anthologised. All the major works have recently been reprinted. There is a Thoreau Society, complete with an anual conference, held in Concord of course, and a quarterly bulletin. Over the world there are Thoreau addicts who read a few pages from the Journal each night before retiring. Every now and then one hears about some follower of Thoreau who has actually built himself a cabin and withdrawn to the woods. No one can dispute the fact that Thoreau has become a vogue.

Why is this true? The answer involves some intangibles, certainly, and some intimations incapable of proof. But one way to the answer lies, I believe, in the fact that Thoreau was a man who knew extremely well the importance of a deed, the value of an act. He had a genius for summing up an idea in an action and then writing about it most persuasively.

Thoreau was one of the most forthright men American culture has recognized and yet he was unusually self-conscious. A glance from a passing eye could cut him like a knife. It is entirely probable that the two outstanding times he struck a public attitude, he did it without guile. Nevertheless, the effect of his doing so has been felt increasingly. In his career there are a number of interesting minor actions — ideas finding a partial outlet as deeds. One occurred when he sent a declaration to the Concord selectmen declining to be considered a member of any incorporated society he had not personally joined; another when he himself clanged the church bell to make his Concord neighbors collect and hear his burning eulogy on John Brown of Kansas. However, the two famous instances are his going to jail for a night rather than pay a poll tax to a state that supported slavery, and his going to live for two years beside Walden Pond.

In reality, of course, the physical action taken by Thoreau is wrapped up inextricably with his artistic treatment of it. The literal details of what he did Thoreau handled with all the freedom we should expect from the artist. His first book, *A Week on the Concord and Merrimack Rivers,* which came out in 1849, the same year as the essay "Civil Disobedience," purports to be an account of one brief river journey made by Thoreau and his brother John. Actually, Thoreau made at least two extensive journeys, selected from each to secure a satisfactory literary synthesis, and then added much new material to fill out his book. *Walden* too is far more than a diary of Thoreau's doings at the Pond. Thoreau again handled his materials with considerable freedom because he wanted to give his Concord neighbors a literary and homiletic work of art, not an exact transcription of two years in his life. In "Civil Disobedience" the detailed account of Thoreau's jailing occupies about one-fifth of the essay and acts as a nucleus for the rest, but even here where Thoreau says flatly, "This is the whole history of 'My Prisons,' " we have evidence that he is still not being literal. He has still distorted and interpreted for the sake of the impression on the reader. The salient fact is that through his art Thoreau has enormously extended the consequences of his action.

Thoreau's action in going to Walden is important because of its far-ranging influence, in various degrees, on many men. His action in going to jail in Concord is particularly important because of its influence on one other greater man than Thoreau.

Mohandas Gandhi was a middle-aged Hindu lawyer in South Africa when a friend gave him a volume of Thoreau's essays which included "Civil Disobedience." Gandhi had become a leader in the resistance of the Hindus in the Transvaal against mounting race prejudice and oppressive legislation. In 1906 the Transvaal government drafted an ordinance which was particularly strict. The English and the Boers joined to frame laws which would force the Hindus — men, women, and children — to register with the government, to be fingerprinted, to produce their certificates of registration on any policeman's demand, and in some cases to pay a £3 poll tax. The idea of nonviolent opposition to these measures had already occurred to Gandhi but early in 1907 he read Thoreau's compelling essay for the first time. His closest ally in the struggle was an Englishman, H. S. L. Polak, who helped Gandhi edit his newspaper *Indian Opinion.* Polak read Thoreau at the same time Gandhi did and testified years later, in a letter to the *New York Evening Post,* that both Gandhi and he were "enormously impressed by the confirmation of the rightness of the principle of passive resistance and civil disobedience, that had already been started against the objectionable laws." "It left a deep impression on me," Gandhi himself said of the essay. "I translated a portion for the readers of 'Indian Opinion' in South Africa, which I was then editing, and I made copious extracts for the English part of that paper. The essay seemed to be so convincing and truthful that I felt the need of knowing more of Thoreau."

Toward the end of 1907 *Indian Opinion* sponsored a prize contest on "The Ethics of Passive Resistance," with special reference to Thoreau's essay and Socrates' writings. Gandhi's readers were asked, in particular, to suggest a key word or slogan which would sum up their movement. The winning term was "Sadagraha," meaning "firmness in a good cause." Gandhi, however, exercised his editorial prerogative and changed it to "Satyagraha," meaning "truth-force" or "soul-force" and implying, according to Gandhi, "moral resistance without the use of physical force." He went on to include the idea of civil disobedience within "Satyagraha." " 'Satyagraha,' " he said, "is like a banyan tree with innumerable branches. Civil Disobedience is one such branch. . . . 'Satyagraha' largely appears to the public as Civil Disobedience."

The Hindu campaign moved dramatically along the lines that Gandhi had laid down and that Thoreau had advocated in his essay. Civil Disobedience succeeded in South Africa. Its victory was formally acknowledged in the Smuts-Gandhi agreement of 1914 and the Indians' Relief Bill of the same year, which combined to give the Hindus freedom from registration, poll tax, and special restrictions.

Then Gandhi returned to India and began his epic struggle there. He had been jailed three times in South Africa for insisting on what his conscience told him were his rights, and in India he was again jailed, once for almost two years, for opposing British control. Repeatedly he was supported in prison by Thoreau's example, and he kept "Civil Disobedience" by him in his cell.

Of all the things he did in India during the long years of the Civil Disobedience campaign, the most remarkable gesture was typical of Thoreau. It was his undertaking of the famous Salt March or Salt Satyagraha. Gandhi and a group of seventy-nine disciples marched from the Indian interior to the seaside town of Dandi. There on the morning of April 6, 1930, he picked up some salt, illegally, on the shore and in this way gave the signal for sympathizers all over the country to make their own salt for table use and break the government's monopoly. Gandhi and his band were arrested, and within a year and a half more than a hundred thousand Hindus were jailed.

Early in the next year Gandhi was released and invited to come to London for a conference on the grievances of the Indians. During part of the trip he was accompanied by Roger Baldwin, for many years director of the American Civil Liberties Union; Baldwin noticed that the only tract visible in Gandhi's train compartment was "Civil Disobedience." There is no need to labor the point. Certainly some part of the credit for Gandhi's success can be claimed for Henry Thoreau.

Significant as the essay "Civil Disobedience" has been overseas, its influence on Thoreau's own country has been limited. Only a relatively few Americans know of his going to jail for conscience's sake. For a long time it was doubtful that many of the Negro and white fighters against segregation invoked his example (though now they do). This action of his has been so little known, in fact, that even the most

sensitive protectors of American patriotism fail to assail him
for it. But his residence by Walden Pond is more widely
known, we may guess, than any other action by an American
writer. It is the gesture that everyone acknowledges as being
the essence of Thoreau.

Yet it seems to me that Thoreau's action in this case has
had an impact far beyond what normally would be expected.
A young intellectual goes off to live in the woods for a
while. What of it? The point is that his action fulfills a
great popular stereotype — the stereotype of "Withdrawal
and Return." If Arnold Toynbee — in his *Study of History*
— is to be believed, the fundamental characteristic of a myth
is that it represents not a fabrication but an attempt to
symbolize a truth that can be expressed by no other means.
Viewed this way, the story of the leader who must abandon
the world for a time to think things out and then returns
to better his people is basically true. He is Plato's philoso-
pher-king who goes from his fellows in the cave to visit the
outer light alone, dwells and matures there, and then comes
down into the dark cave again to teach his people what he
has learned. In the *Study of History* Toynbee gathers two
dozen instances of this stereotype, St. Benedict, Dante, and
Lenin among them. But the great exemplar that Toynbee
discusses is Jesus Christ. He withdraws into the wilderness,
according to the Gospels, and there after forty days and
nights of fasting is tempted by the devil. He is able to reject
the threefold temptation, and He returns from the wilderness with augmented divinity. He now has His mission: "to
preach, and to announce the kingdom of heaven."

Any application of the conception of "Withdrawal and
Return" to Henry Thoreau must be made with considerable
tact. It is a distortion of Thoreau to picture him as a
messianic leader. He was no Gandhi. Nevertheless, it can
at least be said that his withdrawal to Walden has become
remarkably well known not just because it was a dramatic
action in itself but also — and much more important —
because it fell on ground fertile and already prepared.

Following Toynbee and other proponents of myth as truth we can feel that the idea of Thoreau's action has satisfied a longing that people always have. It has fulfilled an unconscious folk expectation.

Moreover, Thoreau's action was performed with a peculiar felicity in its appeal to the American mind. It was exactly right in almost every circumstance — how right can be realized only on analysis. First of all, Thoreau might have withdrawn if not to a desert then to a granite mountain top. He chose instead to withdraw to the kind of place that would be most attractive to American culture. He went to stay in the woods, near a pond. The freshness and life-giving of the water and the shelter of trees combine to make a most pleasant picture. In it there is no Wordsworthian pantheism, nor does there need to be. To replace it, there is something much more generally satisfying. For Americans it is the group of feelings we have associated with the frontier ever since the early days of the republic — with the frontier conquered and adapted, with the "soft" frontier. The woods and waters are good to be near to. They are hallowed by American tradition and are a major asset to American primitivism. In addition, Thoreau built his cabin by himself. He showed enterprise in doing that, and later he showed self-sufficiency by farming and living off the land. Both things are also frontier characteristics still cherished as part of the American ethos. Thoreau's confident activity is clearly more congenial to his countrymen than contemplation in a desert cave.

The attractions of *Walden* are strong and deep, appealing to English readers as much as to American ones. Perhaps even more today, though not always in the same fashion. Both the English and the American public, it may be guessed, find the pull of "Withdrawal and Return" powerful. The two publics also find other things in *Walden* in common. But at least one attraction is modified for English readers and another has recently been added.

It is the appeal of the frontier, it may be hazarded, which is modified in England. The American reader is still more mobile, more apt to try for new frontiers himself than is the Englishman. But the vicarious interest in the frontier is strong in Britain and has long been. The exact nature of the interest cannot be defined but is easy to illustrate. It is the interest that continues to make *Robinson Crusoe* a popular book, that keeps the "Westerns" on British television. The relatively recent appeal has been created by the fact that to the Englishman social security from cradle to grave has become vitally important. Conservatives as well as Labourites support it; public-opinion polls show the mass of voters plainly in favor of it. Yet its very success and universality can be stifling. The individual is apt to feel caught in a net of regulation. As a consequence, he may long all the more for the chance to sit by Thoreau's cabin, in the clear air, with no one to tell him what to do — or to do anything for him even for his own good.

The other attractions of *Walden* are of a different order. We have been talking about what might be called Thoreau's horizontal appeals — that is, appeals to various groups of readers who are on about the same level. But there are also several different vertical appeals — that is, appeals to different levels of readers, in both countries.

In those terms, then, to the simplest beholder Thoreau is someone who threw off his responsibilities and went away to live in the woods for a time. To the mass of men he stands for an escape from the frustrations of dull jobs at dull desks or machines. The more that men are forced to breathe factory dust or repeat one small chore, the better a life at Walden looks to them. Thoreau stands for subtler things to some others; they study the implications of his action, finding their greatest stimulus in the ideas and values it illustrates. A few writers and critics enjoy most the carefully wrought, deceptive simplicity of Thoreau's style. But the best thing to do, perhaps, is to realize that the life and the literary work here go together, that *Walden* grew into a book beside Walden Pond, and that the essay "Civil Disobedience" and the night in the Concord jail are of a piece. As Thoreau himself once said, "Expression is the act of the whole man."

Whitman at Oxbridge

THE LANDSCAPE of American literature, as viewed from across the ocean, has rather a strange look. There are many reasons, some economic, some mechanical, some psychological. But whatever the reasons may be, to the English reader certain American writers are well and favorably known while others — to us equally talented perhaps — are not. At times the results are almost grotesque: a poor writer may become much more widely appreciated than a better one. I remember searching the shelves of the Bodleian one afternoon and discovering more volumes of verse by Ella Wheeler Wilcox than by any other nineteenth-century American poet. Bryant, Lowell, and Whittier were barely represented. Poe and Longfellow to be sure fared better. But the greatest American poet of the nineteenth century, Walt Whitman, could not come up to Mrs. Wilcox. On the other hand, even if the Bodleian fails to house as many volumes of Walt Whitman as we might wish, his popularity has long been great in England, and it promises to endure. Today Mrs. Wilcox is seen to be merely quaint and even the English disciples of Edgar Guest (who was born, by the way, in Britain's Birmingham) fail to buy her works.

The reasons for the renown of Whitman's verse are various. The belletristic ones — the beauty of the idiom, the bardic melody, the majestic rhythm — are, I believe, evident and incontestable. Literary critics have often discussed them. Those reasons are not the only ones, however, for cultural and social factors too play their part. One in particular seems to me worth pointing out. It is that Whitman fulfills the English stereotype of the American writer. It may be argued that if such a stereotype ever existed, it has long since been broken down by transatlantic travel and the easy influx of American books. I am convinced that the effect of all that is much over-estimated and that the stereotype remains, even at the universities and in most of the magazines. This is especially true for nineteenth-century writers. The English critic may very well have read the latest fiction by Faulkner but his grasp of our nineteenth-century literature is apt to be shaky. After all, up to a few years ago no English university made any provision for a systematic study of the American literature of the past.

At any rate it is, in terms of the stereotype, the American writer with a touch of the homespun to him who is most apt to be successful in the English market. He is supposed to write simply, vividly, and for everyone. That means that writers such as Whitman and Mark Twain, Thomas Wolfe and Robert Frost, are the best liked. (Young Southern writers are excused from writing simply as long as they write grimly.) The Whitmans, the Mark Twains conform to the English preconception. On the other hand, certain other American writers are apt to make the English reader uneasy because they do not quite fit. Although he may respect them he rarely relishes them. He enjoys Frost but slights Robinson. He reads Wolfe but ignores Edith Wharton. And he buys Whitman but not the American metaphysicals.

Whitman can be exceptionally stimulating to the English reader. England still maintains a classed society, and Whitman's chant of a thorough-going democracy is more of a novelty to English ears than most Englishmen would admit.

His strong, free lines with their sweep and affirmations are novel too; and Whitman's entire, generous scope is highly attractive to the English public. He looks larger than life, from any angle, and this to the overseas observer is both impressive and American.

Even though copies of *Leaves of Grass* may not crowd the shelves of the Bodleian or Cambridge's big University Library, even though the regional universities sometimes feel it unnecessary to buy much Whitman, he is in England to stay. Interest in him is substantial, as anyone can testify who listens to literary talk in the English universities.

The Sound of American Literature
a Century Ago

ALMOST at once after the new American nation was established a few voices were heard crying for an American literature. They demanded a poetry and prose unmarred, they said, by imitation of British models. As time went on, more voices joined in the cry. By the end of the first quarter of the nineteenth century the call had in a way been answered but not to anyone's complete satisfaction. We were grateful for Washington Irving but he was an international rather than a national figure; he had become a citizen of the world rather than of the American Republic of Letters. Among the novelists James Fenimore Cooper showed the most promise; among the poets William Cullen Bryant was outstanding. Nevertheless, this was still not enough for an American literature and the American critics of the time, such as they were, knew it. A chance remark in the *Edinburgh Review* by the Reverend Sydney Smith so perfectly expressed their feelings of inadequacy that it became embedded in the national consciousness. "Who reads an American book?" he had asked in derision. The answer was loud but hollow.

Yet something was happening by the 1830's which would give Sydney Smith answer enough. Another clergyman had appeared, an American this time, who would not only swell the chorus that called for American literature but would also help notably to provide it through his own writing. This was the Reverend Ralph Waldo Emerson of Boston and Concord, Massachusetts. By May 1836 he was planning a "sermon to literary men"; a little over a year later he delivered it as the Phi Beta Kappa address at the Harvard commencement. Its fame spread promptly and has continued to spread. Today it is known throughout the Western world as the essay on "The American Scholar." In it Emerson put all his exciting hopes. "Our day of dependence, our long apprenticeship to the learning of other lands, draws to a close," he announced. He urged the needs of the new democratic culture, "The millions that around us are rushing into life, cannot always be fed on the sere remains of foreign harvests." These needs must be met by independent American talent. The way to meet them was to take the common, even the vulgar, and raise it into literature by revealing its universal relations. The resulting literature would be bloodwarm, Emerson assured us, for it would comprehend and then transcend our common humanity. But we must look to ourselves; "We have listened too long to the courtly muses of Europe." He concluded with ringing optimism: "We will walk on our own feet; we will work with our own hands; we will speak our own minds."

It was no false dawn that Emerson heralded in "The American Scholar." Within ten years a truly American literature emerged. Emerson's own first books of essays were perhaps the most brilliant accomplishment. But Poe reached the height of his powers, as did Cooper; Longfellow published some of his most appealing poems; Melville's first novels came out; Hawthorne issued his fine short stories; and Lowell, Holmes, and Whittier each appeared in print. All this in ten years. A decade after "The American Scholar" Sydney Smith's remark was unthinkable. And by the time of the Civil War, American literature had won a place, if a modest one, in Western culture as a whole.

Out of the many elements which nourished this antebellum literature, from Emerson's exhortations to the spread of free schooling, I should like to concentrate on one. This one has, I believe, been unusually influential but largely unrecognized. I want to concentrate on the relation between the American public and the American writer in terms of the spoken word. I want to do it on two levels. Like Emerson I want to combine the practical with the Transcendental, the economic with the esthetic.

To explain, I must begin with a description of the American Lyceum. Like American literature its antecedents were English. In London during the 1820's George Birkbeck and Lord Brougham had pioneered in establishing what came to be called mechanics' institutions. These were associations of workmen who wanted to have some technical training. Their volunteer teachers and organizers were educated men who passed on something of their own special knowledge. The principal aim was to teach the workmen to do a better job. At the London institution which Birkbeck helped to found, courses of lectures were offered on chemistry, geometry, and hydrostatics (taught by Birkbeck himself), among other subjects. Almost from the beginning a lecture room, books, and simple scientific apparatus were provided. The London Mechanics Institution flourished from the day it opened. Others followed and prospered in other parts of Britain. By 1826 the mechanics' institute movement had spread to France and then across the Atlantic to America.

In America the movement was fortunate enough to find another Birkbeck. This time it was a Yale graduate with an interest both in teaching and science. His name was Josiah Holbrook and he was in his late thirties when somehow or other — we do not know exactly how — he came across the mechanics' institute idea. It had already attracted a little attention in the United States. Holbrook prepared a manifesto for the movement which he succeeded in placing in a magazine for teachers.

Most significant is the way the manifesto quietly reshapes the mechanics' institute to suit American culture. We no longer see an association where uneducated workers are taught by educated members of the middle class. Instead the keynote is mutual education. Every village or neighborhood will have a club in which the members teach one another. The doctor will discourse on medical science, the minister on moral philosophy, the lawyer on the rudiments of common law, and so forth. Still, the stress will be on applied science and the great bulk of the students will be young apprentices, mechanics, or clerks.

By the end of November 1826 Holbrook had organized the first society, in a town called Millbury in Massachusetts. Then he went about organizing others elsewhere. Soon he began calling his new societies "lyceums" rather than mechanics' institutes. *Lyceum* had a fine academic sound and was a large enough term to embrace more than mechanics and clerks.

Throughout the next decade Holbrook preached the gospel of the lyceum. He proved himself a genius at persuasion. Lecturing had always been a means of spreading knowledge, but through Holbrook's powers the system of voluntary education by lectures became an American institution. The American Lyceum became a notable part of antebellum culture. Holbrook appeared in villages, towns, and cities to tell his story. He was even allowed to address several state legislatures. He traveled as far from Massachusetts as Tennessee and South Carolina. He organized lyceums at local, state, and national levels, and before he was done he had projected a world lyceum. In addition to spreading his gospel by word of mouth, he put into print the most popular pamphlet on the advantages of the lyceum; it was the full-blown successor to his first brief manifesto

in the teachers' magazine. Emerson once said that an institution was the lengthened shadow of a man; he was right
for the lyceum and Josiah Holbrook.

As America developed and changed, so did the lyceum.
The mechanics' institute with its lectures and demonstrations, with its books and apparatus, became a vogue. The
clerks and mechanics gradually found themselves surrounded by a wide variety of fellow Americans; all sorts of
people were sitting next to them in the lecture hall. More
and more housewives appeared, often bringing with them
their husbands and older children. For many an elderly
person the lyceum was a boon. Farm families drove in to
swell the attendance. Ultimately the audience contained
almost a cross section of the population. With this broadening of the audience came a broadening of the local lyceum
policies, which showed itself both in the altered nature of
the lecturers and in their lectures.

The ideal of mutual education began to tarnish. The
change did not occur overnight, but it was striking nonetheless. The first lecturers were often the local minister and
doctor. What they had to say — or read — to their neighbors
and young men was soon exhausted, however. When the
next session of lectures came around, the program committee
began to look longingly at the minister from the neighbor-
ing town or the lively lawyer from thirty miles away.
Distance always lends attraction to a lecturer, and the
villagers, bored now by their local lights, listened readily
to the message of a stranger. As the lecture seasons began to
pass, some men acquired a reputation for being especially
able. They received more than their share of invitations and,
as time went on, even the occasional offer of a fee. As the
1820's became the thirties and forties, lecturing for a fee
developed and spread throughout the land with an inevitable logic. After a while some of the most popular lecturers realized that here was one way to make a living. Or
if not that, then to augment one. Lyceum lecturing could
be depended on to pay its share of debts and bills.

The lecturer began to turn professional or, more often, semiprofessional. As he turned, so did his subject. With the early emphasis on science and neighborly instruction now lost, a wide variety of new topics emerged. The most popular proved to be history, travel, and — to use a term of Emerson's — the conduct of life. "The Story of Mohammed," "Glaciers," "The Discovery of America by the Northmen," "Instinct," "The Practical Man," "Genius": these were among the new lecture titles. And as the subjects changed, so did their treatment. More lectures were read from manuscripts or else delivered with actor-like precision. The stress on learning grew less, the stress on entertainment grew more. Though the lyceum always kept a gloss of education on its proceedings, the truth is that the general tone of the lectures grew lighter. All too often the entertainer edged out the teacher. Yet there were always exceptions and some of them were noble ones. Not the least among them were several literary men. Emerson was the greatest; his company included Henry David Thoreau as well as a number of lesser authors. They kept the highest possible standards. They made it their principle to speak their truest thought, whether they were lecturing or writing. They raised their lyceum audience to the same plane as the reader of their books.

And now I come to my central point, which is that the American Lyceum did yeoman service for American literature. Its contributions ranged from the solidly tangible to the extremely tenuous but in sum total they were impressive. At the one extreme they were as tangible as a ten-dollar bill; at the other, as tenuous as the relation between a writer's turn of phrase and an audience's approving nod.

In effect, the lyceum paid American writers, and paid them rather well, to read the preliminary drafts of their writing to it. That was the most basic service. Again and again writers found that they could earn more money in fees from the lyceum than in royalties from their books. It was not till Emerson, for instance, was past seventy that he could count on a decent income from his writing. Before that if he had depended on his royalties he would have starved. Next, the lyceum augmented a writer's usual public by adding the people who had heard him speak. More persons recognized his name on the spine of his latest book. Finally, it gave him a testing ground for his new work. With an audience before him, he could see what went smoothly and well, what limped or failed. Emerson remarked in his journal that he often tried out a new lecture on an audience of villagers and that, through repeated readings, it was much improved when he delivered it in the city. "Poor men," he said, "they little know how different that lecture will be when it is given in New York, or is printed."

For one or two categories of writers it should be said at once that the lyceum meant little; for others it meant much. I have rarely seen records of American novelists reading their fiction. Melville, it is true, took his South Sea novels to the platform, but audiences found his manner distasteful and his content dull. Then too, he made the mistake of reading from already published works, unlike the successful lyceum lecturers, who read first and published afterward. Not the least of his difficulties was the fact that the genre itself remained disreputable. The novel was still suspected of being mere entertainment. Poetry, particularly when it had a moral or satirical point, was more highly regarded. Though many Americans failed to take poetry seriously, there are grounds for believing that it enjoyed a wider popularity a century ago than it does today. Or, to put it the other way around, the poet was less unpopular then than now. However, for the essayist the lyceum was the promised land and the essay flourished in America as it never has before or since. The informal personal essay was welcome, of course, but the informative or inspirational essay was even more in demand. When that was the evening's fare, the audience could go home feeling that it was the better for having listened. Then it could realize gratefully what Emerson meant in maintaining that the lyceum was his pulpit. For the travel writer and the historian, along with the essayist, the lyceum offered an ample field. The restless, curious Americans were eager to hear about foreign lands as well as about the far reaches of their own. They were equally fascinated by the past. With the intense patriotism of a new nation they heard with particular interest about American history. But they also came to hear about the rich past of Europe, from the time of Pericles down to the time of Napoleon.

Some writers within each category fared better than the rest of course. Most of the best known figures of those days are now forgotten. Who today remembers the essayists E. P. Whipple or G. W. Curtis, the moralists Orville Dewey or Starr King, the travelers Issac Hayes or Elisha Kent Kane? Who recalls the historians John Lord or Joel Headley, the poets Park Benjamin or J. G. Saxe? There are others, however, such as Bayard Taylor, who still receive a paragraph in histories of American literature, and a few at any rate, such as Thoreau, who have found worldwide fame.

Because much of what we have been saying is rather general, it might be well to look briefly at the relation of the lyceum to one specific writer, in this case Emerson himself. To a marked degree, he will illustrate for us the effects of the lyceum.

Emerson made an exemplary personal contribution to American belles lettres, a contribution which continues to be esteemed. In evidence, the latest selection I have seen of his writing came out only a few months ago. The lyceum's role in his life was surprisingly important. It began early and ended late. He read his first lecture in November 1833, when he was thirty. In harmony with the times it was on science but, as always for Emerson, science from a Transcendental point of view. His next two lectures were also on science. Then, however, travel made its appearance as a subject, and after it the sort of lecture which became one of Emerson's staples: the study of a great man with an inspirational inquiry about what made him great. Michelangelo was the first of many to be anatomized and apostrophized. By 1835, when he lectured on Michelangelo, Emerson was becoming established as a popular lecturer. He soon showed himself strong and independent enough to appear before lyceum audiences on his own terms, and they were glad to have him. In 1833 he had lectured only once; by 1836 he could lecture two dozen times a year, and more.

He wrote out his lectures and saved them carefully. As time went on and they accumulated, he rifled them with increasing freedom, drawing pages from them for new lectures and for books. The two books of essays which made Emerson's reputation as a writer were published in 1841 and 1844 respectively. The material for those striking works came chiefly from four series of lectures, the first of which was given in 1836–37 and the last in 1841–42. Paragraph after stirring paragraph, phrase after splendid phrase came from the lectures. First Emerson selected, then he assembled, and then he revised. The major flaw in the resulting essays was a certain lack of structure; this was a lack chargeable in part, though only in part, to his eclectic method. But otherwise the gains were considerable. The tone was heightened, the thought fortified.

Integral with these alterations was a certain shift in the point of view. The lecture had the audience full in front of it. There Emerson's syntax is informal, his examples are familiar, his address is direct. And his images are often homely. This is Emerson as nearly local as he can be. The printed essay, however, has a wider audience. It is addressed to man everywhere and, appropriately, to the individual man, to the man within, not the man without. The difference between lecture and essay is substantial. At the same time, the lecturing remains the basis for the printed prose.

After 1844 the lecturer and the essayist came closer and closer together. The new lectures gained steadily in stature. Emerson's need to revise them before publication lessened, once they had been tested on the lyceum. Consequently, for the next fifteen years he published his books with little revision. *Representative Men,* dated 1850, actually bears the subtitle *Seven Lectures.* If these books were not as consistently notable as the *Essays,* First and Second Series, they still contained some very fine things. And one volume, his *English Traits,* was as good over all as anybody could wish.

In three books, each printed before the Civil War, the essay and the perfected lecture are nearly one. They are the *Representative Men* and *English Traits* just mentioned and *The Conduct of Life. English Traits,* in its brilliant combination of candor and wit, its decent shrewdness and sympathy, is probably the best book written by an American on Victorian England. About the people Emerson says, for instance, "They have a wonderful heat in the pursuit of a public aim." About the land he says, "England is a garden," which is cliché enough, but he takes the curse off by adding in the next sentence "under an ash-colored sky." The chapters of *English Traits* were all proved first on the lecture platform.

Emerson began presenting *The Conduct of Life* to the public in 1851, first in the form of several single lectures and then as a course. As the 1850's went along, the struggle over slavery intensified; the whole weather of American life grew dark. Emerson's response in these lectures was neither to restate the unworldly Transcendentalism of his earlier years nor to preach a political sermon. Instead he took his first principles and applied them to a time of crisis. To his troubled hearers he showed an unexpected awareness of the power of evil, of the strong gods of force. But he maintained that by taking them calmly into account one could emerge with an idealism all the stronger for having been tempered by experience. By 1860, when he finally published *The Conduct of Life* in book form, his attitude was still firm and confident even though the Civil War was less than six months off. Carlyle, going through the book, could see no faltering; to him Emerson was now "more pungent, piercing," than ever. He was right: this was Emerson at his sagest both as a writer and lecturer.

After the Civil War was over, Emerson lost his mental vigor. His gift for selecting the best from his accumulated work slowly faded. Now when faced with the need to give a new lecture he could only leaf aimlessly through his piles of papers. Even when they reached print the postwar essays were structureless, or if they had any structure it was imposed by Emerson's assistants. Even in his prime Emerson's structure had been weak; now in his old age it was gone entirely. In other respects too the last lectures, like the last volumes, show a sad falling off. By the end of the 1870's Emerson was done. For forty years before that, however, the poet-prophet had stood out as the noblest figure on the lyceum and the greatest American essayist. Literary critics have often commented on his felicities, but he could also impress the ordinary listener. Here is what an average young woman in his audience one night in 1857 had to say about his performance, "One of the most beautiful and eloquent lectures I ever heard."

On the whole Emerson gave more to the lyceum than did any other writer. And the lyceum reciprocated, not only by letting him test his essays but also in a more material way: it paid him. During his best period he averaged fifty lecture dates a year. His fee varied from place to place, not surprisingly, but even as early as 1837 he was receiving ten or twenty dollars for a single appearance. And for a series of ten lectures in Boston in that year he netted $571.00. Boston and New York returned him the greatest profit, but otherwise the further he ranged the more he earned. As soon as rail transportation was established he traveled to the Midwest. He went reluctantly, mindful of cold, dirty inns, and tedious journeys; but he went and the result of each tour was a profit of $500.00 or so. Even when he was past sixty he still could produce a best-selling lecture such as "Social Aims." He delivered this one more than seventy times in five years and his fees for giving it exceeded $4,000.00.

It is some distance from Emerson to that thorny individualist Henry Thoreau. Yet he found the lyceum useful too. The important part it played in his literary process paralleled the part it played for Emerson. Thoreau summed up his own method of literary composition one day in the middle 1840's. "From all points of the compass," he explained, "from the earth beneath and the heavens above, have come these inspirations and been entered duly in the order of their arrival in the journal. Thereafter, when the time arrived, they were winnowed into lectures, and again, in due time, from lectures into essays." Some of the essays best known to us today made their first public appearance as lectures. One of them is his outspoken "Life without Principle," which commences, in fact, with a reference to lyceum lecturing. There Thoreau asserts that the lecturer should have perfect freedom to say what he thinks — and is under obligation to say it to the members of his audience. "They have sent for me, and engaged to pay for me, and I am determined that they shall have me, though I bore them beyond all precedent." His classic essay on "Walking" is much more genial but the marks of the lecture are equally plain. Thoreau opens this essay exactly like a lecture. "I wish to speak a word for Nature," he says and then continues in a firm, conversational tone. When the piece is printed the concessions he makes to the reader as opposed to the hearer are negligible. The most influential essay of them all, "Civil Disobedience," is another that started as a lecture.

Much of Thoreau's travel writing also passed through the stage of the lecture. Wherever he traveled he journalized and out of his journal he composed delightful accounts of visits to the Maine woods, to Cape Cod, and to Canada. Then he read parts of these accounts to the lyceum and subsequently turned them into essays which were collected into books published after his death. Of the two books published during his life, *A Week on the Concord and Merrimack Rivers* and *Walden, Walden* is of course much the more important. The *Week* is a unique American pastoral, however, deserving of greater attention than critics have given it. But it has its defects, and it is possible that if Thoreau had read more of it to audiences it would have developed into a better book. Its turgid passages might have been fewer, its narrative smoother. Yet it may well be that he lacked the opportunity to read it aloud. At any rate, we have only one record of his drawing on the *Week* for a lecture. On *Walden*, however, he drew ten times or more. Under such titles as "Life in the Woods," "White Beans and Walden Pond," and "History of Myself" he tested his thesis and polished his chapters. *Walden* still begins with its first, deceptively simple address to his neighbors about why he went away, and throughout the book he talks as directly to the reader as he ever talked to his hearers. There is little doubt that the lyceum affected Thoreau's writing in general, from the world-renowned *Walden* down to so obscure an essay as his "Sir Walter Raleigh." Thoreau's best biographer, H. S. Canby, was not exaggerating much when he asserted that "Nearly everything Thoreau wrote was originally conceived as a lecture."

It would be gratifying to report that Thoreau was enabled to make a living by the lyceum. The truth is otherwise. Though he lectured off and on for a fee and though he served his local lyceum in Concord faithfully, he never managed to earn as much as did a hundred mediocrities who are today forgotten. An occasional ten or twenty dollars would come to him, but there were seldom enough engagements to be of much help. During fifteen years or so of reading his manuscripts on the lyceum, Thoreau lectured about sixty times in all. His luck varied, but he was seldom adequately paid or much appreciated. A few times he fared well. For instance, at the request of Nathaniel Hawthorne, Thoreau read part of the first chapter of *Walden* to the Salem Lyceum for $20.00. He repeated the lecture in Portland and earned another $20.00. On the other hand, when he lectured in Danvers on his excursions to Cape Cod, he required only that his expenses be paid. He lectured about *Walden* in various other places for nothing. Part of his problem was that, more often than not, he lectured with a certain heaviness. "I judge the audience was stupid and did not appreciate him," someone wrote from Philadelphia; when Thoreau lectured in New Bedford, someone else observed judiciously, "I have heard several sensible people speak well of [his] lecture . . . but conclude it was not generally understood." Yet every now and then there was rapport. After Thoreau lectured to a Nantucket group in '54, he said with satisfaction, "I found them to be just the audience for me." Money was far from being everything to him and that was fortunate. It would be rash to guess at the amount of his income from the lyceum but safe to suppose it small. Nevertheless, income is relative, not absolute, and the lyceum was the only regular source of money for Thoreau the writer. He did make some profit from his lecturing, while he lost money on his writing. Regardless of how well he fared, he supported the lyceum gladly. "The one hundred and twenty-five dollars," he noted in his journal, "which is subscribed in [Concord] every winter for a Lyceum is better spent than any other equal sum."

The heyday of the lyceum was before the Civil War, and so we have been focussing on antebellum literature. Yet we should remember that lecturing as such continued after the war. It still attracted some authors — and paid them variously. For one of America's greatest postwar writers it afforded a happy home. This was Mark Twain. His deft wit and raucous humor enchanted a generation of his countrymen. He played the clown but added the satirist whenever he could. In the rather gross culture of postwar America he appeared, for years, at ease on the platform.

Among the prewar writers, after we have cited Emerson and Thoreau, there was no one of Mark Twain's magnitude who found much in the lyceum. Melville bungled his lecture tours. Hawthorne felt too shy to lecture, consenting instead to serve as secretary of the Salem Lyceum. Oliver Wendell

Holmes was too casual. Widely known for his wit, he made many platform appearances but did not regard his lectures as a stage in his literature. Instead he called them his "fireworks" and declined to put them in print. Lowell lectured a little, so did Poe; but the lyceum meant nothing to them as authors. Once we leave writers of the first rank, however, we find many who used the lyceum in their work. They provided the substructure of our new American literature. Bayard Taylor, the gaudy prince of travel writers, was their chief exemplar.

For Taylor the lecture still had much the same relation to the printed book that it did for Emerson and Thoreau, though he was younger than they and came to the lyceum later. When he got there he proved to be a phenomenal success. Taylor lectured on life in Japan, in India, in the frozen North, in Russia. He often dressed up in native costume; the result was magnificent enough to cause any female to sigh. Even when he ventured to make a social criticism of his fellow citizens, he remained popular. Lecturing let him live in state. At his best he could clear $5,000.00 a season and pay for the luxuries he loved; yet he found the lyceum a bore. One rainy night as he sat in a dismal little room in Niles, Michigan, while waiting to lecture, he described his trials:

> Comes a rapping, tapping
>   At my chamber door,
> But, unlike Poe's raven
>   Crying "Evermore!"
> 'Tis the new Committee
>   Any one can tell,
> Come to see the lecturer:
>   "Hope you're very well!" . . .
>
> Finally they leave me,
>   I'm alone, again, . . .
> When again a rapping —
>   (Hope you will not laugh) —

School-boy with an album
　　Wants an autograph!
Next a solemn gentleman,
　　Unctuous of face:
"What's your real opinion
　　Of the human race?"

Thicker than the deluge
　　Pouring out-of-doors,
Comes a rain of questions
　　From the crowd of bores;
"Where's your lady staying?"
　　"What's your baby's name?"
"Do you find Society
　　Everywhere the same?"
"Where are you going to travel?"
　　"What's your future plan?"
"Do you think you'll ever
　　Be a settled man?" . . .

Oh, I want to be
Where, for information,
　　No one comes to me.
I'd be a bloody whaler
　　Among the Kurile Isles,
A tearing, swearing sailor
　　Whom the Captain riles,
Anything but Taylor
　　Lecturing in Niles!

There is no need to labor the point that Bayard Taylor
lectured because he was paid for it. The urge to share the
very best of his thought, the urge which moved Emerson
and Thoreau so much, signified little to him. He was the
professional performer. He was also the most widely read
of our travel writers, however, and to this day occupies a
niche in American letters.

Of the writers on literature H. N. Hudson was representative. He read his essays on Shakespeare throughout the country, and in their printed form still called them lectures. His critical principles were simple ones, obviously appealing to his audiences. He affirmed that literature was intended to teach, that the moral lessons in Shakespeare's plays were manifold. "The peculiar excellence of the poet's works is in their unequalled ability to instruct us in the things about us and to strengthen us for the duties that lie before us." He couched his lectures in what his audiences no doubt believed to be literary language. They heard such sentences as, "It was out of this dark, pestiferous, and lethiferous imbroglio of earth and heaven, of dirt and divinity, that the myriad-minded genius of England was to create the bright, breathing, blossoming world of a national drama." To his impressible auditors Hudson was more than a handmaiden to literature; he was literature itself.

The occasional poets who read to the lyceum wrote as a rule in a debased imitation of neoclassical style. They were given to satire and the heroic couplet. To teach by amusing was their most obvious aim. Before E. P. Whipple began writing essays he produced a poem which was a success from the first time he read it in public. Summing up the appeal not only of this poem but its whole school of verse, the Boston *Transcript* said it was "full of playful humor, lively sallies, and satirical hits in which [he] cut up and used up, with the skill of an old master, the numerous humbugs and abstractions which are emptying the pockets and turning the heads of so many people of the present generation." Park Benjamin and J. G. Saxe became the leaders of this school in which Whipple was a prize scholar. Benjamin's most popular satire is called "The Age of Gold." Here are four typical lines from it:

> Few marvels now the busy mind engage
> In this gold-seeking, gold-discovering age,
> When Love himself forsakes his bowers for mines
> And all our firesides turn to Mammon's shrines.

This was second-rate Dryden, it is true, but better than nothing at all. It may indeed have instructed audiences as well as amused them. After the lyceum disappeared so did the systematic public reading of verse. A poet or two still went bravely about, chanting lyrics to little groups, but the fairly substantial support which the lyceum had given was gone. Little poetry, even of a satirical and entertaining kind, would hereafter be heard from the lecture platform.

During the thirty years the lyceum existed, it was of course only one of many factors shaping American literature. But its effects were far-reaching. At its worst it persuaded an author to simplify his subject and cheapen his approach. It pressed him to pander to its own likes and dislikes — even Emerson had to warn himself once or twice against doing that. At its best it provided a continuing dialogue between audience and author which was inspiring to both. As he read his first drafts to his audiences, he could see what was effective, what was not. Popular taste and the literary artist met and agreed. The rough essay, for example, developed into a work of accumulated, tested excellences. In the process an American literature developed which was not only American in the simple sense of being by Americans but also American in responding to American ideas and attitudes. This was explicitly native literature in which native audiences had played their part.

I myself feel that there is almost a mystique about an audience, even more perhaps a century ago when we read less but listened longer. The author found, I am sure, that the effect of a hundred persons in front of him was tonic. Here was no Gentle Reader in the abstract but a solid group of his fellows. The very fact of the group had its significance, for an audience is more than a number of individuals; the whole is greater than the sum of the parts. The situation demanded that the writer give his best, not his second best. Certainly there were exceptions. But as a rule the experience of the lecture proved effective. It gave the writer a chance to test his sensitivities, to try out his intuitions. The human voice itself, through its odd electricity, allowed a close communion with the audience. That voice too, through its extraordinary command of nuance and appeal, made for a more exact communication of meaning than the printed word.

Sound was indeed important. Thoreau among others knew it well: when he wrote *Walden* he devoted a whole chapter to it. Reading to the audience trained an author's ear. No writer worth his salt would keep a raucous phrase or ugly rhythm after a hundred auditors had heard it. As the lecture season progressed, as the writers read again and again, cadence and measure improved. The sound of American literature grew clear and at times melodious. And I am convinced that it was heard far more widely than it would have been without the American Lyceum.

Hawthorne's *Fanshawe:*
the Promising of Greatness

WHEN Hawthorne published his anonymous first novel in
1828, he followed the fashion of the time and prefixed a
motto. It was a modest one, from Southey. "Wilt thou go on
with me?" it asked prospective readers. Few did, as it turned
out; few have, even to this day. Those who leafed through
the little volume found a moderately unconventional plot.
In its central action a young scholar at Harley College
named Fanshawe was attracted to a comely girl staying in
the house of the college president. His rival was a fellow
student, Edward Walcott. Fanshawe, however, was lucky
enough to rescue the girl after the villain of the book had
kidnapped her. Though she gratefully offered to marry Fanshawe he refused, with regret, because he knew their views
of life were opposed to one another. He soon died and she
married Walcott.

When the book appeared it was almost ignored by the
critics as well as by everyone else. They later — as Hawthorne's reputation increased — glanced at it only to dismiss
it. "Destitute of any brilliant markings of [Hawthorne's]
genius" was the way George Edward Woodberry summed it
up many years ago. "Barely tolerable" was what Mark Van

Doren labeled it in our day. As a matter of fact, the nearest thing to praise it normally receives is a lefthanded compliment like that of F. P. Stearns when he wondered that the sensationalism of the plot had not caused the book to be in greater demand. He observed as a good Victorian:

One would suppose that [*Fanshawe's*] faults would have helped to make it popular, for portions of it are so exciting as to border on the sensational. It may be affirmed that when a novel becomes so exciting that we wish to turn over the pages and anticipate the conclusion, either the action of the story is too heated or its incidents are too highly colored.

By now the elements that go to make up *Fanshawe* have been fairly well identified and separated by students in the field. Librarian George T. Little of Bowdoin College, among them, pointed out as early as the turn of the century that Hawthorne's Harley College bore many specific resemblances to the Bowdoin Hawthorne knew. Mr. Little noted similarities of setting — the trout pool, the old inn, the president's garden; as well as of character and event — Dr. Melmoth anticipated in Bowdoin's Presidents Allen and Appleton, Gorham Deane, second scholar of Hawthorne's class, dying of scholarship and consumption like Fanshawe. P. E. Burnham in "Hawthorne's *Fanshawe* and Bowdoin College" has done more recent and more comprehensive work in the same connection. Another scholar has studied Hawthorne's wide reading among Sir Walter Scott's romances and has commented on the general influence of Scott on characterization and plotting in *Fanshawe*. Still another has discovered in C. R. Maturin's Gothic *Melmoth the Wanderer* the specific source for Hawthorne's plot and three of his major characters. The portion of Maturin's book called the "Tale of the Indians" apparently provided Hawthorne with some of the characteristics of Fanshawe himself, of the villain Butler, and of the heroine Ellen Langton; it also furnished in Melmoth's temporary renunciation of his beloved a suggestion of Fanshawe's self-denial in regard to Ellen.

This is the way that the components of Hawthorne's book have been laid bare. The relative ease with which scholars have been able to analyze *Fanshawe* betrays the simplicity of the volume. The very type of scholarship — capable though it is — that *Fanshawe* has attracted makes the book seem all the more negligible. The demonstrations in the researches on *Fanshawe* just cited are successful ones, and their success is apt to make the reader think even less of the volume than he has before.

There are other faults to be charged against young Hawthorne besides his failure to transform his sources. These ought in fairness to be considered before analyzing the merits of his book. Most of the faults he shares with the great majority of novelists who composed when he did. Not the least flaw is the stilted and melodramatic character of much of the writing. *Fanshawe* is in fact a melodrama and might well have been made into a successful and commonplace stage production. The dialogue has the precise flavor of its period. For instance, soon after fair Ellen has let Butler persuade her to leave with him, her face gives away her regret. The scene between them is complete with stage directions:

"Do you repent so soon?" he inquired. "We have a weary way before us. Faint not ere we have well entered upon it."
"I have left dear friends behind me, and am going I know not whither," replied Ellen tremblingly.
"You have a faithful guide;" he observed, turning away his head, and speaking in the tone of one who endeavours to smother a laugh.

The best example in the book is found a few pages later. Butler by this time has brought Ellen to a cave in the woods and her alarm has been increasing steadily. They are completely alone and Butler tells Ellen harshly that she may shriek if she wishes. No one will hear her.

"There is — there is one," exclaimed Ellen, shuddering and affrighted at the fearful meaning of his countenance. "He is here — He is there." And she pointed to heaven.

"It may be so, dearest," he replied. "But if there be an ear that hears, and an eye that sees all the evil of the earth, yet the arm is slow to avenge. Else why do I stand before you, a living man?"

"His vengeance may be delayed for a time, but not forever," she answered. . . .

"You say true, lovely Ellen; and I have done enough, ere now, to insure its heaviest weight. There is a pass, when evil deeds can add nothing to guilt, nor good ones take anything from it."

"Think of your mother, — of her sorrow through life, and perhaps even after death," Ellen began to say. But as she spoke these words, the expression of his face was changed, becoming suddenly so dark and fiend-like, that she clasped her hands and fell on her knees before him.

"I have thought of my mother," he replied, speaking very low, and putting his face close to hers.

Yet even Ellen's perfectly melodramatic posture of supplication is given some novelty, and dignity, by the way Hawthorne states the problem of evil in the lines she and Butler speak. Nevertheless, most of the conversation is as ornate as scrollwork.

The action, too, in *Fanshawe* is often melodramatic. As a matter of fact, there are several scenes here that were standard on the stage. The villain at the bedside of his dying mother, the pursuit of the abducted heroine, the hen-pecked husband rated by his wife, the fight on the cliff — these were standard fare; and *Fanshawe* has every one.

What then is good in this apprentice piece of Hawthorne's? The answer, perhaps, is: not a great deal but more than might be expected. Furthermore, the contribution lies exactly where critics of *Fanshawe* are apt to find Hawthorne deficient. It lies, I think, in the field of character analysis. This is the place where the general charge of lack of literary merit that is usually leveled at *Fanshawe* can be qualified.

The main character in *Fanshawe* is Nathaniel Hawthorne.

It is true that his classmate, studious Gorham Deane, may have furnished the suggestion for the figure of Fanshawe and that Hawthorne himself was in reality lively and convivial enough to be fined by the faculty for drinking at the old inn. Yet, if the character of the aloof Fanshawe is not Hawthorne at college, it is surely Hawthorne after college — Hawthorne writing by himself, taking his meals alone, studying and composing almost completely without encouragement. He describes Fanshawe returning to his chamber and books after his first meeting with Ellen:

[Fanshawe] called up in review the years, that, even at his early age, he had spent in solitary study, — in conversation with the dead, — while he had scorned to mingle with the living world, or to be actuated by any of its motives. He asked himself, to what purpose was all this destructive labor, and where was the happiness of superior knowledge? He had climbed but a few steps of a ladder that reached to infinity; — he had thrown away his life in discovering, that, after a thousand such lives, he should still know comparatively nothing. He even looked forward with dread . . . to the eternity of improvement that lay before him. It seemed now a weary way . . . and at the moment he would have preferred the dreamless sleep of the brutes.

In this passage Hawthorne makes the earliest announcement of one of his greatest themes: that man must not cut himself off from man. That is the unforgivable sin. Even when committed for the sake of knowledge of the great intellectual past, it will bring deathlike despair with it. The emotions stirred by the sight of Ellen make Fanshawe realize this. One scholar has asserted that Ellen is merely a shadowy composite of the Waverley heroines. Here at least she is much more than that; she is a symbol, a symbol of the world that Fanshawe and Hawthorne are both renouncing. Here Hawthorne is able to add depth to the characterization of Fanshawe through the reflection of his own inner struggles.

Many an author has written out his youthful personal problems precisely as Hawthorne does. Traditionally it is on such stuff that first novels are made, for first novels are, more often than not, ones of character and adjustment. In spite of its heavy drapings of incident *Fanshawe* is such a novel. It deals with the choice of life. Fanshawe testifies to his stature by the way in which, for the sake of the ultimate happiness of the others concerned, he makes the necessary choice. He can do that because of his power — or Hawthorne's — of self-analysis. The book rises to a considerable height when Fanshawe surveys himself, and Hawthorne. Then he displays a cold, even appraisal of himself that is rare in literature and doubtless still rarer in life. The temptation to accept Ellen's grateful love is strong enough to move Fanshawe to tears as he rejects it. He knows what will happen if he isolates himself from man and the common daily concerns of mankind. Yet he knows inevitably that he must live by himself. Hawthorne says of Fanshawe, in the one passage that almost all critics have quoted, that he

had read [Ellen's] character with accuracy, and had seen how fit she was to love, and to be loved by a man who could find his happiness in the common occupation of the world; and Fanshawe never deceived himself so far, as to suppose that this would be the case with him.

Ellen Langton and the pleasant young man she finally marries, Edward Walcott, are both good people in a simple, normal way; and Hawthorne wastes little analysis on them. They are the average and he is not much interested in the average. Fanshawe of course and Butler, also, claim his attention. He spends considerable time in studying the reasons for their conduct and personalities. In Hawthorne's final analysis of Butler, after he has fallen to his death from the cliff, there is the same even, balanced statement that distinguishes Hawthorne's study of Fanshawe. Butler, says Hawthorne in effect, was a wicked man but he was likewise an unfortunate one; his was not a simple case.

A harsh father, and his own untameable disposition, had driven him from home in his boyhood. . . . After two years of wandering, when in a foreign country and in circumstances of utmost need, he attracted the notice of Mr. Langton [Ellen's father]. The merchant took his young countryman under his protection, afforded him advantages of education, and, as his capacity was above mediocrity, gradually trusted him in many affairs of importance. During this period, there was no evidence of dishonesty on his part. On the contrary, he manifested a zeal for Mr. Langton's interest, and a respect for his person, that proved his strong sense of the benefits he had received.

So far, then, nothing more could be asked of Butler.

But he unfortunately fell into certain youthful indiscretions, which, if not entirely pardonable, might have been palliated by many considerations, that would have occurred to a merciful man. Mr. Langton's justice, however, was seldom tempered by mercy; and on this occasion, he shut the door of repentance against his erring protégé, and left him in a situation not less desperate, than that from which he had relieved him. The goodness and the nobleness, of which his heart was not destitute, turned, from that time, wholly to evil, and he became irrecoverably ruined and irreclaimably depraved.

There is no touch of Calvinism in Hawthorne's early view of evil. Circumstances change and persons change in accordance with them. Their actions are not foreordained. As a consequence, Hawthorne's best characters are not static nor are they stereotyped. Often when writing about them he will bring the alterations caused by the passing of time to the reader's attention. Butler changes, it is worth noticing, both before *Fanshawe* opens and afterward. Fanshawe himself changes and so does Ellen. The alteration in Ellen, however, and Walcott is not marked, for both are ordinary characters. Nevertheless, Hawthorne makes the reader aware of it. Sometimes he is so concerned with the explanation of change in character that he not only describes the past development but also predicts lines of change for the future. This is true particularly for Fanshawe, but even Walcott is so analyzed when he is first presented to the reader. "His features," Hawthorne writes, "were handsome, and promised to be manly and dignified, when they should cease to be youthful." This is not a trivial instance in spite of its brevity: how many novelists of that time or today will see anything but eternal youth for their heroes? Hawthorne's opening comment on Fanshawe's appearance is raised above the commonplace by the same concern with the effect of time. "There was a nobleness on [Fanshawe's] high forehead, which time would have deepened into majesty; and all his features were formed with a strength and boldness, of which the paleness, produced by study and confinement, could not deprive them." Here is the effect of the past and the prediction of the future.

Even when Hawthorne winds up his story he is able to dignify the stale and traditional happy ending for the lovers by forecasting in it the effect of change. The pair were to be uncommonly happy but Walcott was to alter, to lose whatever pretensions to a career he might earlier have cherished. "Ellen's gentle, almost imperceptible, but powerful influence, drew her husband away from the passions and pursuits that would have interfered with domestic felicity; and he never regretted the worldly distinction of which she thus deprived him."

However, Walcott throughout most of the book is a wax figure and Hawthorne gives him the scant notice one would anticipate. Several of the minor characters are much stronger and better realized. They show a literary promise that he does not. Hugh Crombie, the inn-keeper, is by no means a simple or typical figure. He responds to his early experiences by changing, knocks about in the world, comes home to quiet down, and in the end marries for comfort. He is not presented unsympathetically. Hawthorne spends more time on Crombie than the story demands, and his characterization becomes almost a virtuoso piece. Crombie is seen to run the gamut from poet to pirate and back, with unexpected inner consistency. He is a full-dress figure, but even when a character appears only once Hawthorne may be able to etch his outline in the reader's mind. For example, although that fat haunter of death-beds, the "follower of funerals," the hedge-priest, takes up only a page, he is memorably drawn. And most readers will not forget "Dolly," the perfectly ugly but good-natured college chambermaid.

Hawthorne's essential devotion to character — and, to a lesser extent in this first book, to theme — at the expense of plot is an indication of his promise as a writer. On the surface, *Fanshawe* is a novel of accelerating and sensational action. Underneath it is a study of personality, and the very choice of title, *Fanshawe*, is in point. Furthermore, Hawthorne is aware of the theme of his novel; and he is always ready to sacrifice plot for the benefit either of character or idea. An excellent example is found near the end of the novel. At the very moment Butler is menacing Ellen at the cave, a rock from the cliff above falls near them. Fanshawe, coming to the rescue, has thrown it. Butler looks up and sees him on top of the crag and mutters "through his closed teeth," " 'By Heaven, I will cast him down at her feet!' " He starts to climb the cliff to get at the slender Fanshawe. Now here Hawthorne is faced by a pretty literary problem. When Butler reaches the top of the cliff and grapples with Fanshawe, one of the two men must win, dramatically. Fanshawe has once before stood off Butler by the sheer power of his mesmeric eye but twice would be too much. In any physical fight the scholar would have normally no chance against his enraged and sturdy opponent. To have Fanshawe win would be thoroughly unrealistic; to have him lose would upset the entire moral structure of the novel. What does Hawthorne do? He vitiates his plot by a spectacular coincidence:

When within a few feet of the summit, the adventurer grasped at a twig, too slenderly rooted to sustain his weight. It gave way in his hand, and he fell backward down the precipice. His head struck against the less perpendicular part of the rock, whence the body rolled heavily down. . . . There was no life left in him.

The probabilities of plot have been violated but character and theme have stayed secure.

The melodrama in *Fanshawe* must be admitted. So must

the literary and historical derivations. Nevertheless, Hawthorne's greatness is foreshadowed through his superior handling of character. The best in *Fanshawe* lies in its characters, and the most memorable character is Hawthorne himself. By way of Fanshawe, Hawthorne poses his own great personal problem and suggests a bitter answer. Hawthorne shows how Fanshawe must choose either a lonely scholar's life or, through force of love for Ellen, a "common occupation." Fanshawe decides in favor of his books — he sees ultimately that it is the only thing he can do — and yet in so doing he commits the unforgivable sin of isolating himself from mankind. Either way he is lost. There is no benign choice in his dilemma and only one way to solve this conflict permanently. Hawthorne himself was not willing to take this way nor in the long run did he need to. But for Fanshawe he could produce the necessary solution: death.

Thoreau's Young Ideas

THE TERROR and tumult in the world today furnish an oblique tribute to the power of ideas. Who would question the cliché which calls the present conflict "a battle for men's minds"? At least two of the ideas of one of America's great writers are as vital as any. Thoreau's doctrine of civil disobedience influenced Gandhi and India yesterday; today by way of Gandhi if not of Thoreau it makes a potent weapon for the African fighting against *apartheid,* for the American struggling against a subtler segregation. And Thoreau's passionate anti-materialism seems to win more converts all the time even if it never seems to win enough.

To comprehend these and other ideas of Henry Thoreau would appear to be sufficiently important to justify a score of studies. There have been only a handful, however, and they have concentrated on his mature works, his far-famed prose. This is proper except that in doing so they have neglected the origins of his thought and particularly the origins as seen in his poetry. When Thoreau was young he thought of himself as a poet. For about ten years — from perhaps 1837 to 1847 — he confided some of the most significant of his early views to poetry rather than to prose.

95

Much of this poetry lacks beauty and grace, so it is understandable that students of Thoreau's writing have hurried past it. But no one interested in Thoreau's ideas has ever stopped to examine them in the poetry as a whole. Surely an examination is overdue.

We ought to begin, however, with a caution. We cannot expect to find a poet who develops his views systematically. "Metaphysics was his aversion," his friend Ellery Channing noted, and by metaphysics he meant systematic philosophy. Thoreau's philosophy plainly has its gaps and omissions. Still, it has a large exactness even though it lacks a small. Years after Thoreau was done as a poet, he acquired the small exactness. He measured the snows in Concord fields. He drew up tables of plants he had seen. But the wider vision was gone.

The prime philosophic term for him is still Transcendentalist. The defining of Transcendentalism has been often and variously attempted. But I believe it will bear mentioning again. This much can be said. It is a way of knowing and a parallel way of being. The Transcendentalist acknowledges that through his five senses he knows the material world. This is tuition. But there is another and finer way of knowing, intuition, which spontaneously teaches him from within. It tells him of a spiritual world. So far as being is concerned, the Transcendentalist recognizes the reality of the material world and also asserts the reality of the spiritual world. He is a dualist but a dualist who yearns to be a monistic idealist, for he believes that the reality of spirit or idea transcends the reality of matter. The Transcendental way of knowing and way of being fuse when the individual, in a mystic experience, merges with God; when the individual soul unites with the Over-Soul.

All this is found in Emerson and Emerson greatly influenced his young friend Thoreau. Yet even in his early twenties Thoreau took only the ideas which appealed to him. For all the impression that these thoughts of Emerson made they are not simply echoed in Thoreau's poems. In point,

Emerson's stirring affirmation of knowledge beyond sense won Thoreau's agreement but never became his preoccupation. The woods and fields (and man) were, if not more important to him, more immediate to observe. Only in a handful of poems, and mainly in "Inspiration," did Thoreau write of the knowledge beyond sense. In "Inspiration" he is concerned, furthermore, not only with the knowledge beyond sense but also with how to achieve it. The title of the poem is particularly significant. In "Inspiration's" rough, metaphorical quatrains Thoreau tells us that material reality has its own virtue but that the God of intuition will raise us — if we will only allow him — to a spiritual reality of indescribable beauty:

> Always the general show of things
>   Floats in review before my mind,
> And such true love and reverence brings,
>   That sometimes I forget that I am blind.
>
> But now there comes unsought, unseen,
>   Some clear, divine electuary,
> And I who had but sensual been,
>   Grow sensible, and as God is, am wary.
>
> I hearing get who had but ears,
>   And sight, who had but eyes before,
> I moments live who lived but years,
>   And truth discern who knew but learning's lore.
>
> I hear beyond the range of sound,
>   I see beyond the range of sight,
> New earths and skies and seas around,
>   And in my day the sun doth pale his light.

"Inspiration" is justly Thoreau's most famous assertion of Transcendental epistemology. Emerson gave it an enthusiastic approval. It is the more outstanding as an expression of Thoreau's thought because of the attention he himself paid to it. He revised and refined it over a long period of time. He felt it important enough to quote from in half a dozen places in the *Week*. Its measured tone adds to its strength of statement. The images do not cohere but the mental narrative holds the poem together and the philosophy is bold.

All the same, the boldness is not — as far as Thoreau is concerned — absolute. Transcendental knowledge comes when the individual rises out of himself and merges with the godhead. Then he knows the deity. Then he reaches the ultimate reality. But the mystic union, the absolute experience of Crashaw, for instance, who died and loved his death and died again, was foreign to Thoreau. He was even less of a mystic than Emerson and all his life kept a tough, grainy realism. Thoreau was, as a matter of fact, a dualist who became almost a materialist. He never could attain complete rapport with any Over-Soul. Even the poems most marked with Transcendental yearning show, on examination, a guarded statement. Thoreau never says he achieves mystic union. He says that he would like to or that he dreamed he had. In his closest approach to a mystic state, he does not have the strong literalness of the most intense mystics. In his poem "The Bluebirds" he rhapsodizes on how he feels at the beautiful time in spring when the bluebirds return. He is, he says, transported. He rises far above the material world and yet he still does not say that "the earth *was* all below" but rather that he *felt* that the earth was all below. No matter how near to ecstasy, he still observed himself. Indeed, he realized that he was doing so, and made it part of his poetics. The poet, he said, must be the observer of his moods.

As a matter of fact, Thoreau saw no real Over-Soul to merge with. The deity he substituted — when he substituted any — was an ambiguous one. His god was a Janus. It presented two appearances in his verse. The first face was that of a god in his own right, God as such. The few times when He appears, He is exhorted rather than adored. Even the god of the poem "Inspiration" is also the "heavenly" "Muse" and thus is demeaned by being useful. The second face was that of god-in-nature. He is the "God who seasons thus the year, And sometimes kindly slants his rays." Such a god is a divine force which Thoreau never tried to define exactly. But the god reveals himself, at least in part, under the guise of "Nature." This is his pleasant manifestation and it is the only one dwelt on. Thoreau could say that "God . . . *sometimes* kindly slants his rays" but he refused to describe any times when the rays were not kindly slanted. Even when the sun fails to shine in the verse, the rain is gay and welcome. The most benevolent aspect of all appears in the demi-deity Thoreau calls "Alma Natura." She is spoken of, in accordance with custom, as feminine. But feminine or masculine, pleasant or unpleasant, immanent or manifest, nature seldom received complete submission from Thoreau. Still, there were times when he longed to submerge in her.

God-in-nature was, early in Thoreau's career as a poet, occasionally mentioned. In such a poem as "The Thaw," he describes his desire for union with nature. Later, though, even this view of deity began to disappear. It lost its identity in the concept of nature as mainly material — uplifting, certainly, and companionable but still material. The pantheism became, in sum, so diffused that it was almost unfelt. Nature as god, by the late 1840's, was being subdued by nature as field and wood. Thoreau was forgetting the deity for the botanical detail but the detail was only beginning to show up in the poetry when Thoreau stopped writing it.

Moreover, even when nature seemed to Thoreau a worshipful deity he still at times yearned for something else, something human but also touched with the spark of divinity:

> I walk in nature still alone
>   And know no one,
> Discern no lineament nor feature
>   Of any creature.

> Though all the firmament
>   Is o'er me bent,
> Yet still I miss the grace
>   Of an intelligent and kindred face.

He misses the man who can be his true friend. That man, in Thoreau's theory, will be the bridge between Thoreau's metaphysics, theology, and ethics. For he will have a reality comparable to the spirit behind nature but nobler than nature because godlike. He will be a manifestation of divinity in whom Thoreau will be readier to believe than in divinity itself. And he will set a standard of inner and outer conduct — conduct in thought, word, and deed — of transcendental strictness. His relation with Thoreau will be one of absolute trust; as Thoreau promises:

> We'll one another treat like gods,
> And all the faith we have
> In virtue and in truth, bestow
> On either, and suspicion leave
> To gods below.

The trouble with such trust, as Thoreau discovered, lay in the fact that it was not for this world. He could find no friend who met his expectations. In the face of this, Thoreau did not lower his standards. Instead he demanded the right to tell his friend when he failed to meet them. Upon his friend's failure to rise to Thoreau's superhuman expectations he reacted with perfect ambivalence, crying out once, for instance:

> O, I hate thee with a hate
> That would fain annihilate;
> Yet sometimes against my will,
> My dear friend, I love thee still.

He did continue to love, perhaps, but it must have been hard for the friend to see it since Thoreau also believed in restraint of his emotion. As he said in another poem he and his friend should be like two oaks, separate above ground but with their roots intertwined.

With restraint and sincerity as its main tenets, Thoreau's philosophy of (male) friendship is an outstanding feature of his thought in verse. Not so prominent but clearly related to the theory of friendship is his theory of love. Simply, love is Transcendental friendship. It has no taint of the sensual — as a rule no touch even of the sensible. And it subsists primarily, by implication, between man and man. Love too is undemonstrative, outwardly aloof, long enduring, deeply mental. Because of its silence and strength, it is often impossible to distinguish from friendship. This is the more true because Thoreau often used the language of love in describing friendship. The long contention of critics, when they disagreed as to whether "Lately, alas, I knew a gentle boy" was addressed to a young lady or really to a boy, is the best evidence.

It is true that Thoreau did write three or four pieces that are demonstratively love poems, normal love poems. "Low in the eastern sky" is their quaint exemplar:

> It was a summer eve,
> The air did gently heave
> While yet a low-hung cloud
> Thy eastern skies did shroud;
> The lightning's silent gleam,
> Startling my drowsy dream,
>   Seemed like the flash
> Under thy dark eyelash.

These love poems grew, almost certainly, out of the emotion he felt for a demure young summer visitor, Ellen Sewall. Yet their relationship was a matter of a few months in the summers of 1839 and 1840, while the poems about brusque friendship continued to be written throughout most of Thoreau's life as a poet.

Although friendship-love was the center of Thoreau's ethics, it was by no means its total. The conduct of life was pervasively important to him. He was always thinking of how to act. The ethical ideal he evolved can be determined fairly easily from his verse; and it is in key with the remainder of his beliefs. It interrelates with his theology and with his regard for nature. Although the true friend is enthroned above even nature, nature still is of use to ethics. If it can add nothing to friendship, it can still help the other virtues. There are two ways it can do so.

The first is of considerable importance. Somehow, nature affords a fertile soil for virtue. Thoreau does not specify how. Instead, as a rule, he simply paints a natural scene and suggests that it is a therapeutic. If the proper scene is not there, then Thoreau by a Wordsworthian process recollects one. Looking on a frozen meadow he remembers it in full verdure. Nature is helpful, furthermore, because it itself is primarily good. Thus Thoreau's ethics here base themselves on a deep although not unvarying belief in the ethical opposition of man and nature. Man is evil, nature is not.

> Man Man is the Devil
> The source of all evil.

This stark opposition neglects the fact of Thoreau's belief in the goodness of some men (of the friend, for instance) and in the evil of certain aspects of nature (nature red in tooth and claw). But Thoreau made no effort, in his verse at least, to work out the inconsistencies. He let the fact stand: nature is good. The second way nature can aid is by example. Nature's own children, such as the birds, can be ethical models for man. Even the little chickadee can set "forth the loveliness Of virtue evermore." Still, the major assistance nature gives comes by man's direct contact with the country instead of with the town. The woods hearten him and they let him think.

Nature is an incentive to virtue in man. Man in his capacity as friend is an incentive to virtue in himself and others. The therapeutic effect of nature is a general one; the effect of human friendship is more specific. It will find itself in the virtues of restraint and sincerity discussed before. One other incentive to virtue is surprising: music. The moment Thoreau heard it, heard even "The Peal of the Bells," he felt like a "hero in coat of mail." It was a whimsically immediate cause of virtue in him. Almost always, in describing its effect, he applied it directly to himself and not just to man in general.

These aids to virtue evidence their power in a general state of probity or else canalize in a few frequently mentioned virtues such as emotional restraint. But to complete the survey of the ethics revealed in Thoreau's poetry, some additional specific qualities need to be noticed. His longest disquisition on the ideal man is called "The Hero." The hero has many fine qualities. He is diligent, tender, and spiritual. He is not, in this poem, martial. As a rule, though, Thoreau's ideal man is a military — or, rather, a militant — one. Not a private about to invade Mexico in the American Army but rather a knightly figure with helm and lance.

The hero has one other important quality. He is independent. When Thoreau was first writing poetry, his ethical symbol was the knight. When he began to find himself, however, the influence of romantic literature was thrown off and the ideas emerged which are today considered characteristic of him. So Thoreau's ethical symbol became the independent man. He is man standing on his own feet, resentful of slight, and facing even God as an equal. Here too, it is not just man in general but Thoreau himself:

> I swear by the rood,
> I'll be slave to no God.

He addresses God directly, as was shown earlier, and lays down terms for him.

This independence originated as a philosophic ethical concept. It developed, under stress of the times (the war on Mexico, the problem of slavery), into a basis for action. Man must not only be independent, he must act independent. The half-way point in Thoreau's transition can be seen in "Wait not till slaves pronounce the word." There he turns on the people who shout for the freeing of the slaves. His stern rebuke is "Are ye so free who cry?" To Thoreau they are not, for true freedom lies within. It is a matter of the mind and the mind is the basis for all genuine freedom.

The philosophy of Thoreau's politics even more than his ethics has become a famous one.

> What is your whole republic worth?
> Ye hold out vulgar lures.

The virtuous man, to keep his virtue, must sever all connections with a debasing government.

> Penurious states lend no relief
> Out of their pelf —
> But a free soul — thank God —
> Can help itself.

The notable statement of his philosophic anarchy is to be found in his prose and not his poems, and in his actions. Yet Thoreau did not ignore it in his verse. One reference concerns his night in jail, his incarceration for refusal to pay the poll tax and so support an unjust government. In a version of a poem mentioned earlier, "The Thaw," he wishes he

> Might help to forward the new spring along,
>   If it were mine to choose my toil or day,
> Scouring the roads with yonder sluice-way throng,
>   And so work out my tax on Her [Nature's] highway.

He would have no objection to working out or paying a legitimate tax for a legitimate purpose. But when it was a tax that helped a bad government become worse, that was a different matter. Here was the doctrine of civil disobedience, refined. It was not to be applied at random; that would diminish its effectiveness and degrade it.

The essence — though not the sum — of Thoreau's philosophy is to be discovered in his verse. There most of the ideas of his maturity can be found. Some of the ideas of his later life cannot, it is true, but those are rare. More frequent are ideas he formulated during his young manhood and then modified when conditions changed. For example, as the slave controversy grew steadily more bitter, Thoreau joined the abolitionists, whom he had previously advised to free themselves first; helped with the Underground Railway; and passionately espoused the rebellion of John Brown. He moved step by step from passive disobedience until he was ready for war. Similarly, the anti-materialism so colorfully displayed in *Walden* is the result of ideas to be found in the poetry only in seed; its noble growth is the product of his maturity. In the poetry Thoreau's deepening conviction that man was too fine to concentrate on grubbing for food or to dedicate his life to material things is not boldly announced, but the intimations are there. They can be found in several of the ideas mentioned earlier: the conception of the independent, self-sufficient hero; the love for nature, which was to have its complement in a contempt for business and the city (God made the country, again; man made the town); and the yearning for things beyond the reach of our senses. And once or twice, though only once or twice, Thoreau does speak out explicitly and bluntly:

> In the busy streets, domains of trade,
> Man is a surly porter, or a vain and hectoring bully,
> Who can claim no nearer kindredship with me
> Than brotherhood by law.

For the way young Thoreau felt about knowing and being, about God and nature, about the friend and the lover, about the difference between the noble man and the ignoble, we can go to his poetry with confidence. There we shall find the first fruits of one of America's most influential minds.

Jemima and the Pattern

THIS is the story of a prophetess who customarily receives one line in histories of American thought, one paragraph in histories of American religion. The story is set in places as obscure as Penn Yan, Canandaigua, and Seneca Lake. The moral of the story for students of American culture is that even when something small is examined through the microscope, its constituents are still regular, its chemistry still comprehensible.

"One religion is as true as another," said a schoolman whom Robert Burton quotes in his elephantine *Anatomy of Melancholy*. Few devout persons, especially in the smaller sects and denominations, have agreed. For many of them their own religion is the sole vessel of religious truth and this same condition of uniqueness is attached to the founder or prophet of their particular group. To her followers Jemima Wilkinson was unparalleled. When she came to upstate New York in the 18th century, no pastor had preceded her. There were still Indians to be appeased; it was as early as that. Not till the next century would the land be well populated by the whites and would their religious leaders appear by the dozen. Meanwhile, to her Jemimakins the Public Universal Friend was a wonder and the rare visitor who came from afar substantiated their amazement. Yet in sober fact Jemima Wilkinson's career was a typical one — typical of one kind of atypical careers. Her story can, it happens, be much better understood and its implications better analyzed if we begin by going back more than a hundred years before she was born. Then there lived another, much better remembered woman, Anne Hutchinson, whose experiences in many ways anticipated hers.

The dour Puritans of Massachusetts were not all pleased when Mrs. Hutchinson arrived from England in 1634 to join them. They had left England as sufferers from religious intolerance but they saw no inconsistency in refusing to tolerate any practices which might undermine their own. Anne Hutchinson, soon after she came to Boston, began to organize church meetings among the other women of the community. At those meetings she criticized the sermons of the Puritan godly and expounded her own liberal theology. Since she was intelligent, outspoken, and confident she soon won a following. She said she preached under direct inspiration from God and most of the women who sat around her at the meetings believed her. She could also count prominent men on her side including the Governor, Sir Henry Vane. But the conservatives united against her, Sir Henry Vane was defeated in the election of 1637, and a year later Anne Hutchinson was tried in court and convicted. She was excommunicated — she was termed a "Heathen and a Publican [and] a Leper" — and banished. Into exile with her went numerous sympathizers. She led them in forming a new settlement where religious freedom was to be cherished. She set up a community first in Rhode Island and then on Long Island Sound, where in 1643 she died.

What was the pattern Mrs. Hutchinson traced in America for Jemima to retrace? It was that of the religious leader, awakened by a mystic experience, who emerges to spread his new vision, shocks the orthodox believers in his community, is expelled or leaves of his own accord, and with his band of faithful followers goes out to found a new community where his vision may flourish undisturbed. Into this general design Jemima was to fit easily. But in addition she was to conform to one of its rarer subordinate patterns, that of the female religious leader whose feminism is perhaps the greatest affront to her foes. Anne Hutchinson can help to clarify Jemima's place in the tradition of American religious protest; and another woman, Ann Lee, with whom Jemima was in great sympathy, can define it still more sharply. This we shall see in a moment.

Jemima was born in 1752 in Rhode Island not very far from the place where Anne Hutchinson had originally settled after her banishment. Morever, she was born into a Quaker family — and this was to be significant. Jemima grew up a motherless, strong-willed girl. She was the eighth of a dozen children. She read incessantly in romantic literature and in 1770 apparently had her direct attention turned to religion when she came across a sermon by the great George Whitefield. Both before and after this event, however, she was doubtless influenced by the turbulently religious atmosphere in which she lived. Then, in 1774, a new and startling prophetess came to New England. She was Ann Lee, and she preached doctrines that shocked her hearers and provoked attention wherever she went. Maintaining that she was Christ in His second coming, she called herself Ann the Word. The group she attracted became known contemptuously as Shakers because they shook while worshipping. Two years after Ann's arrival, Jemima fell ill and almost died. On beginning to recover she asserted that she had actually perished and that in her place the "Spirit of Life from God" (just as in Ann's case) now dwelt in her body. The Spirit was letting her body exist, Jemima felt, because she now had a divine command to go out and preach.

Thereafter, Jemima proclaimed herself the "Public Universal Friend." At once she began to spread her message and was astonishingly successful. Tall, with dark hair and brilliant eyes, she won notable converts — among them the governor of her native colony of Rhode Island — with her youthful zeal and flashing energy. Nevertheless, her influence brought angry attention to herself. The next turn of the pattern was inevitable: the orthodox denominations fought her message and her methods. Clenched fists were raised against her preaching. Tolerant though they usually were, even the Quakers turned against her in large numbers. They demanded that those Quakers who had attended Jemima's meetings ask forgiveness for it. In the face of such hostility Jemima decided to abandon Rhode Island. First she thought of going abroad but then changed her mind. In 1782 she journeyed to Pennsylvania. Her preaching in Philadelphia stirred the city into a sensation. Once again the established churches rose to repel her, and ultimately she came to realize that she must go out with her followers into the wilderness. There her Society would be unmolested; there she could establish the religion and life she wanted.

The Friend pitched on the Genesee country of what is now upstate New York as her Promised Land. By 1786 she had sent one follower, Ezekiel Shearman, to scout the new Canaan. However, he reported that the Senecas there were still hostile and that it would be dangerous to move in. Yet the Friend sent another exploring party out during the next year and in 1788 she had twenty-five of her Jemimakins found a New Jerusalem. They established it in what is today Yates County, New York, on the west bank of Seneca Lake. In 1790 the Friend herself arrived in this Jerusalem, and she brought enough others along to swell the tidy settlement to 260 persons.

Then came a time of prosperity. The harvests were rich, the people busy. But the group that had survived adversity could not as a unit survive good fortune. Trouble came to the Society. A split took place, the reason for which has never been discovered. Two leaders of the group, Judge William Potter and James Parker, disputed with the Friend over either doctrine or property. The bitterness swelled. Parker charged Jemima with blasphemy. Eventually she was arrested on his charge. Like Mrs. Hutchinson she was brought to trial but unlike her she was not convicted. Jemima appeared before the court at Canandaigua, denied that she had said she could work miracles like Jesus, and gave her actual, owned beliefs in the form of a sermon to the court. It must have made a deep impression, for the presiding judge himself was moved to praise it.

That was a victory but merely a temporary one. Although the Society went on, the Friend, growing old and tired, lost some of the persuasive power which had once moved her hearers. More trouble came. The number of her supporters went down, partly for doctrinal reasons, and few young people were attracted to the Society. Jemima saw a fading congregation before her when she died in 1819. Some of its members stayed by during further lawsuits over the land, only to fall under the domination of three incompetent — and male — leaders. When yet another set of lawsuits about its property took place after 1844, the Society never recovered. In each succeeding year the already small number of the Friends shrank further. The faithful vanished from the meeting-hall.

The New Jerusalem was dead. The message the Universal Friend once preached in its confines had faltered and then failed. Certainly it was a message off the beaten track of religion but there had been enough similar messages before it to form a trail of their own. Just as the Friend's career was typical of the new-light "romantic enthusiast's," so were her doctrines. Their novelty lay purely in the combination not in the ingredients themselves.

The chief ingredients in Jemima's message, the chief elements in her creed and system, came from three different sources. One source was the great traditional pattern of Protestant doctrine. Another was the ideas of the Quaker shoemaker, George Fox. The third was the movement led by the ecstatic prophetess Ann Lee, Ann the Word.

The amazing thing about the first source, Protestant biblical belief, was the great extent to which Jemima depended on it. We would expect, from the picturesque quality of her ministry, that her theology would have been the colorful result of her own transfusion. By and large, it was not. We owe much of the information about it to someone who first sat in Jemima's meetings when he was a little boy. His name was Henry Barnes. He was not the acme, it is true, of reliability. For all the melody of the Friend's message, the little boy looked around from time to time. Every now and then, like children in church today, he let his attention wander while he eyed the building about him. Years later he could still describe the crude meeting-house in precise detail. He remembered how many logs there were between the floor and the ceiling; he recalled the exact number of panes in the windows; and he knew precisely how the doors had been hung. But Henry Barnes, as he grew up and continued to go to the weekly meetings of the Jemimakins, also heard and retained a good deal of information of wider interest. It is an extended statement made by him when he was an old man which gives us much of our knowledge of the Friend's theology.

Stafford Cleveland printed Barnes' statement in his Yates County history of 1873. The theology Barnes reported was time-honored enough. Jemima preached her belief in the Trinity: Father, Son, and Holy Ghost. God the Father was the all-powerful creator and judge. He made man; then man sinned and broke the law, bringing death of body and soul on himself. As a result, God required an infinite atonement for the sin. Christ was that sacrifice, and He became the glorious Saviour. What man had to do now was to repent and pray, and live a godly and humble life. Thus the Friend must have outlined her theology; and, as Henry Barnes noted, she tried always to expound "religious doctrine in perfect harmony with the Bible."

Her doctrine was on the whole in accord with that preached in the more rigid New England churches. Only in two notable ways did it depart from Massachusetts Calvinism and incline toward the doctrine of Anne Hutchinson. First, Jemima could not believe in infant damnation, staple that it was of New England theology. In the most popular poem of the previous century, "The Day of Doom," a New England poet had sung that though some of the infants who died would be given "the easiest room in Hell," their destination would still be Hell. But Jemima maintained that all infant souls came from heaven perfect and pure, and stayed that way until their possessors reached the age of understanding; to her no hapless infant ever burned in Hell. Everyone when mature — and here is the second important way the Friend liberalized her theology — could be as good or bad as he desired. Everyone had complete freedom of will, with no tinge of predestination. Lastly, as a corollary to her dogma, Jemima spoke for a life of works: good deeds and retiring kindness. Those were the main tenets of her faith.

A little book printed in 1783 is our other major source for documentary information about the religion of Jemima and her group. It deals more with practices than belief, however. The book is entitled *The Universal Friend's Advice, to Those of the Same Religious Society, Recommended to be Read in their Public Meetings for Divine Worship.* Between its covers the Friend put a rather disorganized homily. It can be summed up in the words "Do good and obey God." It has, nevertheless, amid its exhortations, distinct evidences of the second great influence on Jemima's system, George Fox's Quakerism. One such is the emphasis on being guided by inner light. The Friend too believed that the truth welled up from within a person. Another is revealed in Jemima's advice about what was a characteristic of Quaker meetings: speaking when the Spirit moved one. The Friend told her people, "Those whose mouths have been opened to speak, or to pray in public, are to wait for the movings of the Holy Spirit, and then speak or pray as the Spirit giveth utterance."

Several other ways in which Jemima carried over Quaker practices into her own Society can be found in the little book. Not the least of them was one which the Quakers themselves were not always faithful to. "Use plainness of speech and apparel, and let your adorning, not be outward but inward, even that of a meek and quiet spirit," the Friend admonished her readers. So far as plainness of speech was concerned, her group is said to have heeded her exhortations. For the rest feminine nature, especially, struggled against the drabness of apparel. Yet all in all the Quaker element in the New Jerusalem proved to be a pervasive one. Even speech there followed the Quaker fashion, with its "thee's" and "thou's." So did the written discourse. Nor, obvious though it is, should we forget that Jemima called herself the Public Universal *Friend* and called her Society by almost the same name as the Quakers used for themselves, the Society of Friends.

So the Quaker strand, though gray and quiet, can be picked out clearly in the pattern of Jemima's teaching. That is still more true of the Shaker strand, with its mingled black and red, its combination of iron repression with frenetic relief.

Jemima's kinship to the system carried on by Mother Ann Lee showed itself in many ways. In fact the elements in Jemima's system that nearly duplicated those of Ann's were the spectacular ones. For example, one of the things that singled out the Shakers from among the great mass of Protestants was their uniform. Both men and women wore clothes whose every stitch almost was prescribed by their community. This was particularly so at the peak of Shaker renown. Then the men were assigned the broad-brimmed hats and long, light-blue coats to wear that we see in Shaker pictures. The women wore gowns whose color could vary but whose style of close-fitting bodice and long, pleated skirt was dictated to them in detail.

Jemima had, it would seem, more success with men than women in this matter of regimenting clothes. The trend can be seen in that she managed to enforce a Shaker-like uniformity in men's hats, but she failed in regard to the women's shoes. We are told that the men all became accustomed to wearing broad-brimmed hats much like those of the Shakers. The women, however, at least in such things as shoes, followed fashion's dictates rather than Jemima's. Shaker plainness was no more to their taste than was the Quaker kind. Cleveland quotes a local shoemaker to the effect that he made high heels out of knots of wood for women both in the Friend's group and outside of it, though Jemima herself — the shoemaker added — wore sensible low heels.

To argue much similarity between two groups because a Jemimakin and a Shaker wore broad-brimmed hats seems hasty. But it should be remembered that the outward appearance was intended in part to be the symbol of an inner condition. The fact that the people dressed alike stood for the fact that they really were alike and equal in many subtler and farther-reaching ways. They were equal in the eyes of God. They were equal, in a material sense, in the eyes of man. Moreover, they tried to live under an economic system of "share and share alike." The Jemimakins and the Shakers were communists in their fashion.

Jemima had in her Society both rich men and poor. The rich helped to buy a major share of the land on which the New Jerusalem was to arise. The poor on the other hand were given lands to use. Practical considerations prevented a complete state of equality, however. Jemima's community never got beyond a rather rudimentary state of organization, while the Shaker-like equality of condition she wanted was upset by natural differences in ability and skill. As a consequence, the Friends who settled near the village of Penn Yan never reached absolute communism, though neither did some Shakers. But both societies tried, and the more earnestly perhaps because communism and equalitarianism were in the air. Starting with a religious emphasis and ending with a broadly social one, many groups of the time attempted to build Utopias. They tried in various places, not least of all in upstate New York. Some of the experiments came after Jemima's, and they include the most famous ones such as the Oneida Community. Others were begun earlier. Early and late, nevertheless, they served to show that once again Jemima did something that was not unique but part of a clearly marked current.

The "equal-rights" communism of Jemima and Mother Ann was more than religious and economic. It was also, in one sense, sexual. That is to say, women were given a place on a par with men instead of being subordinated. Indeed, in actual practice both prophets went beyond that. They raised women up over men. They established an organization which depended in numerous ways on their own sex.

The religious, legal, and social position of women during Mother Ann's and Jemima's life was a bitterly unequal one. It was perhaps partly in compensation that both Mother Ann and Jemima leaned toward petticoat government. First of all, the two leaders were themselves women. The one had endured an unhappy marriage, the other had never married at all. Jemima organized her women with especial zeal, dubbing the mainstays of her company the "Faithful Sisterhood." After masculine stalwarts like Judge William Potter and James Parker fell away, Jemima leaned all the more on members of her Sisterhood. They in turn gave her a depth of devotion that the men did not equal.

The background to Jemima's feminism very probably derives from Ann the Word. Jemima clearly went beyond her in practice, but Ann went far beyond Jemima in the religious theory underlying this esteem for womankind. Ann's position as finally set down, after her death, in *The Testimony of Christ's Second Appearing*, was to be explained in this way: Man was guilty of lust in the Garden of Eden and thus brought all evil into the world. However, woman fell first and so was more guilty than he. God thereafter allowed atonement but — and here is the point that most enraged the orthodox denominations — there was to be a male saviour who atoned for the men *and* a female saviour who atoned for the women. The male saviour, *The Testimony* said, was the man now known as Jesus Christ. The female saviour was none other than Mother Ann. The book explained that Jesus had actually appeared much earlier than Ann because man had sinned less than woman and so was open for atonement sooner. Now Ann, the feminine counterpart of Christ, was come to save the souls of all women, just as God had sent Christ before to save the souls of all men. With the advent of Ann the Word, women were once more to be on an absolutely equal plane with men.

On her feminism Ann also based another conclusion. Since the original sinning of the human race had been caused by lust, all physical mating between the truly good people must stop. Ann could not quite decree abstinence for the whole world but she tried for her own Shakers. For them the celibate life was the best way to avoid sexual sin.

Here again, Jemima agreed; she was an enthusiast for celibacy. One of the complaints against her in Rhode Island and Pennsylvania was that she split families in two by demanding that the husbands and wives live apart. It often happened, furthermore, that one member of a family was more impressed by Jemima's preaching than the other; and the result was a broken home. Only occasionally do we read in the records about amiable couples like the Comstocks. Achilles Comstock was a good Methodist who went to church on Sunday while his wife was a Jemimakin who worshipped on Saturday — and neither quarreled with the other. As a rule the results were not so happy. Nevertheless, Jemima clung to her fight for celibacy, particularly among the Faithful Sisterhood; and some of the rancor against her was definitely due to that fact.

Besides these broad bases for sympathy with the Shaker usage, the Friend also followed Shakerism in some other points of doctrine. She opposed the idea, as was mentioned earlier, of infant damnation; so had Mother Ann. She did not believe in the physical resurrection of the body; neither did Mother Ann's Shakers. Lastly, she and the Shakers joined in believing in the ultimate perfectibility of mankind.

It is some distance from Anne Hutchinson to Ann Lee and to Jemima Wilkinson but the way is there, still to be seen. For Jemima, Anne Hutchinson was primarily a prototype but Ann Lee was more than that. The religion of the Public Universal Friend owed much to the prophetess of the Shakers. It owed much too to the Quakers and that other great source, Protestant biblical doctrine. Nevertheless, it also gave something, something intangible but worth noting. Its contribution to the Shakers and the Quakers was that of a sympathetic atmosphere. It performed a similar service for American Protestantism in New York State. There Jemima helped to keep orthodox religion alive during a period when it was in genuine danger. The deism in English thought, with its stress on reason over revelation, the atheism in French Revolutionary thought, and sheer popular indifference combined to smother much of American religion for a generation. Seemingly at least, only radical religious movements like Jemima's fought irreligious radicalism with vigor and thus kept the fires of faith burning. In that way the Jemimakins, depleted by 1820 and moribund by 1850, still managed to keep a place ready for other believers. When the Methodist circuit-rider, for instance, in his tall beaver hat, first came to Seneca Lake, he saw religious ground ready for him.

LITERATURE AND
CULTURE IN THE
TWENTIETH CENTURY

Adversity's Favorite Son

IN DEPRESSION AMERICA it was the first of the big bad books. The date is significant: 1933. The stock market had crashed, and many a fortune with it; the white collar classes were living either on lowered salaries or scanted savings; and more workmen were jobless than ever before. But the great book-buying public still had enough money for a little aspirin, and here it was. More than a little, in fact: 1,224 pages of it. It soothed the pain and offered an escape. In that one way the book was faultless. It was not literature, but it provided all the obvious ingredients for an anodyne.

More than one author, watching Hervey Allen's royalties pile up, must have muttered in envy, "Why didn't I think of that myself"? The envy was justified, for *Anthony Adverse* sold over 10,000 copies a week, at $3 a copy, during its first six months. At the end of its third year it had sold almost three-quarters of a million. And it continued selling well through the rest of the thirties.

Though the book followed a spate of bright bitter novels on modern life by a variety of current authors, it was surprisingly old-fashioned in several ways. It turned firmly to the past, the romantic past, and stood much closer to Sir Walter Scott than to Sinclair Lewis. The action opened neither on Main Street nor Broadway but in the Province of Auvergne, where some peasants clustered while waiting "uneasily in the late afternoon sunshine one spring day in the year 1775." They were waiting, of course, for a coach. It would arrive shortly, carrying the villainous old marquis with a hand like a lion's paw and his beautiful, abject wife. But the wife had a lover, who would soon be run through by her vengeful husband. She would die in childbirth; her baby would be left at a convent; and it would grow up to become Anthony Adverse, the handsome hero of the tale.

The type of plot was as old as the setting, and older. It was picaresque, taking its only unity from the life of the hero. In contrast to the well knit plots of the popular novels by other writers that preceded it, *Anthony Adverse* merely had one adventure after another happen to the hero. However, it was always a slightly different one from those in the chapter before. If at times the author felt bad about the motley nature of the episodes, he made a gesture toward unity by creating a coincidence — the more outrageous the better. When Anthony left the convent he happened to be taken to the house of an old Scottish merchant. The merchant started in astonishment at seeing him: "The truth is . . . he reminded me forcibly just now of — my daughter." And the merchant was, inevitably, the hero's grandfather.

Similarly, once Anthony had grown old enough for passion, he often re-encountered the women he had loved. Faith, Angela, Dolores, Neleta, Florence: he met them all more than once, and usually in circumstances that defied probability. When he met Napoleon, for instance, he found that he had a mistress and the mistress was Angela. Sometimes Mr. Allen introduced coincidence almost for its own sake. He put a crone into the plot and noted in an aside to the reader that she really was old Lucia, once the maid of Anthony's mother. Anthony did not know this nor did anyone else in the book, but the reader was told it anyway.

If the book provided a patent escape in time, it did so

just as plainly in place. It transported the reader over both land and sea. The travelogue was larded with what the author must have regarded as vivid and variegated description. Before the book was half through, Anthony had adventured in Italy, France, Spain and Cuba; had sailed aboard a Yankee merchantman and an African slaveship; and had been a slave trader himself on the African Grain Coast.

After the lurid scenes of the slave trade, something powerful was needed to keep interest in the second half of the book from sagging. It was provided by having Anthony return to France and — the time was now luckily 1801 — come into intimate contact with Napoleon in his prime. The First Consul furnished the proper dynamics. Then Anthony went to England for a while and thereafter to the most romantic parts of the United States: Creole Louisiana and the Spanish southwest. There in the southwest he finally died, by a convenient accident, and the 1,224 pages were done.

The philosophy, if one could call it that, in *Anthony Adverse* did its job well. It comforted the struggler against the Great Depression. The hero took his name from adversity and he always survived his trials. In fact, he seemed curiously unaffected by them. It was not only that when something bad occurred to him something good soon followed; it was that the author never lingered on misfortune. Anthony might lose wife and child in a fire that burned them to death, yet a few chapters later he was married again and begetting a larger family than before. On a lesser scale the same held true; if he lost brown-eyed Angela, dark Dolores emerged to console him.

Not the least appeal of the book was its moral simplicity. Despite American puritanism, the author made a minimum of moral judgments. Anthony could dally all he wished; the author held it no occasion for sermons. Indeed, he displayed a kind of worldliness which is still rare in American fiction. His treatment of sex was generous. "Come," says Angela to Anthony, "lie on my breast awhile"; and hers is by no means the only invitation. Sometimes the action was conveyed with a bit of fancy symbolism about filling tuns of water till they overflowed; but the reader could comprehend.

Most people must not have been conscious of the style in *Anthony Adverse*. Yet it was there. The language was often lush, filled with adjectives and descriptive verbs, and relieved by passages of pure literary vulgarity. In point: "For him the gears of existence were shifted automatically by the signal of Neleta's naked hips." However, it made little difference. When the reader who had bought or borrowed the book went home at night, past the breadlines and soup-kitchens, he could lose himself in faraway times and places. He could swagger about, he could confront Napoleon, he could experience adventures that had nothing to do with getting a living; and who could blame him if he found 1,224 pages too few?

Cappy Ricks
and the Monk in the Garden

ONE OF THE dimmest figures in the limbo of American life is the popular novelist, the purely popular novelist, of a generation ago. Oblivion is his name. On the other hand, the popular novelist writing today is apt to be a nightclub celebrity. But he has his own troubles. Despite the fact that he enjoys the approval of the mass of readers, he is either ignored or castigated by the literary critics. And with justice, from the point of view of belles-lettres. Yet when the popular novelist has been dead for — say — two generations rather than one, he is apt to appear again, this time even in the learned journals, since he has now been dead long enough. The scholar of the future may leaf through an annotated article on "Primitivism in a Forgotten 'Western' Writer, Zane Grey" or "Theological Patterns in the Fiction of Lloyd Douglas." Both the cultural and the literary historians may examine him with fresh curiosity. As a matter of fact, the reputation of the purely popular novelist sinks for some years after his death just as does the reputation, usually, of the good novelist. Each becomes unfashionable and then in due course of time — say two generations again — rises into notice once more.

However, I should like to fly in the face of custom and

say something about a popular novelist of only one generation ago. I should like to rescue him from limbo, if I can,
because he played an unsuspected part in perverting a major
scientific theory and in helping to maintain a highly ques-
tionable American attitude.

A generation before the terms "Aryan" and "Nordic"
were forced on everybody's attention, one of America's leading popular novelists was engaged in writing about some of
the concepts behind them and reflecting those concepts in
his work. He continued to promulgate his theory of race
even after World War II began. His last book bears the
copyright date 1940, his last magazine stories appeared in
1942, and his best-known fiction is still being reprinted.
First serialized in such widely read periodicals as the *Saturday Evening Post, Colliers,* and the *American Magazine,* his
novels went on as a rule to climb towards, if not always into,
the bestseller lists. Thereafter the motion picture industry
increased the public for them. As early as 1919 Paramount-
Artcraft, for instance, a pioneer film company, released its
screen version of one novel, *The Valley of the Giants,* as a
starring vehicle for the now forgotten Wallace Reid.

Peter B. Kyne's novels have earned him ample rewards
almost from the beginning. Buyers for them have run at
least into the hundreds of thousands. In 1910 he started writing for the national magazines with Western and sea stories
that were a cut above the general run of popular fiction,
and it was not long before he went on to widen the scope
of his work and extend its appeal. After *The Long Chance*
(his "first big novel," said *Sunset Magazine*) appeared in
book form in 1914, he limited the flow of short stories from
his ready pen and began to concentrate on the longer works.
That his novels followed a formula became evident fairly
soon. Yet it was a pleasant one in the eyes of many a reader.
The setting would customarily be a Western desert or tim-
berland, sometimes the sea, seldom a city. Before this scenery
a rugged hero would fight for his birthright. The struggle
would mix business warfare with thudding blows on mouth

and chin. Toward the middle of the book a beautiful girl would let herself be won and thereafter she would do her winsome and effective best for the hero's cause. At the end, marriage and large prosperity.

In fiction like Kyne's, one would confidently expect the characters to be types rather than individuals; and they are, with a single outstanding exception. He is irascible little Cappy Ricks of the white mutton-chops and black string tie, who became one of the best-known figures in the gallery of American popular writing. As the bookjacket blurb of *Cappy Ricks Comes Back* implies, Peter B. Kyne's most notable creation was modeled on life. He was probably inspired by a tycoon in Pacific coast shipping of the early 1900's who was colorful enough to invite any facile author's use. Captain Robert Dollar, chin-whiskered and Scottish, was the founder of the Dollar Steamship lines and a man who learned to be equally at home with mandarins and riggers. There is little doubt that he was the original of Cappy Ricks, head of the fictional Ricks Blue Star line and, like Dollar, also the owner of extensive lumber interests.

Cappy Ricks makes his first bow in a short story, "The Devil Ship," of May, 1912, as — simply — Old Hickman. The line of descent is not too plain, however, until the appearance of "The Thunder God" (another short story and not the later novel of the same name) where he has become Old Man Hickman. "The Thunder God" was apparently not printed until after the publication of *Cappy Ricks* in 1916 but it may well have been written earlier. At any rate Old Man Hickman is either Cappy's prototype or his sibling. Hickman is a shipowner, parsimonious and irritable on the surface but generous and warm-hearted underneath. When he argues with a herculean young Viking, his words and actions predict those of Cappy Ricks. "Old Man Hickman shook a skinny fist under the giant's nose. 'Don't you lecture me,' he warned. . . . 'That's right,' [he] shrilled.'" But Kyne's ultimate figure was Cappy himself, conniving against his manly son-in-law Matt Peaslee, for Matt's own good, storming at Skinner, his general manager, and always ready to strike a blow where it would pay him a good return in chuckles and profits.

Along with Old Man Hickman, Cappy Ricks is portrayed with a certain degree of complexity. Instead of being shown as all black or all white, all good or all bad, like the type characters, Cappy is presented — sympathetically — as a lively, likable little tyrant who sometimes overreaches himself and makes mistakes. *Cappy Ricks* is in fact the story of a running battle in which the diminutive shipping magnate suffers one check after another from young Matt Peaslee. Yet Kyne's art is adequate enough to make the reader love Cappy more for his defeats than for his victories. It is this human appeal in Cappy that marks the big difference between him and his main literary precursor in the work of others, Old Gorgon Graham. Graham is the central figure in a volume that once sold many thousands of copies, George Horace Lorimer's *The Letters of a Self-Made Merchant to his Son* (1901). There are definite similarities in the background, attitudes, and social position of the two old men, but if Graham ever admits to his son that he made a mistake, he does so only to point a moral. The reader feels at all times that Graham is in control of the situation. After all, the meatpacking merchant was intended to play the leading part in a commercial man's courtesy book, so his character emerges as a combination of ultimately unbeatable shrewdness and calculating Yankee thrift.

Cappy, however, is the only literary creation of any individual importance to appear in the long series of novels that Kyne produced from 1913 to 1940. The rest are types. All these others, ranging from brave young Bryce Cardigan of *The Valley of the Giants* to lovely Mary Sutherland of *The Dude Woman*, Kyne's last novel, fit their traditional patterns neatly. Kyne provides a varied array of minor characters and major — desert rats and millionaires, horny-handed first mates and cold-eyed bankers, beautiful girls and selfish wives, patently rugged young men and vapid drifters. The minor characters in particular are presented strictly in terms of their stereotypes; and in spite of the fact that Kyne spends some effort on shaping his main characters, of both sexes, he fails as a rule to give depth and individuality even to them. In the case of his heroines he is particularly unsuccessful. They remain mere figurines. Outwardly different, each, it is nevertheless clear, would do almost precisely the same thing in a given set of circumstances as would the others. The girls ride alike, react alike, and love alike. Their eyes may be gentle brown or sparkling blue but they are raised with equal charm and purpose to the hero as he stands before them. The heroes also tend to be of a kind. Although they come off a bit better than do their women and at times show a certain measure of individualization, they are all wiry and courageous, courteous and daring. And they almost never lose a fight. In spite of the fact that the hero's opponent is always a ruffian, as big or bigger than he is, the reader need never doubt who will win. The pattern is fixed.

Yet it should be pointed out that many of the characters, both major and minor, linger in the reader's mind more than do most in purely popular fiction. This is no small achievement. For the writer who aims pointblank at popularity, characterization represents a considerable problem. His characters must be simple and quickly recognizable in order to ensure a broad appeal among the book-buying public. But they must not be too sadly obvious. Normally even a writer like Taylor Caldwell, who was once reported as advancing the claim that popularity is the best critical test of a novel, will try to individualize her characters to some extent. The solution lies in finding the happy medium. It lies in fashioning characters individual enough to make some impression on the reader's intelligence but typical enough so that the reader will not have to ponder them or wrack his mind in an attempt to classify them. Some writers never find an answer to the problem or at best find one only temporarily. Peter B. Kyne was shrewd enough to find his answer early and to hold on to it for almost thirty years.

The answer lay in the theories of "the old monk in the garden" as Kyne calls Gregor Mendel; and his literary debt to Mendel is great. He translated Mendel's Law into a major method of characterization. He made his own interpretation of the law an organic part of his literary method, if not of his entire view of life. When Mendel published the account of his strict and modest researches as *Versuche über Pflanzen-Hybriden* in 1865, it attracted no noticeable attention from scientists, let alone anyone else. Ten years before Kyne began writing, though, Mendel's article was rediscovered by a trio of distinguished botanists and popularized. If Kyne knew that he was guilty of a gross alteration and extension of Mendel's careful study, he gave no signs of it anywhere in his numerous novels.

His debt to Mendel shows itself as early as the time of Old Man Hickman and even earlier. Hickman, in "The Thunder God" again, sees Valdemar Sigurdson and says to him, "Boy, you're the damnedest, finest, white man I've ever seen. Swede, Dane, Norwegian or Icelander?" Viking, pure and unadulterated by any mixture, is Sigurdson's answer: "We have never been disturbed and we have had but slight opportunity to mix with other races." Then Old Man Hickman clinches the discussion. "Ever hear of Mendel's Law?" he inquires of his stalwart. "It's about heredity and the fertility of hybrids and the evolution of species. You're a Viking, . . . a dominant, not a recessive type."

Leaving the field to Cappy Ricks as time goes on, Old Man Hickman disappears from Kyne's stories; but the Mendelian notions he has expounded to his young Viking do not. In one novel, *Island of Desire* (1931), Mendel is mentioned on the very first page and he sets the tone for the whole work. In another, *Golden Dawn,* written in this same period, Kyne has a character define Mendel's Law explicitly. To him it is the "law that like shall produce like," and its violation among human beings can bring bad marriages and disaster. Furthermore, when like fails to mate with like and a mixed marriage takes place, the children will be either throwbacks or half-breeds. Kyne observes that the leading character in a short story called "The Land just over Yonder" "had known many half-breeds in his day — Mexicans and Indians — and he had never known a good one." When the author speaks about the Mendelian theory in other passages, he adds that it shows the danger of mixing different races. So there is danger in mixing races; but there is also, by implication, danger in mixing certain nationalities. Kyne uses the term "race" loosely and it is clear from several citations, including a notable one in *The Pride of Palomar,* that he widens (or rather narrows) the term to include nationalities as well. Consequently, when he is going to give examples of the races of man, he may even mention the Irish, the British, the French, and the Germans.

As a matter of fact, Kyne was interested enough by Mendel's Law, or rather his idea of Mendel's Law, to devote an entire early novel to it. The work was published in 1923 — before *Golden Dawn* and *Island of Desire* — and Kyne entitled it, inevitably enough, *Never the Twain Shall Meet.* The plot of it offers the fullest exposition of the theory to be found anywhere in his long shelf of books. The central character is Tamea, bewitching daughter of a French father and a " 'purebred' " Polynesian mother. Tamea wears a 1923 sarong and wears it well. She enchants the hero, Dan Pritchard, and explains in a careful conversation that "all Polynesian languages are derived from the same Aryan source"; her father too, shortly before his death, underlines the point that the Polynesians are also Aryans. But a staunch friend of Dan's argues against his marrying Tamea. He observes to Dan that although she is a Caucasian, so is a Hindu. That means that the lovely Tamea might bear him brown sons. "You cannot dodge the Mendelian Law, my boy," he says sagely. "Like begets like, but in a union of opposites we get throwbacks." Dan marries Tamea anyway, in the sight of deity if not of man, and goes to the South Pacific to live with her. In the end, though, Tamea comes to realize that never the twain shall meet, so she sends Dan back to civilization and to his reserved but Nordic beauty, Maisie.

To put Kyne's theory nakedly, what is pure-bred and Aryan is good; what is hybrid or pigmented is bad. This is the view that underlies the great body of his characterization. The theory allowed him, for years, to cope with the problem of character portrayal. Kyne could present an assemblage of major and minor characters that would titillate but not confuse the average reader. He could continue to serve the same dish but with a different enough sauce to give his product an individual flavor. There was of course the risk that his method might antagonize some readers and reduce the public demand for his works. However, Kyne was able to minimize the risk involved by presenting his theory most of the time at an innocent, ordinary, and superficial level: by depicting his characters in terms of their commonly accepted national stereotypes, dialect and all.

So his Irish are pugnacious and talk with a brogue one could cut with a peat-ax. Says Terence Reardon, for instance, "As for you, ye devil, faith . . . I thought, begorra, ye was a dirrty Far Down. God love ye, Michael, but 'tis the likes of you I'm proud to be shipmates wit'." Kyne's Scandinavians are customarily simple, grave, and honest, and are sometimes heard to remark, "I ban vant to go home." The Chinese appear only as faithful cooks, excitable and superstitious. Sooey Wan, Dan Pritchard's cook in *Never the Twain Shall Meet,* must speak like this: "Boss, you allee time talkee too damn much. . . . Tonight me go joss-house and burn devil paper." He is the duplicate of Ah Fong in *Lord of Lonely Valley,* who, when his master lies ill with spotted fever, not only burns devil papers but also offers him a broth made from the heart of a wildcat.

Writing in terms of such patent national and racial stereotypes as these, Kyne was also able at times to introduce the more invidious aspects of his theory. These aspects some of his readers certainly might have been expected to resent. Whatever resentment may have been aroused, it was not enough to diminish Kyne's popularity among book buyers. In fact it should be noted that his conceptions agreed with many a reader's feelings; in all probability, such readers were flattered to see their prejudgments confirmed in print. Many a reader would be apt to approve of what was native and supposedly like him, and disapprove of what was foreign to him.

On this basis Kyne could, when he came to certain other national and racial types beyond those mentioned before, further his notion of Mendel's Law and do it without any serious repercussion. He could develop the implications of the theory and be shielded by American nativism. The crasser applications of the idea might be put into the mouth of a character instead of into the author's direct narrative. The result would still be the same. To take a leading example, since Kyne used the Southwest as locale for a number of his novels, Mexicans make a fairly frequent appearance. The type Mexican is shown as shiftless and thieving. After all he is a hybrid, mixing in his veins the blood of Spaniard and Indian, so no good is to be expected from him. He is, in short, a "Greaser." The heroine of *Jim the Conqueror* is said to be surprised that "Texas boasts at least one very intelligent . . . Mexican," while Webster of *Webster, Man's Man* growls, "I don't relish the idea of a Greaser in the same stateroom with me." Kyne adds, "The prospect was as revolting to him as would be an uninvited Negro guest at the dining table of a southern family."

The comparison of the Mexican with the Negro is appropriate enough for Kyne although as a rule he writes little about the Negro in his novels and short stories. When he does so, though, it is in line with his theory. Almost all of Kyne's Negroes are Pullman porters who are to be addressed as "George." Only once is a Negro described at any length in Kyne's writing. He is a villainous mulatto squatter — a hybrid again as well as a member of an inferior race — in *Kindred of the Dust*. He is living in sin with a white woman at the time the hero of the book encounters him. The hero, the "young laird" so-called, identifies himself and tells the mulatto that he must leave a dingy neighborhood called the Sawdust Pile. "We-ll, is dat so?" the "yellow rascal" drawls. "So youh-all's de new la'rd, eh? Well, ah'm de king o' de Sawdust Pile, an' mah house is mah castle." The young laird takes the mulatto's measure, however, and soon "under a rain of blows on the chin and jaw, he sprawled unconscious on the ground."

The young laird's victory is of course inevitable. Nevertheless, one of the contributing causes is that he has what Kyne terms in *Jim the Conqueror* "a superior blood, a superior color." The phrase is a telling one. In its flat assumption of the superiority of one blood and color over another, it epitomizes Kyne's thinking.

Many a villain lurks in Kyne's pages, and more often than not he is of inferior or of foreign blood. In other words he is not white, or if he is white he is also alien. A Frenchman is cowardly and treacherous; a Greek is shown as wicked; a Russian — called by Kyne the "Red," without benefit of quotation marks — is a trouble-maker; a Sicilian comes of " 'Bad people.' " It is unforgivable, for the purposes of Kyne's fiction, to be born in southern or western Europe, even though the person has a white skin.

On the other hand, it should be understood that Kyne's collection of malefactors includes some who are of 100 per cent American stock. It is conceivable, even for the purposes of popular fiction, that one may be a Native Californian and be bad at the same time. But this does not happen very often. If the villain is American, he is apt to hail from some distant and alienated section of the country like the Middle West or the East. For example, Colonel Pennington, the antagonist in *The Valley of the Giants,* comes from the relatively effete Midwest. The Southwest and and West Coast breed the heroes.

Kyne's love for the "native American" extends to the Amerindian although it has to stretch a bit to cover him. There is nothing novel about Kyne's Indians. They grunt instead of speaking in sentences and tread softly through the redwoods or over the desert flats. In spite of being pictured as inferior, they still have a place in Kyne's cosmos. George Sea Otter, in *The Valley of the Giants,* grows up with the hero and throughout the novel remains his man Friday. He is typical. However, he happens to be full-blooded and so escapes the weakness of the hybrid. Pitt River Charlie, in *Outlaws of Eden,* is on the contrary a half-breed. He has the role of professional killer; and, as the action proves, he lacks among other things the full-blooded Indian's traditional stoicism under pain. Yet, all in all, Kyne's nativism and primitivism combine to give the Indian a fairly sympathetic portrayal.

If the villains are usually of an inferior race or nation, the heroes and heroines are conversely apt to be strictly American. One would expect, in terms of Kyne's Mendelian theory, that a considerable proportion would be of Pilgrim stock or of equivalent purity. However, here an interesting complication enters. Kyne's own people came from County Mayo, and he apostrophizes his father as "Dear Exile of Erin." It turns out, not surprisingly, that several of the leading heroes have Irish blood in their veins. The Scottish heritage is also an admirable one; it too is the stock of heroes. So is the Downeaster strain, Cappy Ricks' own, which becomes Kyne's closest approach to the Mayflower stereotype. Moreover, one other national origin is favorable to the production of heroes though it must be blended, curiously enough, with other bloods for the best results. That is the old Spanish, the Castilian. Still, that Spanish must be pure in itself to avoid producing Kyne's "Greaser." Ken Burney, of *The Gringo Privateer,* is one-quarter Castilian, but his Muriel thinks it worthwhile to point out that there is "not the faintest taint of aboriginal blood in his veins." No Indian admixture allowed; no hybrid.

If Spanish is crossed with Irish, however, heroes instead of hybrids can emerge. The result may be indeed as richly endowed a figure as Don Miguel José Federico Noriaga

Farrel, otherwise Don Mike, and after Matt Peaslee the most noted of Kyne's rugged young men.

The Pride of Palomar revolves around Don Mike. This novel had several new editions following its appearance just after World War I, the last being in a 1935 anthology of Kyne's novels issued by Farrar & Rinehart. It is still interesting today, not only because of its hero but because of its villain.

The villain is the Japanese immigrant in California. Just as Don Mike represents the happiest blend of blood strains, the aggressive Japanese potato baron, Mr. Okada, typifies the unblended worst. He is all the more wicked since he represents not an entirely inferior race but one that has proved itself economically superior, a race that is pushing out the whites in California. On this count above all others Kyne rests his novel. In his dedication he calls *The Pride of Palomar* "a book with a mission." He says, moreover, that this work "has, at least, the merit of sincerity." This statement too is notable in its implications. It might otherwise be argued that Kyne's view of Mendel's Law and its operation should not be documented even in part from the words of his characters — after all many a novelist has created criminals in fiction without himself being suspect. Kyne, though, presents this outstanding exposition of his Mendelian views and prefaces it with a public announcement of his sincerity. The book is, he adds, a "labor of love."

The plot follows the Kyne pattern. Mike Farrel, ex-top sergeant in the first World War, comes back to reclaim his heritage. But his courtly father has died, and his Rancho Palomar, in its fair valley, is about to have its mortgage foreclosed. The holder of the mortgage, John Parker, is an Easterner but he is also the father of the heroine and so turns out to be more amenable than others from his region. At the opening of the action, however, he is attempting to lease the rancho and the valley to Japanese farmers through their representative, Mr. Okada, the potato baron. Okada, after a well-deserved horsewhipping, tries to have Don Mike assassinated. The would-be assassin he hires is caught and killed by Mike's faithful retainer, and Okada is forced to give up. Kay Parker soon falls in love with Farrel and helps him in his struggle with her father. By now the action has narrowed into the business warfare to be seen in most of Kyne's plots and Don Mike again wins handily. He out-bluffs and outguesses John Parker, and at the end of the story has married Kay and regained his ranch. And he has converted Parker to his Californian view of the Japanese problem.

As early as the second chapter Farrel explains his own national origins. His family, he points out to his captain just before he leaves the Army, "were pure-bred Spanish blonds" until Don Mike's black-Irish grandfather married into the family. The captain says that Farrel is "clean-strain white," and Farrel himself echoes and amplifies the sentiment by saying that he supposes he is, to sum it all up, an American. Again, when first talking with Kay Parker, Don Mike discusses his Spanish and Irish traits, painting one or two of them just unfavorably enough to add color and warmth to his character. Then he discusses — at the other end of the scale — the Japanese and their characteristics. Some time after his talk with Kay, Don Mike returns to his charges against Japanese blood and Japanese character and presents them in detail during a chapter-long debate with her father. In *The Pride of Palomar* Kyne acknowledges his debt to Montaville Flowers' *The Japanese Conquest of American Opinion* (1917) and much of the material in this chapter and others parallels Flowers. The Japanese use our own national honesty, honor, and sense of fair-dealing to hobble us. They themselves lack those qualities utterly. They do have thrift, industry, and cleanliness — little enough too when weighed against the fact that they are also ruthless, greedy, selfish, and calculating. They are scheming, quarrelsome "disciples . . . of . . . expediency" and "past masters of evasion and deceit." Kyne follows *The Japanese Conquest* further in his description of the Japanese national psychology as it relates to Shintoism and Emperor-worship. The Japs are, in short, the polar opposites of everything that is glorified as native American.

One thing above all singles out the Jap for his bad eminence. That is the fact, it may be recalled, that he furnishes economic competition to the native American — and competition so strong that the Jap is beginning to do to the white man what the white man himself did to the Indian. In consequence, Kyne can summon up some sympathy for "the tragedy of that little handful [of Indians], herded away in the heart of those barren hills to make way for the white man. And now the white man is almost gone," forced out by the "Japanese farmer, usurping that sweet valley" of Palomar. Other intrusions the Aryan has conquered. Aside from "cheap Mexican and Bohunk labor," economic competition has not meant much of a threat to the Native Son up to this time. But here is an alien race, spawning vigorously in spite of opposition.

So with these things in mind Farrel explains, in further conversation with Kay, that he "resents all Japanese" and he dwells on California's lone battle against domination by them. Later the talk turns to the Chinese. "Well then, how about John Chinaman?" the girl asks. Don Mike's face brightens as he answers, "Oh, a Chinaman is different. He's a regular fellow. You can have a great deal of respect and downright admiration for a Chinaman, even of the coolie class." "John Chinaman . . . realizes . . . that he is not assimilable with us, or we with him" and he "admits the wisdom and justice of our slogan: 'California for white men.' There was no protest from Peking when we passed the Exclusion Act." Kay wonders why the Jap is not assimilable, so Farrel asks the traditional question: Would she marry a Jap? Upon her indignant denial, he exclaims, "The purity of our race — aye, the purity of the Japanese race — forbids inter-marriage."

Over and beyond the anti-Japanese material, *The Pride of Palomar* is filled with Kyne's theory of race and nationality. Again and again someone is presented in terms of the stereotype of his origin. Personal characteristics are shown to be the result of national or racial ones. Mike, for instance, is endowed with "a certain curious hard-headedness," says Kyne and he explains parenthetically that it is "the faint strain of Scotch in him, in all likelihood." Half a page further down, Kyne alludes to Mike's father as having had "a large measure of the Celtic instinct for domination." Thus Kyne employs his customary method. In a later chapter, furthermore, he has Farrel himself say, "The racial impulses which I observed cropping out . . . always interested me." Parker agrees, "I think every race has some definite characteristics necessary to the unity of that race."

Best of all races and nationalities, it would seem, is Kyne's own. His Americans and the other Anglo-Saxon peoples are the chosen ones. They have in common a precious possession, "a national conscience." Men, like nations, are by no means created equal — that is a vulgar error. Men of one race, furthermore, are intrinsically superior to men of another. In consequence the races should stay apart. When "a member of the great Nordic race fuses with a member of a pigmented race, both parties," let it be said, "violate a natural law."

Kyne's theory of race and method of characterization work out in union. His writings still occupy the shelf of many a public library, and his books there stay in demand. In testimony perhaps to the effectiveness of his method, the public continues to borrow and occasionally to buy his novels. Apparently his theory when developed in literary terms is not repugnant to his readers. To them, immersed in the story, it may be no more than logical that Don Mike Farrel, representative of the Aryan best, should favor the odious Mr. Okada "with a cool, contemptuous scrutiny" and announce that "We ought to have Jim Crow cars for these cock-sure sons of Nippon."

Today a new group of readers, angered and frustrated by international problems, might be much attracted to *The Pride of Palomar*. American nativism is, I am afraid, by no means dead; in Kyne's books it could find something to sustain it.

Lloyd Douglas:
Loud Voice in the Wilderness

THREE centuries ago a young Puritan minister wrote one of the most popular poems that has ever been published in New England. It was a long didactic work, practically bare — so it has seemed to almost every critic — of literary merit. Yet, as the fullest and best literary history of our country points out, nearly all anthologies of American literature include selections from the poem and nearly all histories of American literature devote a few paragraphs, at any rate, to the minister and his writing. He was Michael Wigglesworth; the poem was "The Day of Doom." In our time one of the most phenomenally popular novelists we have had is another clergyman, Lloyd Douglas. His purpose, like Wigglesworth's, has been purely didactic. Unlike Wigglesworth, however, he is still ignored by both the literary critic and the literary historian. The effects in his novels are often crudely conceived, and so the professional critic may perhaps be excused from examining his fiction. But this is no reason for the student of literary history to neglect it. He can afford to study *The Robe* in the same way that he studies "The Day of Doom." As popular literature both cast light on the popular mind.

It is now clear that Douglas' writing falls rather readily into three general periods. During the 1920's he wrote professional books for ministers. During the 1930's he wrote a series of flashy modern theological novels. During the 1940's he wrote only two books — *The Robe,* a historical novel about the Roman commander who gambled for and won Christ's garment, and *The Big Fisherman,* which deals with Simon, who was to become Christ's chief apostle, and with Christ himself. The fullest period is the middle one, and it actually overlaps the other two slightly. *Magnificent Obsession,* Douglas' first bestseller, came out in 1929 and *Invitation to Live,* the last of the "modern" novels, in 1940.

The first of his books is a jaunty little manual of advice to other ministers entitled *Wanted — a Congregation.* Its main significance lies in the fact that the advice is dramatized by putting the entire book in story form, in a way which clearly anticipates Douglas' bestsellers. The Reverend D. Preston Blue, the main character, is invited to a reunion with two of his old college friends, a successful manufacturer and a successful newspaper editor. They and Blue have just passed their fortieth birthdays (as had Douglas himself not long before), and so they think it an appropriate time to take stock of their careers — to "invoice them," as Douglas puts it. The minister, a bored and tired failure, meets with his friends only after some hesitation. The first half of the manual is devoted to long conversations in which the manufacturer and the editor point out to him what is wrong with current religious practices; and a doctor, the first of many in Douglas' writing, is introduced to do the same thing. Blue is convinced, begins to think positively, and in fact achieves a mild kind of conversion. He no longer regards his role as mawkish and unmanly but goes back to his congregation with the drive of a high-powered executive. The second half of the manual is devoted to the ways in which Blue builds up his church, organizes his laymen, and dominates them.

All this is pictured in a series of loosely connected scenes, with no direct advice to the reader. The story moves along briskly; even the lengthy conversations do not lag. The style is pert and the content easy to assimilate. The book is the product of a natural storyteller. But the level of ideas can be demonstrated through a single example. Toward the end of *Wanted* the Reverend Mr. Blue has effected every practical reform he wishes. He is the shepherd of a large and cooperative flock, and he feels the joy of the pastoral care. He has determined earlier that "the secret of our lack of success in the churches . . . is the absence of crowds"; now every pew is filled and tardy parishioners are turned away. His use of card files, membership campaigns, and newspaper publicity has brought in the crowds he wants, and he has held them with his sermons. Yet he gradually realizes that this is not enough. He asks himself, this once, a basic question, "Exactly why did people go to church? . . . To hear a sermon? Was that all? Was there not another — indeed a primary — function of the church that he, Blue, had completely ignored? Was he helping to satisfy that irresistible heart-hunger of the normal human soul for a closer contact with the Infinite?" Pondering this, Lloyd Douglas joins himself for a moment to a great company including members so diverse as Ralph Waldo Emerson and St. Teresa of Avila. He has finally discovered what he calls the heart-hunger. And what will he do about it? He decides — and this is the final revelation in *Wanted* — that he will make the remainder of his church service more dramatic in order to give it the same punch that his sermon now has!

Wanted was issued in 1920. Four years later *The Minister's Everyday Life* appeared. The significance of *The Minister's Everyday Life* in relation to Douglas' literary work lies mainly in the fact that the minister is advised to broaden his acquaintance with the various walks of life in order to furnish sermon (or story) material. And the written sermon leads naturally into the written story and then into the novel. The interest of Douglas' next book, *These Sayings of Mine: an Interpretation of the Teachings of Jesus,* published in 1926, lies both in the technique Douglas employs and in the subject he chooses. The subject is the parables of Christ. Douglas' method in *These Sayings* is to quote the parables, and then to expand them into novelistic scenes and interpret them. His appeal to the popular taste is forecast by the folksiness and directness of his narrative. The parables lose their biblical richness, their several levels of meaning, and become merely quick-moving moral anecdotes.

But Douglas, it is clear, was troubled by his subject. In *These Sayings* he had begun by asserting that we concentrate on Christ's birth and death too much and fail to stress the stories he told. Douglas himself stressed the stories and also minimized any miraculous element in them. Yet he felt that the miracles in the parables, as well as the miracles of Christ's birth and resurrection, needed to be explained. The conflict between science and religion at this point had to be resolved. Although Douglas was deeply attracted to the figure of Jesus, as he says, he was obviously uneasy in dealing with the basic assumptions involved in accepting Christianity. Within a year after *These Sayings* came out he published his last ministerial book. He called it, aptly enough, *Those Disturbing Miracles.*

In it he admits carefully on the one hand that he cannot interpret Jesus satisfactorily without at least reference to what he terms "the supernormal." On the other hand he does everything he can in the course of this book to explain the miracles in psychological terms. The water, for instance, that Jesus transformed for the marriage feast at Cana did not literally become wine; however, the power of Christ's great presence was such that water drunk with him would seem like wine drunk with anyone else. Or if the appeal to human psychology in that fashion will not do, Douglas turns to an appeal of another kind. The miracle of the loaves and fishes, for instance, was not literally a miracle, he suggests. Instead, many people had a little food with them but were unwilling to share it until a child shamed them by his example. Then they brought out their bit, sharing crumbs with one another, and the sum total was large enough to give a taste to everyone and still have twelve full baskets left over. In spite of the fact that Douglas will profess a moral and a religious purpose for his novels of the 1930's, there will be nothing "supernormal" in them to repel or disturb the lay reader.

Douglas' initial novel, *Magnificent Obsession,* developed out of a combination of a news item with a sermon. In 1920 Douglas saw a report in a Detroit paper about a man who had lost his life by drowning but could have been revived if his own artificial respirator had not been in use across the lake. After mulling over the idea for years, Douglas started the novel in 1927 but found he could not finish it. About a year later he preached a series of three unusually effective sermons on the theme of "secret altruism." At Sunday dinner after the final sermon, one of his daughters suggested that he introduce his striking theme into the book. He did and brought *Magnificent Obsession* to a successful conclusion.

In spite of the popular appeal — apparent to this day — in his energetic mingling of story and sermon, his book was rejected by well-known publishing houses, and the manuscript ended up in the hands of a small Chicago firm called Willett, Clark, and Colby. The first edition, appearing in 1929, was 3000 copies. It was advertised to booksellers among the other religious books the firm published. It sold slowly at the beginning but the date of publication was significant. By the end of 1929 the materialistic values which had characterized boom-time America were suffering heavy blows. Confidence in commercial prosperity was being shaken and the time was apparently right for a novel with a "message." As the depression deepened in the next two years, *Magnificent Obsession* overcame its slow start. It did not reach the bestseller list until a year after publication, but once there, it stayed for eighteen months. In all two million people, according to one publisher's estimate, read the book.

Douglas' literary devices were crude but effective, and the attractions that *Magnificent Obsession* had for the reader are still obvious at a glance. The supposed glamour of medicine, the swift-moving action, the naively but clearly drawn characters, some sex, and, perhaps most appealing, an inspirational message are all to be found in the book. The novel begins with the marriage of a distinguished and elderly brain surgeon, Dr. Wayne Hudson, to a young woman, mainly for the sake of his motherless daughter. The marriage is cut short by his accidental death. His death would not, however, have occurred if a rich, useless young man had not been using Dr. Hudson's own inhalator at the time of the accident. Soon the young man, Bobby Merrick, realizes that he has inadvertently caused the death of Dr. Hudson. He dedicates himself to becoming a doctor in Hudson's place. The rest of the book, stripped of plot complications, is given over to two things. The first is a slick-fiction love story in which Merrick is attracted by Dr. Hudson's beautiful young widow, later saves her life by performing a brilliant operation, and carries her off at the end of the book. Douglas tells the story with the air of a clergyman taking a glass of sherry in public. The other element of importance in the book is Merrick's gradual deciphering of Dr. Hudson's diary. In it he reads, and is finally persuaded by, its philosophy of doing good secretly to others ("let not thy left hand know what thy right hand doeth") and so increasing one's own personal "power." Merrick learns how this system brought fulfillment and fame to Dr. Hudson; he himself now adopts it and the same thing happens. So philosophy and love go hand in hand, and a bestseller is born.

There is seldom, in this novel or those succeeding it, any feeling that the characters grow organically for the author. Galsworthy, for example, has written that at times his characters have taken on a life of their own; all he has done is to describe their course. In Douglas' fiction the characters are simple and plastic. They change obediently from bad people to good ones if the story demands it — and it usually does. Once or twice Douglas achieves an effective caricature; generally, though, everyone moves in a haze of mellow light. The only notable exceptions come late in Douglas' career.

Although characterization in *Magnificent Obsession* and the later novels is simple, the plotting is a bit more sophisticated. Douglas obviously tries to get away from the strictly linear story. He makes use of flashbacks and relatively bold jumps in time. And as he continues to write throughout the 1930's he adopts two particular devices to complicate his plots. His favorite is one that Aldous Huxley describes in *Point Counter Point:* to put different characters in similar situations and similar characters in different situations. *White Banners,* for one, has as a minor theme the relation of parents to their children; and Douglas works it out through several combinations: the hero Paul Ward and his children, the servant Hannah Parmalee and her son by rich Thomas Bradford, Bradford and the son, and so on. There can be little doubt that, whether or not Douglas read the well-known passage in Huxley, he knew what he was trying to do. The other plotting device Douglas uses at times is to begin a story with characters different in temperament whose lives are widely separated. Then, as the story builds up, their lives come closer together and finally meet and intertwine. In the clearest instance of this, *Invitation to Live,* the main characters come to the study of Dean Harcourt of Trinity Cathedral for advice and consolation. The dean acts as a benevolent Olympian and neatly pairs and adapts the characters in order to settle their personal problems. Barbara Breckinridge, an unhappy girl, is sent to a Nebraska farm and there finds a maladjusted young man, Lee Richardson, who has also been counseled by the dean. As they learn to know one another, their troubles dissolve.

This same interweaving of characters is done on a larger,

looser scale in *The Robe* and *The Big Fisherman*. Lacking the patness and coincidence of the earlier plottings, the gradual interrelationships in the last two novels are considerably more convincing. Coincidences still occur but they no longer seem to be the dire result of the novelist's need.

After the absence of literary qualities in Douglas' novels is admitted, it would be unfair not to note the emotional effectiveness of many of their scenes for the average reader. They can be moving. They have no touch of subtlety, no shadow of restraint, but they have all the appeal of sentimental drama. Though the effects are heavy, no one can ignore them. The somber tone of trouble and tears of the old radio serial is lacking; this is a warmer atmosphere. It is one generated, according to a character in *White Banners,* by a "sense of confidence in the integrity of the Plan." In this kindly world, kindly emotions are appropriate. They are what the novelist ought to stress. The same person in *White Banners* who speaks about confidence in the integrity of the Plan at another point lays down a book she has been leafing through and terms it a "meagerly plotted controversial novel wordily dealing with world politics." It is clear that Lloyd Douglas aims to have his literary works the opposite of this. He asks of the novel what his spokesman Dean Harcourt asks of a painting, "Will it benefit society? . . . Will it make anyone a better citizen?"

Drawing on his pipe, the editor in *Wanted — a Congregation* says reflectively to the Reverend Mr. Blue, "Dan . . . next to human blood, black ink is the most redemptive chemical in the world." It is Douglas speaking. The one thing, over all others, that distinguishes his novels from the customary bestsellers is his moral purpose. It took him ten years after writing *Wanted* before he entered the field of popular fiction but once in it he never deviated from his aim. In thirty years no other writer of didactic fiction has been so successful as Douglas. His message is, I believe, worth examining.

The central tenet of Douglas' philosophy, the most important of his ideas, lies in a thoroughly respectable though presently unpopular tradition. It is the stress on the individual instead of the group, on the inner instead of the outer life, and on the spiritual instead of the material. "All other problems will settle themselves," Dean Harcourt tells someone, "when you have set things right — in your kingdom." To the reviewers the most objectionable thing about Douglas' novels of the 1930's was that they actually represented a corruption of this central tenet; and it was not until the writing of *The Robe* and *The Big Fisherman* that Douglas came fully back into his tradition. The philosophy he enunciates in *Magnificent Obsession* is vitiated by the fact that although the inner, spiritual life is preached, it is steadily accompanied by outer and grossly material rewards.

Through a sculptor named Randolph, Dr. Hudson learns the way to personal power. It is to build up his own personality by doing good to others secretly. Randolph says that a person with a small, inadequate personality must build a bigger, better one: "*out* of other personalities? — no, *into* other personalities." And there must be complete secrecy; if "there is a leak along the line of transfer — the whole effect is wasted." Secret good must be done continually, moreover, for good deeds are quickly used up. Again and again, when Dr. Hudson finds himself confronted with someone he has done good to and who wants to repay him for it, he says "I have used it all up." In other words he has fed his personality on the deed; he has already received his rewards.

The material rewards for doing good quietly are various. They may even include the physical development of the doer. Dr. Hudson finds (save the mark!) that doing good "had actually deepened his voice and given it a new resonance." People now defer to him, he notes. "By some I was regarded with wide-eyed curiosity; by others with unusual displays of personal interest and friendship." More solid rewards come as well — praise in the medical journals, a hospital for him to head. This same happy abundance became the attraction of the next half-dozen novels that Douglas wrote. Until the time when *The Robe* was printed, Douglas rang the changes on his major theme. The rewards were always both spiritual and material. For the hero of *White Banners* wealth and a professorship; for the hero of *Disputed Passage* a satisfying medical career and a joyful marriage — and so on. If the inner light was not enough of a guide, then inspiration from the "Outside," from the planners of the Universe, came to the aid of the benevolent.

The man who discovered this way to power, says Douglas, was Christ; and Douglas' philosophy purports to be based on the Sermon on the Mount. Only rarely, however, is the doctrine of abnegation preached in his novels, and it is not the meek but the active and strong who inherit the good midwestern earth. Nor do they turn the other cheek very often, although this would be easy to do in Douglas' fiction because evil is relatively unimportant there. The Devil himself proves to be more of a fool than a knave.

Certainly one of the indexes to the scope of Douglas' mind is the way he deals with the problem of evil, either as a novelist or as a theologian. Positing a benevolent and omnipotent God, as one would expect from his background, he solves the problem of evil in the world simply by ignoring it. Even in his four books for ministers he steers clear of the problem. The closest he gets is in *These Sayings,* where he somewhat doubtfully develops the idea that "Whom the Lord loveth He chasteneth." In discussing the parable of the fruitless fig tree he says, "All this pruning and digging, while not a very pleasant experience, was a distinct compliment to the fig tree. The vine-dresser would not have gone to the bother if the tree had not been worth saving." And in the middle group of novels, there is one instance where Douglas attacks the Old Testament view of God in relation to the problem of evil. A girl praises the hero of *Forgive Us Our Trespasses,* "You've pointed the finger of scorn at a crafty Jehovah who would bring an innocent pair of inquisitive people into the world, and immediately direct their attention to some experiment brimming with tragedy."

Dean Harcourt emerges as Douglas' main spokesman in the novels of the 1930's, and he announces not only that the world is good but also that it is slowly but surely getting better. True, the progress is not always smooth and the ascent is sometimes slow but nevertheless it is a "Long Parade," upward. Therefore the problem of evil, small to begin with, is gradually becoming even smaller. Man, says Dean Harcourt in a book Douglas published in 1935, "is about to make long strides, *morally.*" There could hardly have been a more inaccurate prediction. Douglas did not see fit to modify it, though, in any of his next four "modern" books. But in 1942 *The Robe* appeared and in this enormously popular novel the easy optimism of all Douglas' prior writing is gone. It is replaced by a recognition of the power, theologically, of evil in this world and of its ability to destroy earthly good. Though Douglas still emphasizes doing good deeds, the rewards shift from this world to the next. He comes back to the Christian theology most typical of American religious culture, and he preaches in *The Robe* the same kind of sermon that has been preached in American pulpits many a Sunday morning. Good shall triumph over evil but its triumph may well come in the next world and not in this. In anticipation of the ultimate victory of good, however, the hero and heroine of *The Robe* choose to die a martyr's death at the end of the novel. They die in anticipation of eternal life. In *The Big Fisherman* evil also wins out in this world — Christ is crucified — but the promise of eternal good hereafter has been opened to all mankind. Both in his Roman novel and in his final Galilean one, Douglas confronts the problem of evil fairly directly even though he still does not discuss its implications as much as he did his earlier, easier doctrine.

Thus Douglas' writing becomes both deeper and more traditional. Furthermore, when he accepts a traditional Christian answer to the problem of evil, he finally encounters the conflict of science and religion. In his ministerial works of the 1920's he pays little attention to the miraculous in Christian theology and tries to explain anything that is not normal by using psychological terms. In his novels of the 1930's he does the same thing. When his leading characters are "inspired" they merely pass through a psychological process. They generally undergo conversions and once or twice have mystical experiences, but these are explained in terms that a classic psychologist like William James would have been well satisfied with. By the time *The Robe* has been written, Douglas makes clear that he now believes in "the supernormal." He describes at least one miracle in *The Robe*, Simon's deliverance from prison, but he does so in an ambiguous manner. The deliverance seems to the reader to be part of Simon's dream. Notwithstanding, the miracle, as Douglas sees it, is described. In *The Big Fisherman* he accepts the traditional Christian miracles and describes them literally. There is no longer any attempt at a scientific explanation of them, for Douglas finally makes plain his subscription to the cause of religion at the expense of science. He is far from the author who had a character in *Magnificent Obsession* announce that the Bible was basically the "textbook of a science relating to the expansion and development of the human personality" and that it should be approached with scientific methodology.

Douglas' concept of the ideal man of God also changes significantly throughout the course of his literary career. To begin with, in *Magnificent Obsession* and its immediate successors, he is the physician. No St. Luke, he is rather a brisk and thoughtful healer of both body and mind. His duty is not done when he puts down the surgeon's scalpel. The operation may be over but many a patient still needs spiritual — or rather, psychological — care. Half of the novels that Douglas wrote in his middle period have a doctor either as the main character or as a god from the machine. There are few ministers at first, and they are of little consequence. In *Magnificent Obsession* Douglas contrasts Dr. Bobby Merrick, after his conversion, with the Reverend Bruce MacLaren. MacLaren is a modernist who has freed his congregation from fundamentalism but has given them no true religion in its place. Merrick's practical, scientific faith makes MacLaren's ethical piety look pale and empty. Although MacLaren is not treated unsympathetically, there are other ministerial characters in the later novels who come off less well. Such, for instance, are the Reverend Miles Drumm of *Forgive Us Our Trespasses*, who is weak and untrustworthy, and his daughter Angela, who becomes a golden-haired evangelist in the artful Aimee Semple Mc-Pherson tradition. The hero of *Forgive Us Our Trespasses* skeptically watches her on the stage with some crippled children: "Angela, face uplifted, blue eyes wide, enraptured, called upon her Father, these little ones' Father, to keep His word with her — with them — with us."

One great advantage of the idea of the doctor as minister is that it helps to minimize the conflict between science and religion. In the benevolent medical man as Douglas creates him there is no need to explore unpalatable extremes. There is no offense to the fundamentalist on the one hand or to the materialist on the other.

In his slow swing toward traditionalism, however, Douglas introduces the character of Dean Harcourt. In this dignified but kindly Episcopalian churchman Douglas avoids the things that repelled him in the nonconforming ministry but comes back to a professional ministry nevertheless. Dean Harcourt is supposed to be primarily a man of God, not a psychiatrist. Douglas introduces him in *Green Light* and makes him the central figure in *Invitation to Live,* which was the last novel to appear before *The Robe.* He is much taken with him. The trend toward tradition continues in *The Robe* and *The Big Fisherman.* In *The Robe* Marcellus becomes for a few months a true shepherd to a flock he has gathered around him in a little Roman town. In *The Big Fisherman* Douglas carefully traces the growth of Simon from a simple, rugged, sometimes too hasty human being into the chief apostle. The neat, ready answers and the clever stratagems of the earlier novels are gone. Simon deals with people as if he had learned to love them but did not see through them with medical accuracy. Finally, in Jesus himself, Douglas develops his ultimate conception of the shepherd. He sees him as humble but strong, selfless, and noble. The miracles, furthermore, are all there — no more scientific explanations — but it is apparently a simple human being who performs them. Only once or twice in *The Big Fisherman* can the objective reader begin to apprehend the quality of divinity that our culture normally associates with Jesus Christ. Nevertheless, it is obvious that any attempt to portray Christ meets with great difficulties in Western civilization, and Douglas does somewhat better than might be expected.

Such are the moral and theological doctrines contained in Douglas' novels. His present publishers estimate that over ten million copies of his works have been printed. It would be useless to guess at the number of readers for each copy but at the very least Douglas has gained for himself a parish of millions of people. He said in a magazine article that he did not leave the ministry after he wrote *Magnificent Obsession;* he simply widened his congregation. His parishioners have been a multitude; how many have heeded his sermon no one can tell. But it would be unreasonable to deny either some response or some reciprocity — some response to Douglas' writing on the part of his readers and some reciprocity in his response to his readers' changing interests and demands.

As the times changed, so did Douglas' philosophy. At forty, when he began writing books, he displayed in his ministerial manuals the brisk but conflicting ideas of a modernist minister. In his novels of the 1930's the philosophy is one of doing good for the sake of improving one's personality, with material rewards following consistently if "quite incidentally." In his two novels of the 1940's, the emphasis shifted. In a time of life-and-death struggle, the spiritual rewards of good were stressed. The goal became not this world but the next. Readers today too are receptive, as bookbuying records show, to something more than a materialistic morality play. The result is that Douglas' life of Christ and his chief apostle has sold far beyond normal expectations. *The Robe* has run to nearly two million copies and *The Big Fisherman* was, according to several counts, the top fiction bestseller for at least two years. With its Roman pageantry *The Robe* overshadows *The Big Fisherman*. Yet the latter's message is even more traditionally spiritual than *The Robe*'s and that is probably the major reason for its present appeal. Today man's reason looks considerably less powerful than it did a few years ago. For us, it apparently solved the problem of winning World War II only to be confronted with the massive problems of the postwar period. It may be guessed that a good many readers, losing confidence in their own potentialities, are again turning elsewhere — and in particular to religion of the kind that Douglas dramatized. At any rate, what Douglas has been saying is still clearly more congenial to the American reader than the words of any other novelist with a message.

Finally, I want to say something explicit about Douglas and the unconscious, both because of its importance to him as a writer and because of his exceptional ability to carry the average reader with him in his writing.

At the level of the unconscious the history of Douglas' writing is the search for the father. Fitful and superficial at first, the search gained in intensity as Douglas aged. In the classic Freudian way he fashioned literature, though not very good literature, out of it and its confusions and frustrations. His personal life as a minister was a series of successes yet each left him restless. He knew something was lacking. He made himself the central character of his first ministerial manuals, splitting his personality to do so. He became the bored and baffled Preston Blue, for instance, of the early part of *Wanted — a Congregation,* as well as the two fatherly friends who counseled him and helped turn him into the dynamic pastor of the later part. The manuals failed, however, to give Douglas sufficient scope for his search. It took the freedom of fiction to give him enough room, and it was to fiction that he turned.

In writing *Magnificent Obsession* he based the plot not on

one example of the quest but two. The first has to do with Bobby Merrick. Previously nothing but a wealthy scapegrace, he comes to identify himself so thoroughly with the fine man he has allowed to die that he follows that man's profession, adopts his philosophy, and ends by marrying his young widow. He has, in effect, identified so well with Dr. Hudson that he has replaced him. And Dr. Hudson himself, we are told through flashbacks, once sought and found a father in the sculptor Randolph. This bearded, grizzled man, "an apostle of light," gave young Hudson the guidance he needed when desolated by the death of his first wife.

Throughout the "modern" novels which came after *Magnificent Obsession* the search for the father continued. Often Douglas depicted him as a doctor; in fact the doctor, we may remember, was a vital figure in fully half the novels of the 1930's. The satisfactions he provided for Douglas were doubtless many, but it is all too plain from the records of his personal life that they were not enough. During the 1930's he enjoyed exceptional triumphs. Through the sale of his novels he became a national celebrity. At the same time his family life was marred by a good deal of suffering. He, his wife, and his two daughters all had more than their share of sickness and pain. Turning away in his fiction from the father as medical scientist to the father as avowed churchman, Douglas began to develop the figure of Dean Harcourt. As Douglas defined him he had none of the marks of the pulpit-pounding Fundamentalist whom Douglas despised. Dean Harcourt was shown at ease in dealing with both spiritual and material problems. He moved with finesse in both the cloister and the concourse.

However, in formulating the plots for Dean Harcourt, Douglas made the mistake of over-compensating. The way the Dean did it was much too easy — he solved the problems of life, as presented by the other characters, with too great a facility, too positive an optimism. The contrast with the real world, public and private, was stark. World War II was approaching nearer and nearer; the age of the barbarians seemed at hand. And at Douglas' home everyone appeared to be sick. "I get so tired of nurses in the house," he said sadly one day in 1938. He learned that he was suffering from diabetes in addition to the arthritis which already plagued him. His daughters were in and out of the hospital; his wife herself was not always well. He poured into *The Robe* much of his torment and there at last began to resolve his confusion. Almost grudgingly he began to understand that his search for the father could have only one end, the traditional Christian one. Now he believed in God more devoutly than he ever had before in his long years as a minister. Now he believed in God, but still not quite in His miracles.

Once *The Robe* appeared, he had more blows to suffer. The success of this book was enormous. But his wife broke her back and was put to bed, never to be able to turn again. According to his daughters he endured every spasm with her and became too crippled for a time to walk or even move. Technically this was a case of conversion hysteria; as his daughters saw it, "His was a mysterious illness entirely associated with hers." He recovered, but only partially, and proceeded with the composition of his last book, *The Big Fisherman,* which he had started a few months before. His wife died and he went on writing. There in *The Big Fisherman* he finally found all that he was after. He found his absolute. The father was God, God in the form of Jesus Christ. Laying aside his last misgivings — about the validity of the miracles — he came to full submission. After writing the concluding chapter of *The Big Fisherman* he could say with Dante, "In Thy will is my peace." Now he could tell one of his daughters, "I am very weary, very happy, very humble." And he could add that in writing this book "I feel sure that I had help from The Outside." In his search for the father he had experienced a spiritual conversion. Age, illness, and bereavement had chastened him and made him wise. He lived for two years after publishing *The Big Fisherman*. During most of that time he was bed-ridden; his daughters noted that he died uncomplainingly.

The Buxom Biographies

IN THE last decade several prominent persons have been doing their best to make an honest woman out of the biographical novel. One of them, who happens to look rather like Huey Long, is a New Orleans newspaperman. Another is an ex-college teacher with the face of a reasonably friendly faun. Both have made considerable progress but not, it must be confessed, quite enough. The biographical novel still goes its bosomy way, its flimsy clothing tattered and torn in exactly the wrong places. It has its reasons, though. After all, during most of its checkered history it sinned without knowing. It was ensnared by the fact that new and firmer notions of accuracy grew up. As a matter of fact, the biographical novel deserves more to be pitied than censured.

For us it started mainly with Mason Weems. One of the most engaging liars of his time, he published the first edition of his life of Washington in 1800. He had been, he averred, the rector of Mount Vernon parish; and his readers needed no other credentials from him. The book thrived like a weed. In the fifth edition appeared the fables of the cherry tree, the cabbage, and the colt. Before his death in 1825, Parson Weems had had the satisfaction of seeing some seventy editions of his supposedly biographical work in print. What he produced was not biography in any sense of the word as it is used today. Instead he created a myth. But it was a myth so suited to the American folk-hero pattern that it remains a model of its curious kind. Of the many ways in which the book satisfies popular American demands, one example should be enough to illuminate the rest.

That has to do with the benefits of being good. Though it is part of the official American tradition to consider virtue its own reward, we know that from the arrival of the Massachusetts Bay Puritans to the present, the average American feels unofficially that that is not enough. The renewed vogue of Lloyd Douglas' novels with their insistence that good deeds will return to the doer sevenfold, is one proof of the continuing vitality of the feeling. To Parson Weems, Washington's career was crammed with incidents showing that when he did his duty, even though it might have been unpleasant at the time, he earned an ample recompense. Because Washington put up, for instance, with the constant fretfulness of his ailing half-brother Lawrence, as was proper, he ultimately inherited nearly half of Lawrence's large estate. To use what Weems asserted were Washington's own words, "There exists . . . an inseparable connection between duty and advantage."

During the first half of the nineteenth century the imaginative parson was to find many imitators, and the biographical novel, though it would not yet be called that, would flourish. The American people displayed a love for heroic life-stories which revealed itself not only in the printed book but in lyceum lectures and folk art as well. Notwithstanding, it is a fact that throughout these same decades a few biographies were produced which showed an earnest insistence on truth and historical accuracy. Though the wave of German scholarship with its ideal of citing a source for every statement was still to reach this country, we could already boast of several biographers who wrote the unadorned truth to the best of their ability. A noted and versatile New Englander, the Reverend Jared Sparks, became the most famous one before 1850. His lives of Washington and Franklin received wide though not unanimous acclaim. He was followed in the latter half of the century by an even more outstanding man, our first professional biographer, James Parton. If Sparks dominated the first fifty years of the century, Parton dominated the second. Dexterous and conscientious at the same time, he not only proved that he could carry on meticulous research but also that he understood ideas and social forces. His three-volume life of Andrew Jackson, published in 1860, remains his masterpiece.

But its faults are easy to see. They serve to show why the public often continued to enjoy a biographical novel more than a biography. Parton's book is too full of documents, too thorough, too complicated. What the average reader wanted in 1860, he had wanted in 1800 — and still wants today. He wanted narrative drive, colorful anecdotes, and simple characterization. He wanted every sentence to move. And in all probability the reader with tastes above the average wanted still other things which even a Sparks or a Parton could not always give. He wanted the motivations of the subject to be explored. Just why did Franklin or Jackson do this or that? He wanted the high points of the life described in full, without the disturbing gaps caused by the fact that the writer could not find some of the information he needed so badly. At the same time he wanted the dull parts omitted. And lastly he wanted an orderly, almost a symphonic, structure and a literary richness of style and metaphor to satisfy his esthetic interests.

In other words he set his expectations high and hoped for what is actually found in biography only at its best. Not getting it very often — naturally — he proved himself ready to sacrifice some of the qualities he had wished for. Above all, I am afraid, accuracy. However, he was ready to make other compromises as well, as book-buying records reveal, and so his requirements neared those of the average reader though not coinciding with them. If he could not find the accurate best he was willing to settle for the colorful second-best. If he could not find a good biography he was ready to settle for a good biographical novel.

Because he feels the same today, he still buys a biographical novel more readily than he buys an accurate biography. Thus he encourages publishers to grant the biographical novel a permanent place on their annual lists. The book clubs frequently give the galley proof of such a work at least a calculating look if not more. Several biographical novels have in fact been recent book club choices. Without doubt the biographical novel as a literary type has kept its vigor. Sometimes powerful and often picturesque, it deserves much more attention than it has received from most critics. To let us understand it clearly, it should be seen in its context; we need to know what its literary landscape is like.

The best biographical novelist we have at present is probably Irving Stone (the ex-college teacher) and the next best is Harnett Kane (the newspaperman). Both have been writing for many years. To appreciate what those men, in particular, are doing, and to assess it accurately, we ought to look at the whole landscape now. In the center, for our purposes, we can put one book by each man, his most notable biographical novel so far. Each, incidentally, became a book club selection. One is Stone's story of Mrs. Abraham Lincoln; the other is Kane's novel about Mrs. Robert E. Lee.

To the left of them — and at some distance — we may locate *Whirlwind in Petticoats*. It is the gamy life of a professional harridan of a hundred years ago named Victoria Claflin Woodhull and her overripe sister Tennessee. Dedicated to "all feminists" by its author, Beril Becker, it makes the most of the opportunities for sensationalism that the sisters' careers afforded. From the point of view of popularity, the selection of the subject proved a shrewd one.

Women are interested in the suffering female, and most book buyers are women. (It is worth noting that even the best writers in the field like to write about a woman.) Furthermore, the Claflin sisters were reformers; they wanted to emancipate their sex. That too has a strong appeal for the dishpan and diaper trade. The scenes in the book are vivid; action is laid on with a trowel, and the joys of passion are abundantly discussed and described. From the time Victoria, afire, clings to the first male stranger (on page fifteen) to the time she kisses a giddy Henry Ward Beecher in triumph two hundred pages later, no possibilities are ignored.

If Becker's book represents the worst the biographical novel can do in one direction, two other books of the 1940's still represent the best it can do in others. Both became Pulitzer Prize winners. Robert Penn Warren's *All the King's Men* appeared in 1946. It was a novel, not a biography, yet it revealed the inwardness of Huey Long better than any other book about him. Warren called him Willie Stark. To tell his story and to divine his character, Warren used all the rich devices of literary technique. The thoughtful management of scene, the illuminating dialogue, the characteristic action are all present. And interwoven with them are wisely selected symbols such as the long journey and the mirrored water. The whole story is driven along by the nervous vigor of Warren's style. The only weakness of the book lies in the hasty, huddled ending. It comes after Willie's assassination, and in its cursory assignment of rewards and punishments to the remaining characters it reminds us of a Victorian three-decker.

The other work, Carl Sandburg's study of Lincoln during the Civil War, won the 1940 Pulitzer Prize for history rather than for biography, because of its epic scope. It is primarily a set of books about a single man but the man was so great that he encompassed his time. To compose this biography Sandburg read everything about Lincoln, no matter how tenuously connected, that he could discover. And when his mind had been steeped in Lincoln and Lincoln's life he sat down to write. He wrote without footnotes but there was no need for them. He transcended the outer forms of scholarship.

Because of his achievement as a man of letters Sandburg could add something else to his biography that is rarely found, and that was a felicity of style — a mingling of form and content beautifully suited to his subject. The love of mankind that marks Sandburg's poetry showed in his life of Lincoln. It allowed him to rise to the heights of a great event in a way few other biographers could. When he described how the people felt about Lincoln's death and how the funeral train traveled its slow way through the country, he created a poem out of fact.

These three, then, Becker, Warren, and Sandburg — each in his own fashion — mark out the bounds of the field which Stone and Kane have occupied.

Harnett Kane started out as a legman for the New Orleans *Item*. His first book, *Louisiana Hayride* (1941), is a journalist's report on the Long regime. It is accurate reporting and nothing else. But after writing it he went on to publish three biographical novels, of which *The Lady of Arlington* (1953), about Mrs. Lee, is still the best. He has gradually improved in the thoroughness of his historical research and conveys his information with growing adroitness. He opens his book with a picture of Mrs. Lee shortly before her marriage, and the reader is caught up at once in the career of this long-suffering lady. Family love and family sorrows are movingly portrayed. Illness (Mrs. Lee's agonizing rheumatic fever), frontier hardships, the nagging worries of a soldier's wife, and the losses through death are shown as she encountered them. Kane's style is unobtrusive. His descriptions are accurate, the incidents correct. Most of Mrs. Lee's conversations as well as the things she thought are based on realistic inferences. Dialogue is often a stumbling block to the writer of biographical novels. He is in constant danger either of making it sound like Sir Walter Scott or else like Sam Goldwyn talking to the Queen of England. Kane, though, manages to write it naturally and appropriately. There is one other test of a good biographical novelist which Kane passes with success. He is able to bring in several of the subsidiary historical characters and make them look alive.

All in all, Kane can be commended for a book that combines historical research with a novelist's creativity. He does well, well enough to be widely recognized. But everything Kane does, Irving Stone does a bit better.

One would never have known it from Stone's first book, however. True, it was a biographical, or rather an autobiographical, novel but of the sort to make Stone squirm today. He himself is the hero, under the barest of disguises. *Pageant of Youth,* which found a publisher (now out of business) in 1933, is a panoramic college novel with the saxophone-playing Stone, there called Ray Sharpe, at its center. The theme seems to be sex on the campus. The book begins with Ray's freshman year and then takes him, and the people he meets, on through graduation. Several of the girls resemble the Claflin sisters; some of the young men show with gusto that they can be equally uninhibited. The faults in the book vary in gravity. One of the smaller is a sophomoric use of language which may on one hand confuse "ardent" with "arduous" ("he became arduous") and on the other describe a girl as "desperately quiet, with deep connecting rods of maladjustment soldered between her eyes."

A year after *Pageant of Youth, Lust for Life* appeared. Like the first book it had been forced to wait for a publisher but there the resemblance ended. Stone had learned an astonishing amount between the two books. Having once seen the paintings of Vincent Van Gogh, Stone became obsessed with the man and his turbulent art. He could not rest until he had written a life of him. The result was a carefully studied biographical novel striking enough to be reprinted several times and now included in the Modern Library. The writing is still clumsy in spots but the power of the events themselves in Van Gogh's tragic, blundering career holds the reader.

Five more biographical novels followed. They depicted Jack London, Jessie Benton Frémont, Eugene V. Debs, the painter John Noble, and Andrew Jackson's wife Rachel. Despite their variety, each volume showed advances in novelistic technique. The scholarship deepened too, though less steadily. The peak for the present-day biographical novel was approached with the publication of Stone's book on Mary Todd Lincoln and her marriage. Rather flatly titled *Love Is Eternal* (from the inscription in the wedding ring Abe gave her), it is in other ways a notable piece of work.

The scholarship is just as sound, according to a leading Lincoln specialist, in *Love Is Eternal* as it is in the respectfully reviewed historical biography of Mrs. Lincoln by a trained historian, Ruth Randall. It deserves to be called meticulous. Many an example can be found of Stone's scholarly concern with the life he was writing. Besides the most obvious ones, there are such additional tokens of his interest as the fact that he painstakingly prepared a floor plan of the White House of Lincoln's day — one had never been reconstructed before — as a piece of independent research and that he created most of his dialogue out of skilled paraphrases of historically accurate source material.

Furthermore, the handling of the data is judicious. Mrs. Lincoln is always a controversial figure, and Stone could be excused if he slanted his information one way or the other. But he does not. Rising above his declared intention to vindicate her, he portrays her bedeviled, neurotic character with fairness. As the book moves along through its many pages, she and Abe emerge as memorable human beings, one great and the other not, but human beings both. The minor characters, such as her cousin Logan and Stephen Douglas' wife, who surround them are as a rule still more carefully differentiated than in Kane; very seldom are they merely historical names. The scenes are well handled, with pace and even suspense to some of them in spite of the fact that historians already know how they came out. The descriptions give rich color to the picture Stone creates. The entire book, finally, is written in a style that is, if undistinguished, a smooth-flowing lucid medium for the story.

The aim behind the best writing of this kind is a noble one. It is to see beneath the surface reality of fact and to reveal the true reality to others. It is to use historical data more daringly but more penetratingly than the professional historian can. Of course it is an aim that is rarely achieved. Far too often, the padded and sensational books of the *Whirlwind* kind are all that appear. But every now and then among them there will be a book like Irving Stone's on Mary Lincoln, and then the potentialities of this interesting genre are realized.

It would be pleasant to believe that there is progress in art as well as elsewhere. We would hope that with the encouraging examples in the mid-1950's of *Love Is Eternal* and *The Lady of Arlington* other biographical novelists would do their best to emulate and then surpass Irving Stone and Harnett Kane. We would hope that these two themselves would go on to even better books. What has in fact happened shows otherwise. The genre is still a difficult one.

Among the more recent books by others than Stone or Kane, James Ramsey Ullman's *The Day on Fire* attracted a good deal of attention and can represent the rest. Once a reporter and then a theatrical producer, Ullman moved into the field of the biographical novel after World War II. His best work before *The Day on Fire* was a highly regarded novel about mountaineering, *The White Tower*. He based *The Day on Fire* on the life of the profligate French poet Rimbaud. To his many labors in the library, doing research on Rimbaud's life and associations, Ullman added the actual retracing of Rimbaud's restless travels. He carefully followed Rimbaud from France all the way to Ethiopia. The result was a vivid sense of the North African scene. Throughout the seven hundred pages of his book Ullman tried hard to inform with fiction the many facts he had found. He looked into the minds of the characters, he made them say some catchy things, and he arranged his plotting with an eye to theatrical effect.

Numerous readers appreciated the result; the book went into several printings. Some critics also gave a favorable verdict. But *The Day on Fire* is, I think, a failure notwithstanding. It is partly defeated by the very choice of subject. Ullman tries to show us the trials of a homosexual boy and perverted man. He takes what he can from Freudian theory but it is not enough to reward our understanding or arouse our sympathy. Rimbaud remains repellent. The treatment of the subject as well as the subject itself is unfortunate. The style, in particular, lacks a good deal. Too often it becomes either inflated or overly familiar. Here is the high style: "The body, the flesh was dead, all of it. But out of the flesh, from the putrescence of death, there rose that which was not death; there came that which had never come from Nagunda's belly; there came Life, Life itself. His own belly had burst, and from it poured word and image, dream and vision, rising, soaring, shining, like golden birds." And here is the low style, when Rimbaud is at the point of death: "He smiled at her. He said, 'Hello, princess.' "

Able journeyman that he is, Harnett Kane has kept busily at work. He has added two more heroines to his gallery, the Confederate spy Belle Boyd and General "Stonewall" Jackson's wife. Belle's career lent itself to biographical literature and Kane does reasonably well with her in *The Smiling Rebel*. His writing is neat, with little to distract the reader. He handles his effects capably. His plot is thick with incidents — somehow they cannot help happening to the fiery, glamorous girl. Yet the book reveals no real advance over *The Lady of Arlington*. Ardent though she appears, Belle as a Southern firebrand falls into the shadow of her great fictional prototype, Scarlett O'Hara of *Gone with the Wind*.

Belle was a real woman but in Kane's book she never becomes as alive as the imaginary Scarlett.

For his newest book Irving Stone has chosen his most ambitious subject to date, Michelangelo. In working on it he was able to supplement his own meticulous researches with those of assistants and translators in Italy. Over five thousand typewritten pages of data resulted. He himself went to Italy, staying for several years. While there he benefited from the advice of the great expert on Italian art, the late Bernard Berenson, and enjoyed the use of Berenson's unique library. And to write with the feeling of a sculptor Stone took lessons in the art of carving marble. In other words, he did all the proper things and wrote under the most favorable auspices.

That the result fails to surpass his earlier books, including *Love Is Eternal,* seems to me due chiefly to a single circumstance. Mary Lincoln was a fallible, tormented but otherwise average woman. To understand her required a sympathy which Stone certainly proved he could summon up. Michelangelo was a genius, with that enormous, generous merit which Aristotle termed "magnanimity." To comprehend Michelangelo requires an insight which only a handful of authors can have. I am afraid Stone is not among them. There is another but much slighter flaw in this admirable book: the sometimes uncertain taste which can entitle this solid novel *The Agony and the Ecstasy.*

It seems probable that Stone has reached the peak of his achievement. I do not think this is true of Ruth Stephan. A latecomer to the field of biographical fiction, she entered it after years of experience as a poet, editor, and translator. Her first work, *The Flight,* was issued in 1956. In the troubled figure of Queen Christina of Sweden Mrs. Stephan had a subject which fascinated her. She had collected materials on Christina for fifteen years before *The Flight* and went on after it to publish another and still finer book about her, *My Crown, My Love.* It describes her life after she left Sweden and went to Rome. It is the story in part of

Christina's political intrigues and in part of her note-worthy efforts as a patron of the arts, which culminated in her support of the papal architect and sculptor Bernini. Against the tapestried background of seventeenth-century Rome Christina moves in uneasy magnificence. Mrs. Stephan writes about her with a consistent identification which is one of the book's distinguishing marks. The novel has been put into the form of a memoir, with Christina writing, and the self-revelations are delicately balanced between female reticence and the urge to confess everything. The thread of the story is not very important; the plot though not epi-sodic grows to no major climax. However, this serves in fact to make the memoir the more convincing, the more natural. The style is the book's final distinction. There is an ele-gance in the phrases, unobtrusive but clear, which no one else among the biographical novelists has yet achieved. Mrs. Stephan's is an even excellence and one which could result in more fine books.

Erskine Caldwell:
a Note for the Negative

"THE WORLD'S Fastest Selling Book" — such is the publisher's boast about Erskine Caldwell's gamy novel *God's Little Acre*. It hit the paperback reprint market as early as March 1946 and in slightly over two years 4,000,000 copies were sold. By 1961 the number had risen to 7,600,000 and the book was in its 52d printing. To date its publisher has reprinted twenty-eight different volumes by Caldwell, including *God's Little Acre;* taken together, these have run to the astronomical number of 46,000,000 copies. And they are still selling tremendously. A relevant question would seem to be Why?

Since *God's Little Acre* is a fullblown sample of Caldwell's fiction, the reasons behind its popularity ought to hold as well for the rest of his widely republished novels, *Tobacco Road* and *Trouble in July* among them. *God's Little Acre* has two parts to its clumsy plot. The first deals with an old Southern dirt farmer and his ruttish family, the second with a strike in a mill town near where the farmer lives. One of the leaders in the strike is his son-in-law, Will Thompson. The high point of the book comes when Will beds with a sister-in-law, the gorgeous Griselda, and then (ah, symbolism!) goes out and turns on the power in the strikebound mill so that the strike cannot be broken.

The slabs of social significance in the novel (fashionable in 1933, when it was published) are today merely interruptions to the narrative. They allow the publisher to murmur something about the sociological importance of Caldwell's writing, but it is inconceivable that they helped to sell the book in the 1940's or '50's. They did not need to. Sex did the job. Caldwell used it very effectively. With an instinct amounting almost to genius, he matched his characteristic kind of writing with its perfectly appropriate locale. How appropriate the back-country South, with its cornshuck mattress and its privy, was for his setting can be realized only if we try to substitute another section of the United States. New England, the Midwest, the Far West — none is as good. Nor is the big city, although James Farrell's Chicago and Norman Mailer's Harlem probably come as close as anything else. Certainly, as many people have pointed out, Caldwell's is not the true South. But the important thing for the multitude of customers in the reprint market is that it is true enough for them. And it invites them to feel superior to it.

Along with sex Caldwell supplied a feverish narrative. Something is always happening in *God's Little Acre* and the other books. One action swiftly succeeds another. As Caldwell said years ago in the preface to one of his short stories, "Finally, the reader is so dizzy that merely the sudden cessation of motion is sufficient to send him on his way physically reeling and emotionally groggy." Death — either murder (Will Thompson, for instance, is finally shot by the mill company's guards) or of the "Look-it, the hawgs et Grampaw" kind — is frequent, and always under sordid circumstances. Fighting is even more frequent. And all kinds of other events take place, many with a grotesque exaggeration that smacks of tall tales and Southern folklore. The reader cannot stop for a moment, if Caldwell has his way.

His publishers' figures show the remarkable extent of his success.

God's Little Acre and the rest of Caldwell's hot and shoddy novels make much money for him but add nothing to his literary reputation. This is not true for his short stories. *The Complete Stories of Erskine Caldwell* gives us a chance to see him to better advantage.

Most of these tales are set, as one might expect, in the same South as *God's Little Acre*. A few of the remainder are set in New England, where Caldwell spent several early years trying to sell what he wrote. The rest of the stories are un-localized. The Southwest — he now lives in Arizona — fur-nishes him with no material at all. His characters in these narratives are rarely individual. The poor whites act much alike. Similarly, although some of his stories of social injus-tice are as moving as anything he has ever written, it is hard to tell one suffering Negro from another. It we had to fix the time within which these beaten-down white and colored sharecroppers move, it would apparently be the depth of the Great Depression. Caldwell has selected the period as he has selected the place, which offers him the best chance for grimy melodrama. The pressures of poverty and exploita-tion weigh on his people. Actually, the New Deal, World War II, and the postwar boom in the South have all come to relieve those pressures to a degree, but Caldwell wisely continues to ignore this fact.

When he abandons his picturing of the impoverished South, his writing nearly always suffers. His conclusion to "The Lonely Day," for example, the story of a Maine farm girl, is pure mawkishness. "The first light of day broke through the mists and found her lying in the road, her body made lifeless by an automobile that had shot through the darkness an hour before. She was without motion, but she was naked, and a smile that was the beginning of laughter made her the most beautiful woman that tourists speeding to the Provinces had ever seen." When he tries to philoso-phize about Life for the women's magazine market, he sounds just as false, though in a different way. In "Here and Today," first printed in *Harper's Bazaar*, he takes up the problem of the eternal triangle. The solution he recommends pontifically is that the wife who wants to keep her husband must make herself more alluring than the other woman. Says the heroine to her wandering husband, "I've been fighting you all this time, trying to take you from her and bring you back to me. I know now that it is up to me to make you think I'm the most attractive." With supernal wisdom, the husband agrees.

Half a dozen authors in the prizewinning short story annuals, almost any year, write better than Caldwell. Yet he has achieved some reputation and he once won a literary prize himself. The hard words he has received are not always justified. He has the ability to put vivid sense impressions into simple terms, the ability — mentioned before — to keep the action moving, and finally — in his short stories at any rate — the ability to stop before the reader has caught up with him. A fair share of his short stories are memorable ones, although that is partly the result of his matter rather than his manner. Even his crudely constructed stories linger in our mind when they are tragic enough, though a visit to the morgue will too. In general, however, the sagging architecture which weakens all his novels does not develop in the short stories. They are the better for being brief.

Among the collected stories, "Candy-Man Beechum" clearly proves Caldwell's power to portray pathos and dignity; this is a sharper, keener story than the better known "Kneel to the Rising Sun." "The Medicine Man" is a first-rate sample of what some people have called his Rabelaisian humor, although it is really pornography with a horse laugh. And "Evelyn and the Rest of Us" compresses into three pages the whole story of the loss of childhood innocence. Nor are these stories the only excellent ones.

In the last seven or eight years even the short stories have begun to run down. Caldwell published a rather miscellaneous collection in 1956 called *Gulf Coast Stories,* which proved to be slicker and more superficial than the *Complete*

Stories. They showed a practiced ease of movement but gave the impression that their author was running short of breath. In 1957 he published another collection, *Certain Women.* Here he turned from the Gulf Coast to the back-country South he had helped to make notorious. Each tale focused on a sexy Southern heroine and her steamy emotions. *Men and Women* (1961) is a tissue of reprints.

Caldwell's latest efforts in the novel have been equally unrewarding. His *Claudelle Inglish,* for instance, seems more mechanical than almost any other of his book-length tales. Set in the Piedmont of Georgia, it follows the career of a jilted country girl. As the publisher's blurb puts it, "The knowledge that Linn wasn't coming back to her changed Claudelle's life — and the life of the whole crossroads." For the disillusioned girl paints her face now and swings her hips as she walks past the gawking rednecks. When she becomes the crossroads trollop her father in desperation sends her to the local parson, the Reverend Horace Haddbetter of the Story Creek Free Will church. Starved by his wife, Haddbetter is an easy conquest when Claudelle comes to him for counsel unclothed. Later he urges her to go away with him and so gives the fickle Claudelle a chance to utter the classic line, "I despise you, Horace Haddbetter." Though Caldwell has the gift of making rustic evil look funny, and uses it here and there in *Claudelle Inglish,* he manufactures a tragic conclusion for the book by having the hapless Horace shoot Claudelle. The result is no more impressive to the reader than if Caldwell had ended with a piece of thigh-slapping farce.

There is a place in the world of literature between William Faulkner and Les Scott. Mythologist of the South and holder of the Nobel award for literature, Faulkner was a great novelist. Les Scott, whose works attracted the animated attention of several censors and at least one Congressional committee, is well represented by such a labor of commercial love as his novel *She Made It Pay.* Between these two men Erskine Caldwell can be set.

Lloyd Douglas
and America's Largest Parish

"I AM NOT abandoning the ministry, but expect to give my time to a larger parish than may be addressed from a pulpit," Lloyd Douglas wrote years ago as he underlined the religious and moral purpose of his fiction. Whatever its purpose, literary critics have not as a rule taken Douglas' work seriously. This is because his writing is too often gaudy in its emotional effect, superficial in its characterization, and marked by lapses in literary taste. Though it should be added that he improved in his last two novels, *The Robe* and *The Big Fisherman,* many of his deficiencies were permanent. It is enough here to say that most reviewers have either ignored Douglas or else scoffed at him, and in terms of pure literature they are probably right. However, for anyone interested in the relationship between contemporary American religion and contemporary American culture, Douglas' value is considerable.

In sheer popularity he towers above any other American writer of this century with a religious bent. Led by *The Robe* with its nearly two million copies, several of his novels have been fantastic popular successes. And from the first one, *Magnificent Obsession* (1929) to the last, *The Big*

Fisherman (1948), all his stories have enjoyed popular esteem. After appearing in book form, most have been made into motion pictures. In the days of radio more than one of the novels was dramatized on the air. On television today *Dr. Hudson's Secret Journal,* in particular, has been seen in half-hour segments over a national network.

Magnificent Obsession showed Douglas' appeal from the outset. In the book he referred to a certain page in the Bible without naming the page. During the first year after publication, when the book was not yet selling at a breakneck pace, more than two thousand readers took the trouble to write him personally asking about the number of the page. Without doubt some who read *Magnificent Obsession* ignored the "message" and simply followed a rather unusual story. Nevertheless, the bookshops always had a large variety of novels in stock — novels without a religious purpose — and only a handful of them surpassed in popularity *Magnificent Obsession* and its successors from Douglas' pen.

An attempt to find out exactly what kind of religion Douglas was preaching in his novels both directly and indirectly ought to cast light on current American religious attitudes and desires, particularly among the middle class, from which most book buyers are drawn. It should tell us something about what they want and what they respond to. He once said that Americans are "spiritually wistful," and it can certainly be argued that the success of his novels shows that he is right. It is also true that no one can determine exactly what a people's attitudes are but that fact should not keep suggestions about them from being made.

Specifically, then, Douglas' books are useful in two ways; they help to answer two major questions. The first is, What kind of religious message do middle-class readers find most acceptable? The second is, What kind of minister do they find most appealing in the religious fiction they read?

To convey his message Douglas employs the novel form as if it were a traditional sermon adorned with examples, but the examples of course bulk far larger than the text of the sermon. Instead of stating his doctrine to the reader directly, he gives the exemplification of the doctrine dramatically. He demonstrates it through the actions of his characters. In this way his impact on the reader is personalized and is greater than it otherwise would be, and his message is normally apt to be remembered longer. As a matter of fact, Douglas uses all the instruments at the popular novelist's command — suspense, sharp change of action, alternation of mood, and the technique of the flashback, among them.

The sermon Douglas first preached to his readers came from the Sermon on the Mount. In *Magnificent Obsession* he centered on the verses in Matthew 6 where Jesus speaks about doing good without expecting reward and without making the good deed public: "Let not thy left hand know what thy right hand doeth." Through the figure of Dr. Wayne Hudson, described as a brilliant brain specialist, Douglas developed and dramatized this idea. It is the key to the full life, Dr. Hudson was told by a sculptor, one Randolph. However, where Jesus had preached abnegation and self-denial for the sake of life after death, Douglas — although disclaiming any debasing intention — made it clear that service to others would be followed by success for oneself. Virtue, in other words, was more than its own reward. The good deeds that Dr. Hudson did had to be kept secret, but their favorable effect on his career was manifest. So, to quote Douglas, "Doctor Hudson . . . became obsessed with an idea . . . that his professional success depended on certain eccentric philanthropies which had to be kept secret to be effective." Similarly, he risked his professional future by doing a precedent-breaking brain operation on Natalie Randolph, the sculptor's daughter — this, by the way, being in a later book, *Doctor Hudson's Secret Journal*. The operation succeeded and it received three pages of laudatory notice in the next Medical Encyclopedia.

To the harried middle-class reader at the depth of the Great Depression this made welcome reading. In place of the relatively stern, denying doctrine he could hear in most of the churches, *Magnificent Obsession* and its successors painted a vivid picture for him of the fact that the universe meant well and that human nature was basically good. Given these assurances, the reader was told that he could generally work within himself to conquer the spiritual and economic ills that beset him. God appeared as a rule under the guise of "the planners of the universe" or else was simply referred to as "They." At crucial moments, in several of the novels, a character was enabled to make contact with Them; then he was inspired and could draw on the strength outside of him for a new invention, for example, or a new trick of surgery. Or he might even have a mystical experience, of a sort. This constituted the acme of Douglas' religious representations and occurred very rarely. But it did occur; and there is an excellent example of it in *Magnificent Obsession,* by way of the case of Dr. Robert Merrick, who had inherited Dr. Hudson's responsibilities. In a crisis it seemed to Merrick "as if a pair of great double-doors, somewhere at the far end of a dark corridor in his mind — in his heart — in his soul — somewhere inside of him — had quietly parted, shedding a soft, shimmering radiance upon the roof, walls, and pavement of the long hall." Thus Merrick received the impulse he had longed for.

This mild kind of venture upon mysticism was as far as Douglas would go for many years. Moreover, it was not until the writing of his last two novels that he touched on the supernatural. He avoided the conflict between science and religion during most of his career as a writer by minimizing the biblical miracles and referring to parts of the Old Testament as legends or stories. In this way there was no burden placed upon the reader's belief, and through the tutelage of Douglas' fiction he was able to dismiss everything supernatural except what was sanctioned by psychology; he was freed from adherence to a literal Bible.

Douglas went on to give his reader still another assurance. Having demonstrated the benignity of the universe to him, he also demonstrated the fundamental benignity of the individual human being, both from a psychological and a religious point of view. No serious problem of evil existed in any of Douglas' novels up to the time of *The Robe.* Few people were bad in his fiction; and if they were, they customarily reformed before the end of the book. His view of human nature was the complete opposite of the Calvinist's. In *The Robe* and *The Big Fisherman,* however, the problem of evil was faced more frankly. There Douglas recognized evil through his very choice of subject. He pictured the martyrdom of St. Stephen, for example, in *The Robe* and the sufferings of Jesus in *The Big Fisherman,* and added depth to his writing by doing so. In place of a reassurance emphasizing this world, he began ultimately to emphasize the next.

It might be expected that this facing of realities in *The Robe* would diminish Douglas' appeal for his readers. It has not, and there are at least two different reasons for the fact. One is the undeniable appeal made by the pageantry, a standard attraction of the historical novel, to which Douglas has added a false freshness. The Romans parade in burnished armor but talk just like the characters in his earlier novels. The other is the fact that we were at war by 1942, when *The Robe* was published. It is difficult indeed to calculate the effect of a changing climate of opinion; yet it can be maintained that in that time of death and threatened national disaster, the reading public was ready for more than a happily ending morality play.

In *The Big Fisherman* the problem of evil is presented to an even greater degree. In this story of Christ's developing ministry and of Simon (the "Big Fisherman") and his gradual conversion to belief in Jesus, Douglas paints a picture of suffering and death — and, incidentally, of the supernatural. Furthermore, his message to his readers has altered entirely. The easy promise of material success is gone and its place is taken by an exemplification of the whole Sermon on the Mount.

Over all, it can be seen that Douglas grew as a didactic

novelist in his last years. His teaching lost its ready optimism and its naive appeal. It came to conform with traditional Christian theology, especially in *The Big Fisherman.* That book rounded out his development.

Self-portraiture is characteristic of many a novelist, and Lloyd Douglas could certainly be pardoned if he developed an ideal minister for his novels in his own image. It would be no surprise if the main character turned out to be an energetic Protestant clergyman, leader of a large parish and active in his community. The interesting thing is that this did not happen at all.

True, Douglas had at least one reason, which he stated when writing about his first novel, *Magnificent Obsession:* he did not want to repel the layman by anything ecclesiastic. Consequently, the only man of the cloth in that novel, the Reverend Bruce MacLaren, occupied a minor position. He and Dr. Merrick held a long conversation in which Merrick's mystic psychological experience was intended to make Mac-Laren's intellectualized religion seem pale and futile in contrast.

It was actually Dr. Merrick, and before him Dr. Wayne Hudson, who had the real religion. One of the most interesting aspects of Douglas' ideal minister lay in the fact that he was by profession a physician — a scientific minister to both body and mind. Douglas was attracted by the medical profession to an almost obsessive degree. He had mastered some of the more common medical terms and worked them into his writing wherever he could. He had acquired some acquaintance with medical schools, and one novel, *Disputed Passage,* dealt mainly with the process of medical training. *Green Light,* like *Magnificent Obsession* and *Disputed Passage,* had a physician as hero — young Dr. Newell Paige — and Dr. Wayne Hudson of *Magnificent Obsession* was also, it may be recalled, given another novel all by himself, *Doctor Hudson's Secret Journal.* In a space of ten years, half of Douglas' novels dealt with doctors.

In *Disputed Passage* Douglas subdivided the profession and made quite clear what type of physician was most to be admired. The central character was Jack Beaven, whose progress as medical student, intern, and specialist was described in a wealth of detail. The antagonist to Jack was his long-time instructor in medical school, stubby, harsh Dr. Milton Forrester. Because Forrester was mechanistic in his approach to life and research-minded in his approach to medicine, he became a maladjusted man. The proper foil to him developed toward the close of the novel in the person of Dr. Bill Cunningham, who was a general practitioner, a healer of mind as well as body, and therefore shepherd to his informal flock. Jack Beaven was allowed to see that Cunningham was on the right path and Forrester was not; and *Disputed Passage* ends with even Forrester experiencing something like a mild conversion.

The desideratum for Douglas was a physician — a scientist — who had felt the emotional force of religion and was thereafter qualified to act as minister in ordinary. By the use of the physician as symbol, moreover, Douglas was able to smooth over the conflict between science and religion for his readers. It became one of his most effective devices.

In his obvious desire to ignore the customary Protestant minister as a leading figure and vehicle for his message, Douglas developed not one but two general conceptions as time went on. The first, just discussed, was that of the doctor as minister. Gradually another emerged to balance it, but again not that of the expected Protestant pastor. It was instead embodied in the figure of Dean Harcourt, an imposing Anglican churchman, of Trinity Cathedral. The dean was an aristocrat among his kind; yet he revealed great human sympathies. To him came people different in many ways but alike in that they needed counsel. Dean Harcourt gave it with unvarying success.

Although the dean played a role of some importance in one of Douglas' earliest novels, he was the outstanding character in *Invitation to Live,* which was published in 1940. He occupied an almost godlike place as he benevolently manipulated the lives of those who came to him. As a matter of fact, his wisdom and common sense as noted in *Invitation to Live* ran higher than average for a counselor in Douglas' fiction. Not surprisingly, the advice he gave in his oak-paneled library had little to do with the Thirty-nine Articles. Instead he preached the customary doctrine of service to others — with reward for self — under the inspiration of a kindly universe. As he said once about his own experience to Dr. Newell Paige, "I have suffered — but I know that I am Destiny's darling!"

That Douglas was taken with the character of Dean Harcourt for several years is easy to see. He represented formal, professional religion but religion without any of the folksiness that Douglas had learned to dislike. In *Doctor Hudson's Secret Journal* he commented wryly on the "joyful noise" of most Protestant services in contrast to the ecclesiastical dignity of Dean Harcourt's service. Indeed, in another novel Douglas traveled further from Nonconformity and described a Roman Catholic service with considerable sympathy. Anyone watching a Catholic or Episcopalian ritual, Douglas also remarked, knew that he was at any rate in a church, not in a Y.M.C.A. or ethical club. It is evident that the so-called democracy which Douglas had observed in Protestant practices made less and less appeal to him. Although he himself had served large Nonconforming congregations, he maintained in a little manual of advice for ministers which he wrote years ago that the average minister holds himself too cheap. He bows to the businessmen and busybodies of his congregation; he demeans himself by asking weakly for money; and in most ways he is content to sit below the salt.

Douglas continued to feel strongly about the dignity of ministers, and this is noticeable even in *The Robe,* which appeared almost a generation after the manual just mentioned. In *The Robe* he once describes Simon's asking the Ecclesia for money shortly after Jesus' death. Stephen criticizes Simon to the man next to him. "Did you notice that weak solicitous smile on [Simon's] face as he entreated them to be more generous with their gifts?" he asks.

Otherwise, however, Simon was characterized in *The Robe* as a strong, sincere shepherd; and in *The Big Fisherman* his growth into an ideal minister of the Gospel is traced with care. He is shown at times to be impatient, slow to believe, and — once at least — quick to deny. Nevertheless, his stature increases steadily, and he emerges as a dignified and powerful figure, one destined to guide his flock and protect it. Here then in *The Big Fisherman* Douglas displays his final conception of the model Christian leader. It is a picture that was partly anticipated in *The Robe* by the hero Marcellus in his brief, idyllic ministry in the little Roman town of Arpino, but in *The Big Fisherman* we have a full-scale and notable portrait. The doctors and the dean are forgotten and in their place Douglas puts a figure of great strength and constantly growing understanding. Just as Douglas' view of Christianity in his novels deepened with the passage of time, so did his view of the ideal minister. Both the message and the messenger revealed a new earnestness.

The importance of the role Douglas has played in the relating of contemporary American fiction and religion can be underestimated too easily, by the critics and, incidentally, by the clergy. A greater realization of what religion means to Americans today can be gained by studying him. And yet that realization may not be entirely pleasant, for Douglas has something uncomfortable to say to the American ministry. As Dean Willard Sperry of Harvard has noted, "Douglas is a comment upon the failure of the professional ministry to state its case in an effective popular form that appeals to laymen — we offer them only a stained-glass figure of Jesus, drawn in a formal theological pattern." A good many people still read Douglas and go to church as well but it is fairly clear that many more read him instead of going to church.

Farewell to Hollins Street

H. L. MENCKEN died in his famous Baltimore row house sometime during the early morning of January 29, 1956. He was 75. His last waking hours were spent in a way that is perhaps worth particularizing since it carried the lingering flavor of his once full-bodied life. Toward the end of the winter afternoon he stretched out on the couch in his second-floor office, listened to a portion of *Die Meistersinger* on his radio, and then took a nap. On awakening he came down to supper. His brother August had built a cheerful fire as usual, and there was an old friend present. Mencken complained to them of not being well, but according to August he drank two scotch highballs and felt better. The conversation was good. Shortly after 9 he went back upstairs to his bedroom, listened to his radio again (this time to a symphony), and then went to sleep. He died about 3 or 4 a.m. Long before his death he had, characteristically, specified the only eulogy he wished: "If, after I depart this vale, you ever remember me and have thought to please my ghost, forgive some sinner and wink at some homely girl."

Mencken's family moved to the row house on Hollins St. when he was three. His father, half-German August

Mencken, Sr., owned a cigar factory in the city; his mother, Anna Abhau, had been born in Baltimore of German parents. Young Harry and the other children in his family grew up pleasantly and uneventfully in the Hollins St. house. He was considered bookish and a bit shy but not inordinately so. A good student, he survived the strict discipline of Professor Friedrich Knapp's school opposite the City Hall and went on to graduate from the Baltimore Polytechnic Institute at 15. He was, naturally enough, promptly deposited in his father's cigar business. However, the itch to write proved so strong that he eagerly joined the staff of the *Baltimore Morning Herald* as well, even though it meant devoting his nights to the job after his days at the cigar factory. But he had no tedious apprenticeship to serve. His abilities showed themselves almost at once. By 1903 he was city editor of the *Herald* and by 1906 he was managing the Sunday edition of the *Baltimore Sun,* having already made what was to be a life-long connection with that noted newspaper.

"Baltimoreans with long memories," wrote Hamilton Owens, for years editor of the *Sun,* "will recall the impact of the boisterous youngster on the columns of the paper." He became known for his pungent descriptions of the local scene. "The politicians, the policemen, the magistrates, the judges, and all such worthies were depicted with much more robustness and much less veneration" than before. And "the humors of the corner-saloon, the free-lunch counter, and the crab feast emerged." Using his vigorous wit as one of his main weapons, Mencken joyously began his long battle "against frauds and stuffed shirts."

Mencken was to remain a social critic (though he might reject that heavy term) throughout his life, yet he found so much to laugh at in American habits that he could never become a fire-breathing reformer. For that matter, he expressed his criticisms in such roaring generalities that many — though emphatically not all — of the objects of his satire probably said in innocence, "Who, me?" Mencken started on the American people as a whole and then proceeded to anatomize them part by clownish part. As he once said in the third series of his *Prejudices,* it was his conviction that "the American people, taking one with another, constitute the most timorous, sniveling, poltroonish, ignominious mob of serfs and goose-steppers ever gathered under one flag in Christendom since the Middle Ages." Then he worked out from that.

Literary criticism like social criticism also attracted Mencken from the time he was a young man, and his liveliest, best writing appeared when he combined the two. In his early days with the *Sun* he often wrote about the theater. His articles and reviews contained praise for such European dramatists as Ibsen and Shaw balanced by slashing criticisms of the clumsy dramatic performances he sat through in America. He wrote *George Bernard Shaw — His Plays* (1905), which though brief gained enough attention to make him known to literary circles in New York. He became friends with the publisher Alfred Knopf, and with another and shrewder drama critic, George Jean Nathan. A New York magazine called *The Smart Set* was the brightest periodical of its time; Mencken went on the staff as literary critic and then helped Nathan edit it during its prime from 1914 to 1923. In 1924 the two friends started *The American Mercury,* with Knopf as its publisher. It flourished phenomenally. During the next nine years Mencken grew to be the most vigorous and influential literary journalist in the country as well as the tart-tongued guardian of the individualism of the '20's. He cultivated what he called "a certain ferocity" of expression and used it against all forms of "tribal impulses," though he still retained the right to be a social conservative.

He was not a conservative in literature, however. He fought with happy fervor against the fraudulent popular successes among the established writers (the Harold Bell Wrights, for example) and for such newcomers as Theodore Dreiser, Sinclair Lewis, and Scott Fitzgerald. It was as critics of American society that they made their basic appeal to him. In their various ways they pointed out the fatuousness of American culture, and he approved of that. But he also approved of the fact that their writing belonged to this country instead of being an imitation of foreign models.

During the Harding-Coolidge era he maintained his supremacy brilliantly. However, the history of American taste shows that it has taken many a turn, and Mencken's reputation suffered an eclipse throughout the 1930's. Two causes brought this about. The first was the Depression. People found very little of the ridiculous in an economic catastrophe, and so Mencken's view of life as a circus — a view which remained essentially unaltered despite bread lines and mass unemployment — lost much of its appeal. The new taste-makers were distinguished by their consuming interest in economic reform, sometimes Marxian, more often not. But at any rate they focussed on matters of most concern to the depression-ridden public. Mencken, on the other hand, scoffed at the New Deal measures of the '30's just as heartily as he had at the tribal puritanism of the '20's. He offered the WPA the same contempt he had offered Prohibition. The second reason for the dimming of his reputation lay in the Germanic flavor of his writing. The rise of Hitler's Third Reich meant a corruption of the many good traits in German culture. Hitler blackened the reputation of all things German throughout the world, and this — it may be suggested — had its effect even on the standing of Mencken. Mencken himself, moreover, made the mistake of taking Hitler too lightly, just as he had the Kaiser. It took some time for him to see that Hitler was not simply a buffoon.

With the coming of the '40's and then the first half of the '50's Mencken re-established himself through his growing eminence in a field where few would have expected it. His energy in writing and his wit had been admitted from the start but hardly anyone realized the orderliness ingrained in the man. Out of his interest in American writing had come his interest in the American language, and as early as 1919 he had published the first results of his orderly culling of that writing for Americanisms. Many critics were doubtless surprised to discover him at work on something both time-consuming and scholarly. Yet he did not stop. With each revision and supplement *The American Language* gained in stature and authority, until it could justly be said that the Baltimore newspaperman stood out as the leading student of his native tongue.

A byproduct of this same orderly method was his *New Dictionary of Quotations*. In his research for the first book he had made a practice of filing the proverbs and sayings that he came across. As the years passed, his files thickened and by 1942 he could issue a work as thorough as any in its area.

Of less value are his treatises. He published these in mid-career. They are systematic assemblages of his opinions, buttressed by the reading he relished. They add up to an interesting minority report, and they always have the thrust of his style. *Notes on Democracy* (1926) is an example. It frames an indictment of the flaws in democracy with a zest no political scientist could command. It contains many a sentence still relevant today. In point: surrounded as we are by the clamor to solve foreign problems no administration can solve, we see vividly what Mencken meant when he jeered, "It is one of the peculiar intellectual accompaniments of democracy that the concept of the insoluble becomes unfashionable — nay, almost infamous. To lack a remedy is to lack the very license to discuss disease."

In his final literary phase Mencken turned to autobiography. Here his contribution cannot perhaps be rated as high as in criticism and philology; notwithstanding, his three volumes afford a colorful, even sentimental, view of the man and his times. *Happy Days* (1940), *Newspaper Days* (1941), and *Heathen Days* (1943) describe his life from his birth in 1880 to 1936, and they provide a mellow contrast to his earlier writings.

In spite of these diversified contributions, there was one kind of writing he always returned to. That was newspaper reporting, of an opinionated, witty, and choleric sort peculiarly his own. He maintained his generally pleasant connection with the *Baltimore Sun* for over forty years. From 1912 to 1917 he conducted a column called "The Free Lance" which had all the sharpness its title implied. For years afterward he contributed a Monday evening article with the same astringent tone as his former column. He also took on special assignments every now and then. The Republican and Democratic national conventions always yielded him more than his share of guffaws and so he covered the sessions regularly. The most famous single spectacle he attended as a reporter was the John T. Scopes trial in 1925. When this young Tennessee schoolteacher was charged with teaching Darwinism instead of Genesis to his science students, the noted agnostic Clarence Darrow defended him and William Jennings Bryan led the prosecution. Mencken enjoyed the contest keenly, cheering and hooting as it went along.

He reported likewise on many a less sensational event for the *Sun*. Through its columns he often influenced his native city, and he swayed the policy of the *Sun* itself. Indeed, he "exerted an immeasurable influence," according to Mr. Owens. "His hatred of pusillanimity and sham was not exhausted by his attacks on outsiders; he insisted that the paper to which he had given his allegiance live up to the standards for forthrightness, courage, and, above all, vitality, which he had set for himself."

As a matter of fact, the words of the *Sun* the day after he died are perhaps his best valedictory. Writing of Mencken and his effect on his fellow workers, the *Sun* said, "To those who exerted the effort, even when their product fell short of the ideal, he was sympathetic, helpful, and encouraging. To many outsiders who had been scourged by his pen, he was the embodiment of evil, as their anguished efforts at reprisal showed, but to those of his colleagues who knew that his battle was waged against sham and hypocrisy and not against individuals as such, he was simple, compassionate, and even humble. In short: a warm, loyal, and understanding friend. We shall not soon see his like again."

Auditor's Report: POETRY

[The first four of these pieces were written for a British audience, the last two for an American one.]

1959:
The Poems across the Way

THE HALLMARK of current American poetry is its vitality. This American vigor clearly manifests itself in the constant experimenting with new modes of saying things, in the diversity of forms, in the probing of language, in the attempts to search meaning to the utmost. The contrast with current British verse is sharp. Anyone who reads a good deal of that will be impressed by its common sense, lucidity, and restraint. No one shouts; no one yells. There is no Beat Poet howling in England, or if there is one, he howls alone. At its worst the American energy results in chaos. At its disciplined best it gives us something as strong and elegant as the lyrics of Wallace Stevens.

On both sides of the Atlantic, Stevens is the American poet most fashionable with the critics. With the single exception of Robert Frost (who confounds most generalizations), he is the subject of more essays and very probably of more serious attention than any other poet. His verse is fluid and disciplined, and often obscure. But his obscurity is worth studying because it is the evidence of subtlety rather than confusion. Already certain of his pieces suffer from being reprinted too much; nevertheless, a lyric as carefully inwrought as "Sea Surface Full of Clouds" or as "The Idea of Order at Key West" gives fresh pleasure to many of us.

In his poetry Stevens tries again and again to determine what is real in the world and what is not. And to him one of the major signs of reality is order. He wants it to be of a platonic kind and so jeers at the everyday world with its materialistic, upside-down scale of values. As he puts it in the first stanza of one of his most popular poems, "The Emperor of Ice-Cream":

> Call the roller of big cigars,
> The muscular one, and bid him whip
> In kitchen cups concupiscent curds.
> Let the wenches dawdle in such dress
> As they are used to wear, and let the boys
> Bring flowers in last month's newspapers.
> Let be be finale of seem.
> The only emperor is the emperor of ice-cream.

It would be idiotic to accept a universe in which ice-cream is king, he feels.

In spite of his great current popularity, Stevens was for some years an enthusiasm only of the few; this is still the case, regrettably, for Marianne Moore. Her very fine verse is as strictly controlled as his, and as formal. His seems far larger, however, and free despite its subtleties. Her neat, tight stanzas speak precisely. Here is the world of the spinster with the cat, but a world which deals with certain universal values and, often, with universal crotchets. Birds and animals walk through her poems and assume oddly engaging attitudes.

Among the other poets, the one growing fastest perhaps in British esteem is Theodore Roethke. He represents a whole school of American experimentalists, all of whom would deny that they belonged to any school whatsoever. Notwithstanding, Roethke, Richard Wilbur, Robert Lowell, and Randall Jarrell have much in common. The differences are easy to see but the similarities are for us the significant thing. These men all write a poetry of tension, a poetry which has that intellectuality tightened into obscurity which marks so much of American verse today. It would be presumptuous to guess how much their work reflects a world of strains and baffling complexities; but, at any rate, no one of them lives in the tranquil mode of the pastoral. In Roethke's case at least, we can argue that the greater the tension in his poetry, the better the poem. A very nice example can be found in the two versions of "Cuttings." The early one is quiet and delicate, opening with "Sticks-in-a-drowse droop over sugary loam" and closing in the same gentle way. Contrast this with the second version, full of struggle and sexual overtones:

> This urge, wrestle, resurrection of dry sticks,
> Cut stems struggling to put down feet,
> What saint strained so much,
> Rose on such lopped limbs to a new life?
>
> I can hear, underground, that sucking and sobbing,
> In my veins, in my bones I feel it, —
> The small waters seeping upward,
> The tight grains parting at last.
> When sprouts break out,
> Slippery as fish,
> I quail, lean to beginnings, sheath-wet.

Not the least sign of the pulsing vitality of American verse is that it sometimes demands a new stance from the reader. A novel subject or a strange combination of emotions is met with more often in American verse than British. Jarrell's poem "The State" is an instance. Its beginning line sets the tone: "When they killed my mother it made me nervous." And the work of Gregory Corso contains other striking examples. He is the Beat Poet whom Allen Ginsberg termed "probably the greatest" in America. We might pick out a poem from Corso's volume *Gasoline* almost at random. Here is one he entitles "Italian Extravaganza"; it offers an interesting test:

> Mrs. Lombardi's month-old son is dead.
> I saw it in Rizzo's funeral parlor,
> A small purplish wrinkled head.
>
> They've just finished having high mass for it;
> They're coming out now
> . . . wow, such a small coffin!
> And ten black cadillacs to haul it in.

What should we say to this? Is it poetry or not? The poem also raises some subsidiary questions which can be debated. But for this reader, at any rate, the answer to the main question is "Yes."

We have left the best poet for the last. He is Robert Frost. Of all the American poets of our time, he will probably be read the longest. His are the poems with the happiest blend of the universal and the particular. No one can deny his universality. His reputation was first established in Great Britain, not in the United States, and his poetry continues to be cherished there. The visit he paid in 1957 was a triumph; he became the only American poet of the century to be awarded honorary degrees by Oxford and Cambridge both. Yet even if his appeal is international, he is as much a poet of New England as any nineteenth-century Yankee rhymer. In Frost subject and style develop together from New England soil. Such variegated lyrics as "Birches," "Two Tramps in Mud-time," and "Mending Wall" all speak with a Yankee accent. And the words are shrewd, kind, and wise.

Frost is also a poet of New England in one almost unnoticed way. Although the New England inheritance includes a Calvinistic sense of guilt, the stereotype of Frost presents us with a genial Olympian. The stereotype is not quite accurate. At intervals we can find such a poem as "The

Subverted Flower" in which there is a sense of sin so strong that it damages the poem. This is a set of verses about a brutish young man and his attempt to force a bitter young woman. But its murky puritanism is rare; most of Frost has the balanced wisdom we ordinarily associate with him.

He goes on writing memorable poems though he is now in his mid-eighties. Perhaps the one which sums up, as well as any, all that we admire in him is the golden sonnet on Eve:

> He would declare and could himself believe
> That the birds there in all the garden round
> From having heard the daylong voice of Eve
> Had added to their own an oversound,
> Her tone of meaning but without the words.
> Admittedly an eloquence so soft
> Could only have had an influence on birds
> When call or laughter carried it aloft.
> Be that as may be, she was in their song.
> Moreover her voice upon their voices crossed
> Had now persisted in the woods so long
> That probably it never would be lost.
> Never again would birds' song be the same.
> And to do that to birds was why she came.

1960:

The Changing Face of American Poetry

ONE OF the most interesting things about American poetry for the last year or two is that it has begun, in several important ways, to resemble current British poetry. This is not to say that British poetry has had much influence on American; as a matter of fact, the ignorance about it among American poets is almost sublime. But American taste has been changing recently and the change can be detected in a number of directions.

First of all, American criticism has been changing. In most countries it would be ridiculous to think that the literary critics could strongly influence literature itself. Yet in the United States the New Criticism — now a generation old — has been powerful indeed. The leading New Critics have not only written literary criticism. More important, they have been able to dominate the editorial policies of the chief literary magazines, of which the quarterlies the *Kenyon Review,* the *Sewanee Review,* and the *Hudson Review* are perhaps the most respected. The poetry their editors printed was the poetry which lent itself best to the purposes of the New Criticism. The poets whom the New Critics and editors applauded most were the poets of obscurity. They wrote verse which was compacted with images, difficult in its rhythms, and often personal in its references. They wrote verse whose riddle the New Criticism was best equipped to read. It would be nonsense to charge that there was a conspiracy. There was, however, a happy coincidence.

It is hard to disentangle cause and effect but it is certainly worth noting that within this last year the most respected of the New Critics, John Crowe Ransom, has retired as editor of the *Kenyon Review* and has been succeeded by an alert young English writer, Robie Macauley. When he took over, there was a distinct atmosphere of change in *Kenyon* circles. True, the lead article in the first issue under the new editor was by Mr. Ransom but this was patently a graceful gesture. The academic gossip and printed announcement both strongly suggested that the magazine proposed to serve a widened audience. It would appeal to critics of various schools and persuasions, and even to the enlightened general reader.

The boldest attempt to change the face of American poetry has been Karl Shapiro's. During World War II he was the most remarkable new poet we read; since then he has written less and less poetry but more and more criticism.

In a widely noticed article in the *New York Times Book Review* and in his book *In Defence of Ignorance,* he has thrown all his weight against what he calls the "culture poets" and has demanded a fresh poetry of much greater clarity and order. For some years now, he has been editing the *Prairie Schooner,* a midwestern literary journal to which he has brought new life and zest. Here he has printed the poetry which has pleased him. Much of it would not have pleased the New Critics.

The change is manifest in other ways. There is, for example, the case of the American magazine *Poetry,* which occupies a unique position in the English-speaking world. Its record of publishing good poets before they become popular is hard to equal. From the time of its founding it has been alert to new trends, sensitive to fresh talent. For a decade it has been printing a good deal of verse which could have appeared equally well in the literary quarterlies of the New Criticism. But of late there has seemed to be a change in *Poetry.* In its number for January 1960 it welcomed ten poets who were new to its pages. Not a one specialized in the lyric of tortured meaning.

I would not argue that the shifts I cite have affected existing reputations very much. Still, even here it is possible to note some impressions. I feel that Robert Frost's reputation is higher than ever. In its luminous simplicity his verse has always run counter to the demands of the New Critics. But he has so obviously been a great poet that he has escaped their hostility as a rule. Now his verse is well in the coming mode and his books have the esteem not only of critics in the public eye but also, apparently, of the bright young academics who are usually on the scent of something new. On the other hand, I must also mention an exception, Wallace Stevens, the idol of the obscurantists. He is probably more popular than ever before. His subtle, often baffling verse is much discussed. His riddle has not yet been read, so there is some of the same excitement in studying Stevens that there was in studying Eliot before the war. But aside from Stevens, those poets whose reputation is now being consolidated write more clearly than the rest. Prominent among them is Stanley Kunitz, whose *Selected Poems 1928–1958* won the Pulitzer Prize last year. He had been around for a long time before getting his due. Now, however, his acute and sensitive intelligence is being generally appreciated. The strong first stanza of one of his most popular poems, "Open the Gates," helps to show why:

> Within the city of the burning cloud,
> Dragging my life behind me in a sack,
> Naked I prowl, scourged by the black
> Temptation of the blood grown proud.

Richard Eberhart has just been honored by reappointment as the Library of Congress's Consultant in Poetry and by election to the National Institute of Arts and Letters. Many a lyric poet withers early but not Mr. Eberhart. His *Collected Poems* will appear in the autumn. In form his lyrics range from free verse to the traditional regularity of the sestina and villanelle. His rhythms, however, tend to sameness. It is not a sameness of regular iambics or dactyls; it is one of roughened beats and hard juxtapositions. We have in his lines the closest American parallel to Hopkins's sprung rhythm. In method Mr. Eberhart is most effective when he takes something in nature and makes an emblem of it. He does this, for instance, in one of his favorite poems, "For a Lamb:"

> I saw on the slant hill a putrid lamb,
> Propped with daisies. The sleep looked deep,
> The face nudged in the green pillow
> But the guts were out for crows to eat.
>
> Where's the lamb? whose tender plaint
> Said all for the mute breezes.
> Say he's in the wind somewhere,
> Say, there's a lamb in the daisies.

Despite his modern idiom Mr. Eberhart is a traditional Romantic, loving nature, mindful of death, and true to humanity. He acknowledges the early influence of Wordsworth on his poems and the influence of William Blake both early and late.

This year's Pulitzer Prize for poetry has gone to a shock-headed young midwesterner named W. D. Snodgrass, for *Heart's Needle*. The book falls into two parts. The first is made up of poems about the returned soldier, the unfaithful wife, the restless student. The lyrics are taut, ironic. At times they seem patently clever. In their choice of the unexpectedly common metaphor they resemble Karl Shapiro's wartime poems. In fact Snodgrass plays much the same role for the Korean veteran that Shapiro did for the conscript in World War II, though Shapiro played it better. But the second part of the book has genuine distinction. It is a group of poems itself called "Heart's Needle," about a small daughter (or, once or twice, a son) of his. He is separated from her most of the time, apparently because he is divorced from her mother, but on occasion the child is allowed to visit him. Lyric after lyric is based on the ordinary happenings involved in this situation but Snodgrass develops his poems about them with a hard pathos which is most moving. The style is so direct as to seem almost matter-of-fact. The surprising but not uncommon metaphors are here again; the previous tendency toward the rather self-conscious wit valued by the New Critics is absent from the lyric sequence. The opening stanza of the third poem in the sequence is characteristic. Here the divorced parents are together for the moment:

> The child between them on the street
> Comes to a puddle, lifts his feet
>   And hangs on their hands. They start
> At the live weight and lurch together,
> Recoil to swing him through the weather,
>   Stiffen and pull apart.

The metaphor seems to me exactly right. With the nicest economy of means he implies an entire situation. The language is like Wordsworth's in its almost doctrinaire simplicity. The stanza has its pivot just as does the whole poem; here it is "Stiffen," which not only carries the greatest weight of sense but is onomatopoetic. So is the whole last line in fact. Its sound lengthens like a rubber band with "pull" and then snaps with "apart."

Throughout the series there is this same unobtrusive skill. Yet skill alone would not move us as do these lyrics by Mr. Snodgrass. The poetry — to revive a remark about some poems of the First World War — the poetry is in the pity. The American poet Robert Lowell has called these poems "a break-through for modern poetry." I think he is right but the break-through is taking place at more points than the one that Mr. Lowell indicated.

1961:

The Mixed Romantics

IT HAS BEEN a stimulating year. For the first time a president of the United States has invited our most noted poet to take part in the Inaugural ceremony. The glare of that occasion proved too bright for Mr. Frost but the symbolism was happy. More prizes for poetry are being offered, and more grants. The audience for poetry seems to be widening as well. On the other hand, the millennium has not arrived. The American foundations, incredibly rich though some of them are, seem to use all kinds of expedients to keep from simply supporting good poets. William Meredith, for example, was one of several younger ones awarded a Ford grant, not to write poetry, however, but to do the lyrics for an opera. The Guggenheim Foundation alone continues in its steady sensible way to award yearly fellowships to keep poets alive. Some day federal patronage will, I hope, help to support literature and the arts. It did so in the depression-ridden 1930's; it could do so even better now. But the same strong forces which oppose federal aid to anything connected with the mind would with pleasure oppose government grants to poets. I can hear Congress now. Conditions for poetry are better in Britain but I doubt if there is much cause for self-congratulation even there.

Still, there is no doubt that things are looking up. The impulse in America toward making poetry clear has grown. Last year the Pulitzer Prize for poetry went to a man, W. D. Snodgrass, whose lucid, compassionate lyrics can be understood and felt by many rather than by few. His *Heart's Needle* has now been issued in England, with all the critical approval one could wish. This year the Pulitzer Prize has gone even further in the same general direction. Looking back we can see that American poetry of the period from 1945 to 1957 or 1958 was particularly marked by two things, its obscurity and its taut seriousness. Our poetry was in fact nervous. Laughter in it looked almost as out of place as lucidity. Now, however, the prize has been awarded to a writer of light verse. She is Phyllis McGinley and her book is called *Times Three*. Her tone is dry, her jokes restrained. She lacks the low-comedy sense which Kingsley Amis shows in his poetry as well as in his fiction. She lacks the richness of texture and the wry self-deprecation which characterizes John Betjeman's lighter verse. But she has a wit both deft and gentle, well demonstrated by "Christmas Eve in Our Village":

> Main Street is gay. Each lamppost glimmers,
>   Crowned with a blue, electric star.
> The gift tree by our fountain shimmers,
>   Superbly tall, if angular
>   (Donated by the Men's Bazaar).

Verse like this Miss McGinley can write as well as anyone in the United States. Her Pulitzer Prize is an understandable tribute.

Such recognition seems to me all the more valuable because it promises to extend still further the circle of readers of our poetry. And yet I have the uncomfortable feeling that in choosing Miss McGinley's book an injustice was done. A far better, if uneven, and far more serious work was slighted. Richard Eberhart's *Collected Poems* appeared last fall. The gathering of thirty years of work by a major poet, it lost to the delightful trivialities of *Times Three*. His writing lies full in the Romantic tradition but still remains his own. With its rough rhythms and sharp insights, it often forces the reader to respond. The old poems and the new are both good. Here is the whole of an older one:

Now is the air made of chiming balls.
The stormcloud, wizened, has rolled its rind away.
Now is the eye with hill and valley laved
And the seeds, assuaged, peep from the nested spray.
The bluebird drops from a bough. The speckled meadow-lark
Springs in his lithe array. Fresh air
Blesses the vanished tear; the bunched anguish.
The laughing balls their joyful pleasure tear.
Renewed is the whole world and the sun
Begins to dress with warmth again every thing.
The lettuce in pale burn; the burdock tightening;
The naked necks of craning fledglings.

Two other American poets, unknown I believe to the British reader, have been steadily extending their American reputation. They are William Meredith, whom I just mentioned, and Chad Walsh. Both as a poet and theorist of poetry Meredith displays a remarkably resourceful mind. He can nicely compromise technical problems which other poets are apt to fumble with. His poems are as deft as his poetics.

On the surface their rhythms appear almost old-fashioned, their phrases routinely Romantic. He can even say "Ah" in a poem; he can still write a verse about the stars. Notwithstanding, the result is rarely a cliché. The subject is often the ancient country of the self but the exploration is new. It is new because Meredith, while recognizing his humanity, speaks to us as a unique individual. His poetry and his poetics come together in what is perhaps the most often anthologized of his poems, "A Korean Woman Seated by a Wall." A stanza or two from it can show something of his skill but it should be said first that he excerpts badly — the whole is frequently greater than the sum of the parts. He seldom achieves that transcendent phrase or passage which Matthew Arnold called a touchstone and which Emerson thought of as a luster. Still, the opening of "A Korean Woman" makes its impressive point, I think:

> Suffering has settled like a sly disguise
> On her cheerful old face. If she dreams beyond
> Rice and a roof, now toward the end of winter,
> Is it of four sons gone, the cries she has heard,
> A square farm in the south, soured by tents?
> Some alien and untranslatable loss
> Is a mask she smiles through at the weak sun
> That is moving north to invade the city again.
>
> A poet penetrates his dark disguise
> After his own conception, little or large.
> Crossing the scaleless asia of trouble
> Where it seems no one could give himself away,
> He gives himself away, he sets a scale.
> Hunger and pain and death, the sorts of loss,
> Dispute our comforts like peninsulas
> Of no particular value, places to fight. . . .

In Chad Walsh's poetry there are two poles. One is a steady determination not to be taken in; the other a sensuous love of order. They are linked by his Christian faith. Americans shy away from most expression of religion in verse; the only kind currently admired seems to be the troubled, tense Catholicism of Robert Lowell. It almost looks today as if a poet can be irreligious or Catholic but not anything in between; perhaps Anglicanism — and Walsh is an Anglican — seems too pale and polite. Quite possibly, the acceptance of Walsh's verse has been delayed because of this situation. Some of the tenderness and perception in his work comes no doubt from his Christian compassion. There are other influences, of other kinds, on his poetry too, however. Among them he especially acknowledges the writing of Yeats and Auden. Yeats helped to teach him controlled harmony; Auden showed him how to confront his time. But the result is Walsh's own and can be as personal as his childhood near the Blue Ridge mountains. Among his poems a favorite of his is "Christmas in the Straw," which moves lightly but reverently:

> This is the dance the fiddler danced when Eve
> Danced to her feet from Adam's wounded side.
> This is the song the fiddler sang at eve
> Beside a cradle and his Jewish bride.

The joy pulses through the square-dance. The nativity hymn is sung with zest.

Aside from what I have said about Miss McGinley's verses, I realize that I have been interpreting current American poetry as largely Romantic. Eberhart, Meredith, Walsh: each looks like a Romantic to me. I hope I have not been distorting the American scene, yet I confess that even among the Beats I see Romanticism. After the initial shock of their poetry disappears, the Romantic and even traditional elements begin to stand out, I suspect, for many readers. The accomplishment of their poetry begins to look both better and worse than it did before. Gregory Corso and Lawrence Ferlinghetti, for example, no longer seem startling, though

Corso has been moving more and more into a kind of semi-automatic writing that resembles nothing so much as the abstract painter's scumble. Allen Ginsberg himself has not exceeded "Howl," which has begun to enter the anthologies. Its origin and structure have been the source of more than one essay. Teachers have been instructed by an article called " 'Howl' in the Classroom," which certainly must have made Ginsberg take thought. "Howl's" boldness now looks Whit-manesque and the four-letter words — the ones Sinclair Lewis called "the nine Anglo-Saxon physiological mono-syllables" — in its text are printed with increasing readiness. And as the reputation of the poem has solidified, its Romantic elements have stood out all the more strongly. The rebelliousness, the sexual swagger, the cult of the individual, the glorification of youth, the stress on the emotional; these I think we can all term Romantic and "Howl" has them.

In an odd way one of the symptoms of the Romantic rebellion has been the public use in the work of Ginsberg and other Beat poets of the previously forbidden four-letter words. Writers and publishers in America have fol-lowed the *Lady Chatterley* case with a good deal of interest. With the court victory won, the feeling is no doubt that another shackle to self-expression has been removed. But regardless of the *Lady Chatterley* case it is probable that some of the Beats would have persisted in breaking the old boundaries of the language for poetry. The perfect example is the sex rhapsodist Michael McClure. He uses the four-letter words as if they were neon signs. They appear so often they tire the eye. But McClure's intention seems to me quite as honest as D. H. Lawrence's. McClure wants to use them to describe sexual ecstasy, to communicate the incom-municable.

It is some distance from Robert Frost to Michael Mc-Clure; the gulf between them is not small. The distances between the other poets I have mentioned are substantial. They are a mixed lot. Yet all, except for Miss McGinley, have something in common which is difficult to define strictly but can be called the Romantic temper. What is being written in America under the rubric of this Romanticism has, it seems to me, considerable power and much promise as well.

1962:

The New Battle of the Books

THIS story starts in Nashville, Tennessee, and ends in New York's Harlem. Not long after World War I, a little magazine appeared in Nashville called the *Fugitive*. It fled, according to the editorial foreword, "from nothing faster than from the highcaste Brahmins of the Old South." Its editors and principal contributors were from a local university. Their chief was a professor of English. They printed some unusually good poetry as well as some mediocre prose. Today their magazine would be forgotten except for the fact that the *Fugitive* group went on in the next decades to dominate most of American literary criticism, much of American poetry, and part of American fiction. Nor did they stop with this country. Their influence has been felt in Cambridge and Oxford, Heidelberg and Paris. If this claim sounds exaggerated, let me give a few particulars about the main members. The leader, John Crowe Ransom, went on from Nashville to a professorship at Kenyon College in Ohio and the editorship of the highly influential *Kenyon Review*. With credentials which included some of the best minor poetry of his time, he almost inadvertently founded the still prevailing school for literary taste, the New Criticism. His onetime student Allen Tate, through his complex critical essays, his carefully constructed poetry, and his frequent lecturing, became the New Criticism's principal propagandist. Robert Penn Warren, another former student of Ransom's, who composed a string of Southern stories, became its major novelist. His best novel, on Huey Long, received every kind of acclaim, from a Pulitzer Prize to a motion-picture production. These men, and most others in the group, sooner or later left the South and moved to key posts in Northern universities. One or two, Donald Davidson and Andrew Lytle in particular, stayed home and looked around them with mixed emotions.

To their New Criticism the Fugitives attracted many followers as well as several noted allies, among them I. A. Richards and F. R. Leavis. In spite of their differences over detail, all agreed that the critic must concentrate on the text of the poem or novel, not on its historical background and not on its author's life. The service they did for American literary scholarship was substantial. We were rescued from some remarkably recondite researches on, say, Milton's aunt's inheritance or Wordsworth's letter to the Bishop of Bangkok. On the other hand, it soon became obvious that the New Critics preferred the poem or book they had to focus on the longest. They relished the murky novel, the metaphysical lyric. They exalted the symbol. And they were able through the quarterlies they controlled, through the honors in their giving, and through the very vigor of their preachments to rule over the academic side of American literature for a long time. Only in the last few years have they had much opposition from other established critics and writers, opposition led by the poet and editor Karl Shapiro. This has been academic warfare, however, of a kind the New Critics can generally counter; and they have not succumbed. But now they are being subjected to a fresh attack, from a new quarter. With this they cannot seem to cope. My guess is that they are both angry and uncomfortable.

The irony is that these latest opponents are almost accidental ones, who hardly care that the New Critics exist. They are the Beats. Crude and boisterous, they have in passing pushed the New Critics from the center of the stage, and this with antics of a most ungentlemanly sort. They have simply outdone — and shouted down — the New Critics.

Having ruled as Southern gentlemen, the New Critics were completely unprepared for the clownish tricks of the Beat generation. They acted much like parasoled ladies spattered by vulgar boys. Allen Tate once intimated in print, during a controversy over a prize for Ezra Pound, that he stood ready to fight an opposing critic — "Courage and honor are not subjects of literary controversy," he wrote, "but occasions of action" — yet how could he compare with Allen Ginsberg stripping off his clothes on the public platform? How could a gentleman compete with a clod?

The New Critics were outdone in another direction. They had become known for the graceful way they appreciated each other's work — and complimented it in print. Tate would praise Ransom, Ransom would praise Tate; but the compliments would be judicious. Minor members of the group might need to praise a little louder to be heard, it is true. Notwithstanding, the Fugitives passed into and through their prime in an atmosphere of mutual appreciation. But this was nothing compared to the barbaric yawp of the Beats as they cheered one another. Ginsberg hailed Gregory Corso as the best American poet now writing: "a scientific master of mad mouthfuls of language." Corso hailed Ginsberg in return. Ginsberg hailed Michael McClure. Michael McClure, etc. The Beats became their own best evangelists. The peak was probably reached by one Paul Carroll in the *Evergreen Review* for January-February 1961, when he trumpeted that Ginsberg was the best poet America had known in its whole history. Still, I may be wrong about that peak. Soon no doubt some scraggly-bearded bard will hail his bedfellow as the greatest poet in the cosmos.

But the most vital advantage the Beatnik has had over the Fugitive is in the attitude toward the Negro. Though at the outset the Fugitives asserted that they were fleeing from the Old South, they gradually changed their tune. Before the decade was over, Tate announced that he had criticized the South for the last time. In an anthology of social comment, *I'll Take My Stand,* published in 1930, the Fugitives viewed with regret the passing of the agrarian, almost feudal Old South. In that world the Negro and the white man both knew their place. With the coming of the new industrialism and dislocation, the problem was to restore order. In seeking the solution to the problem the Fugitives consistently looked at it from a white man's point of view. They probably could not help it. To this book Warren contributed an essay called "The Briar Patch." He said in it, "The Southern white man . . . wishes the Negro well; he wishes to see crime, genial irresponsibility, ignorance, and oppression replaced by an informed and productive Negro community." The keynote of *I'll Take My Stand* was in fact Ransom's essay, "Reconstructed but Unregenerate."

The contrast with the attitude of the Beats toward the Negro is awesome. "The Negro," according to Jack Kerouac, is "the essential American." The other Beats, almost without exception, join Kerouac in his homage. But the man who has hymned the Negro loudest is a neo-Beatnik, a latecomer, who has tried to become the shepherd of the Beat flock. He is Norman Mailer. Mailer, after a highly successful war novel, *The Naked and the Dead,* saw his career collapse into drugged futility. In desperation he grasped at the Beat movement and in it found something of what he wanted. Most of all, it led him to the Negro.

His essay "The White Negro" appeared in a periodical called *Dissent* in 1957 and has since been widely circulated and reprinted. There Mailer views American culture in a bleak light; our society is hell-bent for totalitarianism. Our only hope is the Hipster, the man who can be cool even to calamity. And "the source of Hip is the Negro," who for two hundred years has learned how to live at the edge of disaster. He is the American existentialist and he has devised the Hip jargon, largely from Negro jazz, to express his emotional disengagement from the outside world. Within his own world he makes choices and urges them into action. His favorite word is "Go"; the message is movement. The

White Negro must take the cue from him since he has long lived in a world the white man is only now inhabiting. As Mailer sums it up, the Negro Hipster "holds more of the tail of the expanding elephant of truth" than anyone else.

The influence of Mailer's view has not, I think, been slight. He and the Beatniks have contributed to a climate of opinion in which the Negro is exalted. The white intellectual — and especially the white intellectual who belongs to the New York culture-cartel — now identifies with the Negro to an ineffable degree. The only one unimpressed by this exaltation of the Negro is the Negro intellectual. The playwright Lorraine Hansberry, author of *Raisin in the Sun,* has coldly dismissed Mailer's doctrine as "the new paternalism." The Negro novelist James Baldwin has remarked that he would hate to be in Kerouac's shoes if he ever read his rhapsodic prose about the Negro to a Harlem audience. On Mailer himself, Baldwin has quoted from Negro jazzmen to pronounce Mailer's epitaph: "a real sweet ofay cat, but a little frantic." And the key word is "ofay": foe.

So the battle has gone on. But the real casualties have been the talented writers of the median. Not esoteric enough for the New Critics, not bawdy enough for the Beats, they have often been ignored. Or if not ignored, then given less attention than they merited. This is especially true for poets, poets such as Chad Walsh or William Meredith. Another good example, to my mind, is Daniel Hoffman.

Hoffman's first volume, *An Armada of Thirty Whales,* was picked by Auden for the Yale University "Younger Poets" award in 1954. In general it received respectful notices and the *Saturday Review* — unfortunately a journal without much critical reputation — called it "the year's best poetry book." *A Little Geste* came out in 1960. It should firmly establish Hoffman's high standing and would, I believe, make him internationally known if his voice could be heard above the battle cries. In both books his technique, often, is to take a trivial incident, explore it with the reader, and then widen it with a universal application. A professor of

English, he writes verse which leans at times toward the academic. His references or sources may be mythological or literary; he may write of Cytherea or Taliesin. His humanity transforms the antique references into something we need to know in order to understand the human condition today. In his latest poems, not yet collected into a book, Hoffman says that he has not "dealt as directly with myths" but has "written more from an involvement with contemporary events."

What his poetry has above all is charm. I know that "charm" can be a weak, even a derogatory word. Yet if it means grace and gentleness without sentimentality, if it means attractiveness without commonness, if it includes all that we mean when speaking of "a charm," then I think we can accurately apply the term to Hoffman's poetry. I find it best in such a poem as "In the Beginning," most of which I want to quote:

> On the jetty, our fingers shading
> incandescent sky and sea,
>
> my daughter stands with me.
> "Boat! Boat!" she cries, her voice
>
> in the current of speech cascading
> with recognition's joys. . . .
>
> She points beyond the jetty
> where the uncontested sun
>
> wimples the wakeless water
> and cries, "Boat!" though there is none.
>
> But that makes no difference to Katy,
> atingle with vision and word;
>
> and why do I doubt that the harbor,
> in the inner design of truth,

is speckled with tops'ls and spinnakers,
creased with the hulls of sloops?

Kate's word names the vision
that's hers; I try to share. . . .

Child, magician, poet
by incantation rule;

their frenzy's spell unbroken
defines the topgallant soul.

Here at times is the touch of Emily Dickinson, though the
poetry is paternal.

Auditor's Report: PROSE

1961:

Mr. Salinger's Franny and Zooey

THE most remarkable thing about Salinger's pair of stories is how old their kind turns out to be — medieval at the least. "Franny" is a Dialogue between Body and Soul in terms not much changed since the Middle Ages. And "Zooey" is a theological tract. In "Franny" the only significant departure is a modern one: Body and Soul are here so disassociated that little give and take results. Though the Soul displays some respect for what its antagonist says, to the Body the dialogue as dialogue can hardly be said to exist. This disassociation Salinger makes profound. It shows not only in words but in attitudes and actions. The great extent of it makes the story all the more current. The medieval moralist could paint his fat lecher, for instance, in lurid colors but there was something appealing in his grossness, his triple chin, the sheer gusto of his appetites. Not so in "Franny." What strikes us here is how bitterly Salinger hates the Body.

A college man named Lane Coutell waits at the station for his girl, Franny Glass, a guest at the big football weekend. When she arrives he takes her to a restaurant for drinks and lunch. During their stay at the restaurant they bicker and Franny becomes so overwrought that she flees to the restroom. There she cries convulsively. When she rejoins Lane their dialogue, raised now, begins again. It ends when Franny leaves the table for a second time and faints. That is the plot of "Franny."

Lane is so ordinary that Salinger does not bother to describe him. The only physical attribution is unpleasant: Lane's long fingers are his vanity. We know him, and know him well, through what he does rather than through how he looks. We know him through his actions. These are never really good, they are seldom neutral, and they are often offensive. From the start of the story Salinger takes the privilege, relished by Victorian writers but rarely used today, of criticizing what one of his characters does. "Lane himself lit a cigarette as the train pulled in. Then, like so many people, who, perhaps, ought to be issued only a very probational pass to meet trains, he tried to empty his face of all expression that might quite simply, perhaps even beautifully, reveal how he felt about the arriving person." Salinger's indignation is sharpened by his irony. His hostility is so open that the effect is overdone. After Franny's arrival and throughout the long luncheon Lane remains repellent. There are degrees — he is more so at one time than another — but he never makes much claim on the reader's regard.

But Franny we are invited to love. She looks beautiful and acts beautiful. Even when she is distraught. Just before her paroxysm of crying she presses the heels of her hands against her eyes. Salinger says, "Her extended fingers, though trembling, or because they were trembling, looked oddly graceful and pretty." When she returns to Lane's table she looks "quite stunning." The extent of Salinger's commitment to her is shown by the frankly naive quality of his praise. There is something far from sophisticated in his descriptions of her — "quite stunning" is schoolboyish — just as there is in his descriptions of Lane's offensiveness.

She is both beautiful and good. To a marked degree she represents embodied Soul. But in this story she is lost and trying to find her way. She has been looking around her, with more and more desperation, for the absolutes. In her search she finds it far easier to detect what she is not after than what she is. Like Holden Caulfield in *The Catcher in the Rye* she can tell the phoney from the genuine, though she is never as offhand and intuitive in doing so as he is. She is subtler but more apt to be confused. Yet she knows, for example, that the "section men," the glib graduate students who take over the literature classes in the professors' absence, are frauds when they tear down Turgenev to build up their own favorites. As the luncheon goes along she sees that Lane, who postures like them about a paper he wrote on Flaubert, is also a fake.

Her testing for the beautiful is of a piece with her testing for the true. The English department at her school includes two widely heralded poets, Manlius and Esposito. Lane is impressed. Not only are they two of the best men in the country, he says, they are poets. "They're not" is her flat answer. She tries to make clear to him what the beautiful is. It is not the much reprinted poems of Manlius or Esposito. These two leave nothing beautiful behind them. They and their sort write verses which at best "may just be some kind of terribly fascinating, syntax *droppings* — excuse the expression." These men may reach the mind but never the heart. Franny fails to make Lane understand, however; the more so because she herself remains unsure of what the beautiful is and how to find it.

She is a little clearer about the good. She says that through her Religion Survey course she has come upon a small book by a "Russian peasant, apparently," called *The Way of a Pilgrim*. He wanders about Russia looking for someone to tell him how to pray without stopping. Ultimately he meets "a starets — some sort of terribly advanced religious person" who directs him to a wonderful collection of the writings of the Church Fathers, the *Philokalia* or "The Love of Spiritual Beauty." There he finds his answer and learns how to pray incessantly. Then he goes about teaching others. His message, which so appeals to Franny, is that even though you start by merely praying words, if you persist the word will become the reality. The good, the beautiful, the true will grow apparent. You will, Franny explains to Lane, "purify your whole outlook and get an absolutely new conception of what everything's about."

Striving for the Pilgrim's knowledge has made Franny change. She has given up her work in dramatics, which before meant a great deal to her. She has surrendered some of her comfortable ideas of excellence; for example, she used to think Manlius remarkable but now she writes him off as just another poor fellow. She has lost most of her illusions about Lane, leaving in their place, however, enough of a feeling of guilt to make her demonstrative. The less highly she thinks of him the more warmly she holds his hand. Just before the story opens she has written him a letter full of affection; in the course of the story she admits solemnly, "I had to strain to write it." Throughout the luncheon the strain of her search and the compulsion to apply her new standards are always present. She tries to stifle them but is only briefly successful. Twice the tension in her comes to a peak. The first time is when she leaves the table and sobs in the restroom, the second when she collapses and loses consciousness.

During the meal she tries tensely to show Lane what she is looking for. While she pleads with him — indirectly — for understanding, he sits and eats. She cannot bring herself to touch her own slight meal. Her forehead glistens with sweat, she turns pale, her hands shake. But Lane plods with workmanlike pleasure through his food. He has ordered snails, frogs' legs, and a salad. Salinger makes us watch while Lane cuts all this up and stuffs himself. As Franny sits in torment he finishes everything on his plate. Then, "thoroughly relaxed, stomach full," he dismisses all that Franny has had to say — and she excuses herself only to faint.

As the story ends, Lane intimates that he will attempt to reach her by a back stair, when she feels better, and sleep with her. Then he leaves. Franny, now lying in the restaurant manager's office, looks at the ceiling and moves her lips in the Pilgrim's prayer.

The second story, "Zooey," is the complement of "Franny." Much longer, it is, on balance, just barely as good. Essentially it is a theological tract, of three sections which easily fall apart but which taken together constitute the answer to the question asked in "Franny." They give Franny herself what she is looking for. Salinger takes care to deny that "Zooey" should be considered a tract — or as he puts it "a mystical story, or a religiously mystifying story" — and calls it a love story. It is not. Or if it is, so is the New Testament.

A better and shrewder technical term for the story is the other one he uses: a home-movie. In form and content both "Zooey" seems home-made, family-style. The Glass family are the cast. Only three appear in the film but the rest are often invoked. The parents are Bessie and Les Glass, a pair of ex-vaudevillians. We never see Les but Bessie brilliantly plays herself through the picture. Their galaxy of children ranges from the oldest, Seymour (now dead nearly seven years but still a strong influence), to Franny, the youngest. In between come Buddy, a kept writer at an unnamed college; three other children with no direct bearing on the present story; and Zooey, described as one of the most popular leading-men in television. Nearest in age and spirit to Franny, he plays the main role. Salinger insists on the remarkable excellence of the Glass children's minds. All the children have in their time been regulars on a noted juvenile quiz show, "It's a Wise Child." There and elsewhere all have shown extraordinary powers. One of the younger boys, for instance, once got over an unhappy love affair by trying to translate the Mundaka Upanishad into classical Greek. And Franny is not only beautiful but so talented an actress that even her brothers admire her acting.

"Zooey" opens with a piece of professional posturing. Salinger puts mirrors face to face; between them the narrator preens. Buddy Glass, the older, "writing" brother, tells the story. In the pompous introduction he implies that he is both the author of a long letter, which will be reproduced, and of the narrative to follow. As Salinger has him put it, "The style of the letter, I'm told, bears a considerably more than passing resemblance to the style, or written manner-isms, of this narrator, and the general reader will no doubt jump to the heady conclusion that the writer of the letter and I are one and the same person. Jump he will, and, I'm afraid, jump he should." One argument can be made for this posturing: it is fairly consistent throughout the story.

It appears in the style itself. Buddy is bound to remind his readers that he knows a cliché when he sees one. Even near the climax he writes self-consciously. "This was the first time in almost seven years that Zooey had, in the ready-made dramatic idiom, 'set foot' in Seymour's and Buddy's old room." The posturing appears still more in the content of "Zooey," especially when Salinger wants to impress us with the depth of the Glass erudition. Again and again he has Zooey, in particular, pour out a fund of religious informa-tion, usually esoteric, in the matiest possible accents. "This is Kaliyuga, buddy," he will remark, "the Iron Age." Or he will burst out, "I feel like those dismal bastards Seymour's beloved Chuang-tzu warned everybody against." It can be argued that this is Buddy writing rather than Salinger just as it was Holden Caulfield speaking in *The Catcher*. But Zooey shows off in dialogue which Buddy is reporting and not composing. Some of this pretentiousness is clearly Salin-ger as Salinger anyway, as we can see from his other Glass stories. And it is this pretentiousness which is largely re-sponsible for the mixed effect "Zooey" gives. "Seymour's beloved Chuang-tzu"!

The three sections of "Zooey" differ considerably from one another. The first, after the affected introductory letter, is a delightful tour de force. It presents Zooey and Bessie in the Glass bathroom. While Zooey bathes and shaves, Bessie beetles her way around, worrying about

Franny, who is now back home. The dialogue alternately rushes and meanders; the comedy timing is admirable. Salinger describes Zooey's and his mother's actions with loving care. The writing turns at times almost hypnotic, for Salinger can list the contents of a medicine chest and make us read every word. The effect of the dialogue and brilliant stage directions is much like that of some play by Samuel Beckett, say, "Krapp's Last Tape."

The second section takes Zooey from the bathroom to the living room, where Franny is sleeping on a couch. After some theological backing and filling, he quizzes her on her breakdown, her praying, and her religious feelings. She becomes more and more harrowed as he goes through his maneuvers. The second section climaxes when she says, almost inaudibly, "I want to talk to Seymour." Zooey proceeds with his questions and answers, however, probing as far as he can into her mind. He continues, in fact, for another twenty pages after Franny says she wants to talk with her dead brother. It takes that long for Zooey to know that he is beaten. Then: "In an instant, he turned pale — pale with anxiety for Franny's condition, and pale, presumably, because failure had suddenly filled the room with its invariably sickening smell."

In the final section Zooey calls her on the telephone, pretending that he is Buddy — that is, the best surrogate for the dead Seymour. To answer the phone Franny returns to her childhood and to the womb. As she goes down the long hall in the apartment, she appears "to grow younger with each step." By the time she reaches her parents' bedroom door her "handsome tailored tie-silk dressing gown" looks like a small child's woolen bathrobe. She takes up the phone in the bedroom and there listens while Zooey disguised as Buddy tries to make talk and defend himself. The upturn of this discussion comes when she realizes that Zooey is speaking. Zooey, now desperate and inspired, reassures her about her praying but tells her that the phoniness of the world is none of her concern. She must keep her own standards in spite of it. She must do her best for the Fat Lady — Seymour's term in radio days for the audience, invisible, doubtless horrible, and yet completely dependent. Actually, Zooey continues with rising pitch, the Fat Lady is everyone. And he concludes with the revelation. *"Don't you know who that Fat Lady really is?"* he demands of Franny. "Ah, buddy. Ah, buddy. It's Christ Himself. Christ Himself, buddy."

Franny is overjoyed at the revelation. Peace comes to her in a moment. She gets into her parents' bed and smiles quietly just before falling asleep.

There is the message, the answer to Franny's question. The false is finally just as true as the true because God is everywhere, in everything. The phoney and the genuine equally deserve our love because God manifests himself in both. All must be good and true, if not always beautiful.

It is even possible, though guesses are risky, that this is the answer to Salinger's own question too. He would not be the first author to work through his problems by way of his poetry or prose. The rumors of Salinger's troubled emotional life have been widespread. It may be that here we have his personal Pilgrim's Progress, for the distance between the end of "Franny" and the end of "Zooey" is substantial. Salinger finished "Franny" with a spasm of quiet hate; Lane Coutell leaves looking even more detestable than when he entered. As he goes, it is hinted that he is as gross and persistent in his loving as in his feeding. He hasn't been alone with Franny for a month. He shakes his head. "That's no good. Too goddam long between drinks. To put it crassly." However, by the time we reach the last page of "Zooey" this perfectly specific manifestation of hate has turned to a message of universal love. "There isn't anyone *any*where," Zooey proclaims to Franny, "that isn't Seymour's Fat Lady." That, presumably, includes even Lane Coutell. The hate of "Franny" is gone; the love of "Zooey" prevails.

And Salinger may have worked out his own solution and reached the same answer, his own answer, even if he may not yet be sleeping as quietly as Franny.

1962:

Miss Porter's Ship of Fools

IF YOU ARE OLD enough you can remember the occasional cocktail party comment in the middle 1930's about the new novel Katherine Anne Porter was writing. She had started it in 1932 and the fact was not long in becoming known. She worked painstakingly and finished a draft in August 1941. At intervals during the next two decades, preliminary versions of scenes appeared in a variety of magazines ranging from *Accent* to *Mademoiselle*. They whetted the reader's curiosity but gave little indication of the scope of the book. It was more than once suggested that the book might, in the grim tradition of the aged and failing artist, never come out at all. But it has, and its long delayed appearance has been accompanied by much critical, and noncritical, acclaim. Here and there you have a half smothered dissent but in general the praise is loud and lusty.

I am not sure that it should be. To me *Ship of Fools* lacks the flawlessly finished surface of her three short novels which preceded it. The richness, the decorative beauty of those books is gone. So is the mournfully elegant symbolism; it is replaced by a compound of images either too obvious or too vague. So is the sureness of tone of the prior books. Now the tone is usually hard but sometimes cloying. For example. In a prefatory paragraph where Miss Porter acknowledges her debt to Sebastian Brant's *Stultifera Navis* of 1494, she adds that the central idea was not new even when Brant wrote: even then "it was very old and durable and dearly familiar." I think the whole clause cloys and the last phrase is almost sweet. And when she says of the Ship of Fools, with a patness accentuated by the sentence rhythms, "I am a passenger on that ship," the effect is forced.

We all know that there is such a thing as too much revision; here apparently is such a case. And yet the book as a whole is powerful despite the fact that some of the life has been written out of it. The subject itself is strong. Evil makes more impressive reading than good; folly is more entertaining than wisdom; and Miss Porter's vessel is as much a ship of knaves as of fools. There is a wickedness in most passengers in addition to some foolishness, and a sickness in every passenger. Before the vessel — it is called the *Vera* — leaves the Mexican port of Vera Cruz for the dock at faraway Bremerhaven, each passenger has had to be vaccinated and now "all alike were feverish, with a crusted, festering little sore above the knee or elbow." Beyond all this there is constant ugliness. Miss Porter sets down detail after detail that is simply unpleasant. Here for instance are two besotted passengers, a man and a woman, joining in song: "They bent towards each other until their noses almost touched and sang the whole chorus into each other's mouths."

In this ugly microcosm of a ship in which nearly everyone is either ridiculous or hateful or both, the exceptions have an unusual importance. They include two major characters. One is Miss Porter's persona, Mary Treadwell, a sophisticated, sensitive divorcee in her mid-forties. Her disengaged life is too delicate to be merely a drift but it is certainly an existence without much satisfaction. The other is Miss Porter's spokesman, Dr. Schumann; he is — of course — the ship's physician. A man of judgment and principle, he stands out as the only person either among the passengers or crew who is eminently good. Appropriately enough in this universe, he suffers from a heart ailment which threatens him with death.

During a Washington interview given a reporter after *Ship of Fools* was published, Miss Porter leafed through a number of reviews and remarked that none of them quite saw the point of the book. The point was, she said, "that evil is always done with the collusion of good." She explained that she considered the theme of the book to be "the budding of an evil. All the wrong that is being done is done through the moral inertia, carelessness, and indifference of what are usually thought to be upright citizens." Dr. Schumann believes both in Original Sin and the Real Presence. In the most important philosophic passage in the book he observes dryly, "It takes a strong character to be really evil. Most of us are too slack, halfhearted, or cowardly — luckily, I suppose. Our collusion with evil is only negative, consent by default, you might say. I suppose in our hearts our sympathies are with the criminal because he really commits the deeds we only dream of doing!"

In *Ship of Fools* the amount of evil varies greatly from person to person. In Dr. Schumann there is almost none. In Mrs. Treadwell there is only a little. But among the rest, aside from a doll-like Mexican bridal pair, wickedness flourishes. At the opposite extreme from the good doctor Miss Porter puts some Spanish gypsy twins, a boy and a girl six years old. They call themselves Ric and Rac after some comic-strip terriers. They are original sin personified. In all they do, from pouring ink on a carpet to causing a man's death by drowning, they breathe with brute malevolence. Their mother and the other Spanish gypsies are evil too but not absolutely and unrelievedly so, partly because life has beaten some circumspection into them. Somewhat less evil but thoroughly doltish are another group of passengers on board, the Germans. Heavy animals, they sin almost automatically. Cruelty has been their lot since childhood; prejudice has become second nature. The most ominous of their sins is anti-Semitism. The time of the voyage is significant, August 1931, and the destruction of the Jews in Germany is clearly foreshadowed. When the *Vera* takes on a set of wretched steerage passengers Herr Rieber the German publisher has a suggestion, "I would do this for them: I would put them all in a big oven and turn on the gas." And when a German passenger sitting at the Captain's table admits to having a Jewish wife, he is ejected from the group and the rest draw together in mutual satisfaction.

As the ship sails along Miss Porter weaves her characters into elaborate and suggestive patterns. From character and action two generalizations about evil can gradually be deduced, generalizations which cut through national lines and have nothing to do with being German or Spanish or American. These are, first, that the young are more wicked than the old. This idea, at its ultimate in the twins Ric and Rac, is not only implicit but explicit. Dr. Schumann, when discussing the noisy malice of some Cuban medical students who are among the passengers, says sadly, "It is hardly to be believed, the malignance of the young." Older people, he argues, sin and know it and sometimes repent. But the young "sin and they do not even know it; or they know it and they glory in it." The second generalization is more tentative and never openly announced. It is that men are more evil than women.

The key characters designed to show this are two American painters, Jenny and David. They are lovers who alternately enjoy and abrade one another. Though both are, on balance, harmed by their relationship, Jenny clearly suffers most. Under David's cold eye she lets herself become colorless and nearly plain. The change in her painting is marked. Before meeting David she had produced gay, bright-colored canvases. Now her palette is muted. She is even turning from oils to charcoal and India ink. And all her warm, outgoing impulses are being frozen by his influence, for David is an inverted puritan moving joylessly through life. He loves Jenny best when he has damaged and hurt her. "The sight of her weakness and defeat gave him pleasure like no other": such is Miss Porter's damning dismissal of him on the last page of *Ship of Fools*.

The basic charge against men is, however, both more and less than this. It comes, rather clearly, from Miss Porter's personal experience. It is that men want to own their women. "Total demand" is her term for it. She has been married three times and in the Washington interview quoted earlier she noted carefully, "I am very fond of men and have had good and lifelong friends, but it is a disaster to have a man fall in love with me, because they aren't content to take what I can give; they want everything from me." As part of this demand David must always open the letters Jenny gets and when she argues against it saying "I don't open your letters," he asks with mindless egoism why she should. He has no respect for any of her privacies. Everything in her ought, he thinks, to be open to him; but he jealously guards his own private world. The resentment of women against this gross male proprietorship is epitomized in one of the most curious acts in the book. Mrs. Treadwell has been mistaken for one of the Spanish slatterns by an oafish young Texan, William Denny. Denny, drunk, tries clumsily to attack her. She pushes him over and then hits him with the stiletto heel of her shoe until his head is covered with ugly cuts and her arm aches. Afterward "in her joy and excitement" she kisses the bloodstained shoe.

Here in *Ship of Fools* is the world as Miss Porter has come to see it. When the voyage nears its end Dr. Schumann says defensively to the *Vera's* captain, "There are still some very decent persons on board." The captain promptly challenges him to name one — and he has no answer. Sordid as this world seems, however, Miss Porter thinks it her duty to report it faithfully, to write "straight." She declared in the Washington interview, "I am not as good an artist as I hoped I would be, but I am a straight one. I am that if I am nothing else." Hers is the classical artist's urge for clarity; and unswerving honesty is her aim. In the book she makes Jenny say, "I want things straight and clear or at least I want to be able to see when they're crooked and confused." But love, sexual love, puts dust in people's eyes. Once again, as Jenny says for the self-possessed author of the book, "When you are in love, it is nearly impossible to make yourself see straight, isn't it?" Different in mode though they may appear, these two kinds of straightness, straight writing and seeing straight, are one to Miss Porter.

Ship of Fools is an honest, disheartening book. It is not over-written or overblown. Quite the reverse: it has been revised downward. Its basic image is old and plain but as the author develops it, it becomes modern and more complex. I do not believe that *Ship of Fools* reaches the heights of Miss Porter's earlier work but I am sure it will find a place, if a small one, in American literature.

E. E. Cummings
and Exploded Verse

EDWARD ESTLIN CUMMINGS was buried with a burst of eulogy. His death in September 1962 caused many critics, mainly of the more popular variety, to look back over his career and sum it up in admiring phrases. *Time* magazine, long one of his apostles, noted that he was being apostrophized as "the greatest innovator in modern poetry," the man who perfected "the idiom of American common speech," an American writer whose place was beside Thoreau and Whitman, and so on.

There is no doubt that his verse earned him an impressive amount of recognition. For one thing, he was productive. He wrote steadily for over forty years, his last volume *95 Poems* coming out in 1958. In a country where poets are frequently forgotten, his very industry helped to keep his name alive. Before he died nearly all other poets of his generation had fallen silent, and more than one poet of the succeeding generation had found his inspiration gone. Throughout his long career Cummings accumulated honors. He received the Dial Prize, two Guggenheim Fellowships, membership in the National Institute of Arts and Letters, the Bollingen Award for poetry, a fellowship from the Academy of American Poets, and a handsome grant from the Ford Foundation. More than one respected literary critic admired him too. The early praise equalled the late. Theodore Spencer, whose untimely death deprived us of an unusually sensitive mind, could hail Cummings as "the most truly delightful lyric poet in America." Lloyd Frankenberg could term him "one of the major poets of our time." Horace Gregory, no mean poet himself, could assert that in Cummings' poetry "one is refreshed by the revival of courtly music and compliment, of poetic wit, and the art of burlesque." These early advocates set the tone; it has maintained itself for decades. At first glance it seems to maintain itself even now.

And yet something more has remained to be said. The pages of *Time* are indicative. When *95 Poems* appeared *Time* termed Cummings' poetry "fresh, singular, vivid and intense." The poems themselves were "the flowers and fancies of a unique lyricism." But when *Time's* eulogy was printed in 1962, there was a note of doubt and reservation in the praise. Was it possible that even at the middle-class level, which *Time* so well represents, Cummings was being reconsidered? Regardless, there is little doubt that the time for reconsideration has arrived. Cummings' work is finished. On the one hand, we have before us all his poetry plus his autobiography. On the other, we have a shortage of substantial critical studies. There have been three or four good articles, and a useful monograph, Norman Friedman's *E. E. Cummings, the Art of His Poetry* (1960). The only biographical study, Charles Norman's *The Magic-Maker* (1958) is as uncritical as its title suggests. So a candid reappraisal might be in order, and the notes that follow might perhaps contribute to it. It ought to start with Cummings' initial volume.

Tulips and Chimneys, issued in 1923, was the first book of poems he published. A surprisingly good case can be made for saying that it was also his best. Some of the verses

buried there were never to be exhumed. No later collection
of his work, and no anthology, would ever include such a
piece of derivation as his "Epithalamion," with its rhetoric
about

> Thou aged unreluctant earth who dost
> with quivering continual thighs invite
> the thrilling rain.

Nor would we be apt to read in reprint the commonplace
couplets of "Puella Mea" ("Lovely as those ladies were,
mine is a little lovelier") or the lines of "Nicolette" ("right
wildly beat her heart"). All that these poems reflect is the
enthusiasm of the college student who has earned an A in
his English literature course.

But once we read past the tributes to Nicolette and other
ladies of great beauty we begin to see several of the pieces
which were later anthologized. Their advent is marked by
the first, tentative use of the little "i" and of fragmented
typography. "Thy fingers make early flowers" and "the Cambridge ladies who live in furnished souls" are particularly
worth looking at. "Thy fingers" reveals a mainly traditional
tone and rhetoric, but we also discover the new typography,
the delight in playing with the poem on the printed page:

> Thy fingers make early flowers of
> all things.
> thy hair mostly the hours love:
> a smoothness which
> sings, saying
> (though love be a day)
> do not fear, we will go amaying.

This is certainly a lyric of mixed qualities. Its theme, of
love and death, is thoroughly traditional, as is the tone. The
syntax is more nearly unconventional; it is loose and informal though it is also marked by old-fashioned inversions for

the sake of proper rhyme. The imagery is mild and not very memorable — except for the bold opening image itself, "Thy fingers make early flowers of all things." On the other hand, the sonnet about the Cambridge ladies, though traditional in its imposed form, is sharp and individual underneath. Cummings was a Harvard professor's son and the scene is of course Cambridge, Massachusetts. Cambridge's scale of values is the reverse of his own; he establishes the fact with an attractive blend of irony and wry indignation. His final image exactly defines the level of this lyric, remaining one of his most often quoted. But here is the whole poem:

> the Cambridge ladies who live in furnished souls
> are unbeautiful and have comfortable minds
> (also, with the church's protestant blessings
> daughters, unscented shapeless spirited)
> they believe in Christ and Longfellow, both dead,
> are invariably interested in so many things —
> at the present writing one still finds
> delighted fingers knitting for the is it Poles?
> perhaps. While permanent faces coyly bandy
> scandal of Mrs. N and Professor D
> . . . . the Cambridge ladies do not care, above
> Cambridge if sometimes in its box of
> sky lavender and cornerless, the
> moon rattles like a fragment of angry candy

Cummings' problem almost seems to be the fact that he could achieve originality either in the form of a lyric or in its content, but seldom in both. It is as if he had only so much individuality to spend and had to husband it for each poem. He could either compose a lyric of unusual form and commonplace content like "Thy fingers" or a traditional sonnet like "the Cambridge ladies" with an exceptional content. In those few times, perhaps a dozen in all, when he developed an original and organic unity of form and content, he gave us some truly memorable poems.

In *Tulips and Chimneys,* then, we find some of the best

as well as some of the worst of Cummings' poetry. The kind of poem he managed in the course of time to make widely recognized is already present. We see the sonnet, for instance, whose conventional form is disguised by pushing the words and phrases apart and by abandoning punctuation and capital letters—though it should be added that he would later on go further in those directions than in *Tulips and Chimneys*. Then there are the free-verse lyrics which represent an extension of this technique, a reduction of it at times almost to absurdity. Not always, however. The much quoted "in Just-spring," for example, turning as it does on the epithet "goat-footed" for the balloon man, extends far beyond childhood and the moment.

The tricks of technique, or, if you will, the stylistic devices, appear in both crude and complex forms. One that Cummings particularly likes is paradox. Ultimately that was to become a considerable barrier between Cummings and the reader because it defeated even the most persistent attempts to make out the poet's meaning. Perhaps the most interesting thing, if we want to comprehend his long career as a composer of verse, is to see the first simple use of the device. There is a poem in *Tulips and Chimneys* which begins "my love is building a building" and here this technique is to be found at its crudest. The building in question is "strong fragile," "skilful uncouth," "precise clumsy," and "laborious, casual." In his succeeding volumes the device becomes less simple but not much less. Normally the advantage of paradox for a poet is that it increases the tension of his poetry. In Cummings even later it is often merely a case of opposites which cancel out, leaving neither meaning nor emotion behind them.

Cummings' discontent with traditional rhyming can well be appreciated. *Tulips and Chimneys* marks both his departure from it and his characteristic deviation afterwards. He takes masculine rhyme, feminine rhyme, internal rhyme, and assonance, and mixes them all loosely together. His rhyme effects are sometimes vivid, sometimes not, but they are never restrained. Nor in general are the sound patterns of his verse. Two of the most noted instances of his bold use of sound also serve to show his lack of subtlety. They are the "angry candy" in the sonnet about the Cambridge ladies and "the bigness of cannon is skilful," which opens one of his free-verse poems about World War I.

His humor is of a piece with his metrical effects. It is bold, earthy, simple. At its pungent best it is mingled with anger, and that combination has produced several strong poems. The sonnet about Kitty is among the most memorable in *Tulips and Chimneys:*

"kitty" . sixteen, 5′ 1″, white, prostitute.

ducking always the touch of must and shall,
whose slippery body is Death's littlest pal,

skilled in quick softness . Unspontaneous . cute.

the signal perfume of whose unrepute
focusses in the sweet slow animal
bottomless eyes importantly banal,

Kitty . a whore . Sixteen
                          you corking brute
amused from time to time by clever drolls
fearsomely who do keep their sunday flower.
The babybreasted broad "kitty" twice eight

— beer nothing, the lady'll have a whiskey-sour —

whose least amazing smile is the most great
common divisor of unequal souls.

This is, in fact, one of the finest sonnets ever written by Cummings. Later on, the same mixture of humor and indignation, with an extra measure of contempt, produced "Poem,

or Beauty Hurts Mr. Vinal," his most acid attack on the genteel art of boom-time America. It is an awkward poem to
reprint or quote from because time has dulled the edge of
its criticism of America and American poetry for most readers — the poem is filled with references to advertisements and
literary fashions of over thirty years ago. Yet something can
be gained from it through the force of Cummings' feeling,
which cuts through the old sales slogans:

> take it from me kiddo
> believe me
> my country, 'tis of
>
> you, land of the Cluett
> Shirt Boston Garter and Spearmint
> Girl With The Wrigley Eyes (of you
> land of the Arrow Ide
> and Earl &
> Wilson
> Collars) of you i
> sing: land of Abraham Lincoln and Lydia E. Pinkham,
> land above all of Just Add Hot Water And Serve —
> from every B. V. D.
>
> let freedom ring
>
> amen. i do however protest, anent the un
> — spontaneous and otherwise scented merde which
> greets one (Everywhere Why) as divine poesy per
> that and this radically defunct periodical. i would
>
> suggest that certain ideas gestures
> rhymes, like Gillette Razor Blades
> having been used and reused
> to the mystical moment of dullness emphatically are
> Not To Be Resharpened.
>
> · · · · · · · · · · · · · · · · · · · ·

littleliverpill —
hearted-Nujolneeding-There's-A-Reason
americans (who tensetendoned and with
upward vacant eyes, painfully
perpetually crouched, quivering, upon the
sternly allotted sandpile
— how silently
emit a tiny violetflavoured nuisance: Odor?

ono.
comes out like a ribbon lies flat on the brush

More important perhaps than anything else in Cummings
is his treatment of words in themselves. It is utterly casual,
and that is the major charge against him.

In the closest study made of his verse, "Notes on E. E.
Cummings' Language," the critic R. P. Blackmur shows beyond any doubt that Cummings' chief flaw is that he uses
words without a particular meaning. He is especially apt to
take a general term — his favorite is "flower" — and then to
try to conceal its emptiness from a reader by attaching a
paradoxical adjective to it. He may be aiming at metaphysical wit; if so he does it erratically. His metaphysical conceits
nearly always seem slapdash. They come near the mark; they
give the reader a general notion of what Cummings meant;
but they never have the absolute rightness that the images
of the best poets have. The mind of the reader can usually
find a connection between image and idea or, say, between
Cummings' noun and the adjective he uses to qualify it; the
point is that the connection is seldom found to be fundamental. For example: "this taxi smile or angle"; "blond
absence"; "fat colour." Or among the conceits, to pick a
popular one: Mame's eyes "are newly baked and swaggering
cookies of indignant light." It may be that we as readers are
at fault in not gauging the fullness of the poems; yet if
Cummings has ever shown the sort of subtlety that rewards
close reading, few critics have noticed it. From *Tulips and*

Chimneys down to his latest collection of verse, there seems to be little to discover.

It is always possible, notwithstanding, that we have not seen all the evidence. Perhaps the pages of his off-beat autobiography *i: six nonlectures* will yield additional data. The value of a poet's autobiography lies in the light it casts on his poetry, and so we can turn to the *nonlectures* to find out what they have to say.

Regrettably, they say nothing new. They report simply on a man whose verse is, at heart, the sentimental celebration of the individual. Beneath the cynicism and the physicality, beneath the broken lines and small letters, there is a surprisingly old-fashioned lover who — without neglecting to sing about his own self-discovery — hymns the praises of his mistress. The later chapters of the book have many references to Cummings' belief in the importance and uniqueness of the individual: "Even success . . . cannot concern him otherwise than as a stimulus to further . . . self-discovering." "Selfhood" and "self-transcendence" are the key words. And as to love between man and woman: "I am someone who proudly and humbly affirms that love is the mystery-of-mysteries."

The most significant passage on his poetry in the *nonlectures* is actually a quotation from a play which Cummings called *Him*. In this piece of dialogue the main speaker is the poet as acrobat. The other speaker is the girl who loves him and what he does. "Him" speaks first:

HIM: Damn everything but the circus! (*To himself*) And here am I, patiently squeezing fourdimensional ideas into a twodimensional stage, when all of me that's anyone or anything is in the top of a circustent . . . (*A pause*)

ME: I didn't imagine you were leading a double life — and right under my nose, too.

HIM (*Unhearing, proceeds contemptuously*): The average "painter" "sculptor" "poet" "composer" "playwright" is a person who cannot leap through a hoop from the back of a galloping horse, make people laugh with a clown's mouth, orchestrate twenty lions.

ME: Indeed.

HIM (*To her*): But imagine a human being who balances three chairs, one on top of another, on a wire, eighty feet in air with no net underneath, and then climbs into the top chair, sits down, and begins to swing . . .

ME (*Shudders*): I'm glad I never saw that — makes me dizzy just to think of it.

HIM (*Quietly*): I never saw that either.

ME: Because nobody can do it.

HIM: Because I am that. But in another way, it's all I ever see.

ME: What is?

HIM (*Pacing up and down*): This: I feel only one thing, I have only one conviction; it sits on three chairs in Heaven. . . . The three chairs are three facts. . . . I am an Artist, I am a Man, I am a Failure. . . . I breathe, and I swing; and I whisper: "An artist, a man, a failure, MUST PROCEED."

Here is an unexpectedly humble and disarming poet, offering us his poetics in a fable. He reminds us that a touch of sympathy must go with any critical appraisal. He reminds us that we still may not have approached his poetry properly when evaluating it; we still may not have asked the right questions about it.

Blackmur's essay, despite its acuteness, is weakened by an inadequate approach. The probings into Cummings' verse have all the delicacy, all the sensitivity, we have learned to expect from Blackmur. His method, however, is the one he usually uses with other and more thoughtful poets. Used on Cummings it provides us with a limited insight. We see deeply but narrowly. The essay on Cummings came out in 1930; a year later Blackmur's appraisal of Wallace Stevens appeared. Blackmur's careful reasoning and his close searching of Stevens' language produced rich results; Stevens' poetry was properly approached. But the similar analysis of Cummings produced only the critic's conclusion that here was a trivial versifier. Granted, Blackmur from his point of view was right. I suggest, however, that we approach Cum-

mings now from another point of view — and on a simpler
level.

To do this, we must begin by considering that he is not a
poet who thought about every word before he printed it. His
work is not intense, not concentrated. He is by no means
an intellectual poet. It is possible to guess that he seldom
revised his writing very much. Consequently, the virtue recently most fashionable in American poetry — intellectuality
tightened into obscurity — is not his. The most important
thing Cummings has to offer in its place is a delight, at times
too simple, in the sound of words.

For the sake of sound he seemed willing to sacrifice both
clarity and complexity. That, I think, is the reason for
"angry candy" and other well-known exhibition pieces.
Often of course there will be an approximation to meaning
— at intervals there will be more than that, much more —
but ordinarily sound rather than any real sense is the prime
consideration. In a way there is a resemblance between Gertrude Stein and Cummings. According to Professor Leon
Howard's theory, Gertrude Stein thought of words as things.
In terms of medieval philosophy, she was a realist rather
than a nominalist. Cummings too may have thought of the
very sounds of words as things and in this way let himself be
captivated by them.

In its use of sound "and this day it was Spring" is exactly
typical of Cummings. It reads:

and this day it was Spring . . . . us
drew lewdly the murmurous minute clumsy
smelloftheworld. We intricately
alive, cleaving the luminous stammer of bodies
(eagerly just not each other touch) seeking, some
street which easily trickles a brittle fuss
of fragile huge humanity. . . .
                              Numb
thoughts, kicking in the rivers of our blood, miss
by how terrible inches speech — it

made you a little dizzy did the world's smell
(but i was thinking why the girl-and-bird
of you move . . . . moves . . . . and also, i'll admit——)

till, at the corner of Nothing and Something,we heard
a handorgan in twilight playing like hell

There seems to be an almost childish pleasure in such
sounds as "drew lewdly" and "murmurous minute." And
then there is the senseless attraction in the assonance of
"trickles a brittle" as well as the more meaningful, if trite,
coupling of "bird" with "girl." At times the chiming is faint
enough to be accidental though usually one guesses it is not.
The complex of sounds, "intricately alive, cleaving" with its
mingled "l's," "v's," and "c's" is a case in point; so is "fragile
huge humanity." Often alliteration alone is heard but generally Cummings creates something a little more complicated
than that.

If we take this love of sound and add two other things to
it, I believe we have the technical basis for Cummings' poetry. The one is the radical pattern of the poem on the page;
the other, already mentioned, is his love of paradox. The
paradox, like the appeal to the ear, is apt to be simple. It is
often merely a reverse. Lectures become nonlectures; Cummings himself is an unthing; he is a poet who chatters un-
poetically. Or, at the extreme, in the lyric "this mind made
war," we read such a stanza as:

> unfools unfree
> undeaths who live
> nor shall they be
> and must they have

This is the world of the simple switch; this is the world of
"un."

The look of Cummings' poetry on the page is its most
famous characteristic. It is like the exploded view of a ma-

chine. The parts are separated so that we can see each one more clearly. The important syllables are made salient, the unimportant ones huddled together. The typography reinforces the arrangement of the parts on the page. Capital and small letters are used for extraordinary discrimination. The reading of the page is directed, both for those who will read aloud and those who will read silently. Cummings shows how slowly or swiftly he wants his words and syllables pronounced. Vachel Lindsay put his explicit instructions in the margin of the page; Cummings prefers to be oblique. The typography is in part a trick but one that Cummings has made his own. I once heard Roderick Jellema argue that Cummings would never have achieved what he did if the typewriter had not been invented for him. Regardless, the exploded verse is his trademark.

Does all this help to make him a major poet? To a degree perhaps. Yet even at its best it fails to result in a substantial amount of first-class writing.

Cummings himself believed that only twenty of his poems truly showed his work as a poet. It may be hazarded that perhaps half that number will continue to be reprinted. In his own defense he said that poetry must be read with love. And yet the question for all but a few of his poems is whether they are worth the loving. He is still a poet who is more esteemed than he deserves to be, a man who has made his vogue out of a good deal of rather casual, at times semi-private, writing.

However, he still is acclaimed. And he still is read. There must be other reasons, of a wider-ranging kind, for his continuing popularity. My guess is that they are to be found particularly in the formal experimentalism of his verse. I would maintain that Americans are attracted by experimentalism, especially of the bold, superficial kind to be seen in Cummings' writing.

This is of course shaky ground. Anyone who makes a statement about national characteristics is apt to be met with a lifted eyebrow, a look of disbelief. Yet I feel that they exist. If we think of them not as absolutes but as clusters or frequencies, we may be close to the truth. Americans may well have some traits that distinguish them from other nationals. And when a writer can appeal to one or more of these traits he is apt to achieve popularity to an otherwise unaccountable extent.

Such I think is the case with Cummings. His bold experiments with form are compatible with a feature of the American character which has in it several elements. One is the interest in the new for its own sake. The quaint American custom of buying a new automobile every year is a good example. Each new model has — must have — some changes over the old. The changes may be superficial; they may be merely a novel grill or six headlights where two grew before. But that is enough: at least the surface has been altered.

With the new, however, goes the desire to find something better. The typical American is constantly looking for improvement — in his material conditions but also at times in less superficial things. It is not only that he wants a better salary than he has been paid before; he often wants to better himself, so to speak. He has his aspirations, his sentimental dreams. To them too Cummings appeals. He celebrates love and the individual and the caustic but yearning human character.

Along with the American wish for the new and better, there has always been an American restlessness. This likewise is an element in the complex which responds to Cummings' verse. More than a century ago the French visitor Tocqueville, one of the most penetrating observers ever to write about the United States, noticed our restlessness. To a certain extent it was physical. We could not sit quietly. We drummed with our fingers, we tapped our feet. To a certain extent it was psychological. We wanted to leave wherever we were and travel somewhere else. Vaguely dissatisfied with ourselves, we wanted to see the new as well as to be it ourselves. The best book to come from any of the recent "Beat" writers, Jack Kerouac's feverish novel *On the*

Road, is filled with aimless movement. From the beginning Americans have been travelers and seekers.

It is probable that all this has favored experimentalism in American literature. Of course other countries have had their experimenters, great and small. I shall name only one, a great one, James Joyce; and I shall be the first to admit, with all the valor of ignorance, that the Irish are not an experimentally-minded nation. The point I wish to make is not that one nation is devoid of a desire to experiment and another consumed by it, but rather that experimentalism appears more often in the United States than in, for instance, Ireland.

I would argue, further, that this tendency to experiment is found in the best American literature as well as in the worst. A dozen poets, of different sorts, spring to mind. Whitman, Emily Dickinson, Amy Lowell, Hart Crane, Wallace Stevens: these are among them. And the fact that some of them were slower to be appreciated than others does not, I believe, invalidate my argument. We can call on prose writers in evidence, as well as poets. Though experimentalism in American fiction is not as frequent as in verse, it is not hard to find. Among the generally important novelists of the twentieth century most critics would include Theodore Dreiser, John Dos Passos, and of course William Faulkner. Anyone who has read the work of these three will recognize their daring departures from standard practice. I can cite a number of novels, but perhaps one important work by each man will be enough: Dreiser's *An American Tragedy,* Dos Passos's *U.S.A.,* and Faulkner's *Absalom, Absalom!*

This is the context in which we ought to place E. E. Cummings. If we do so, I think we can assess him better than before. We can understand that few American anthologies will ignore him; most will print a few of his poems. These poems will be distinguished by their experimental surface but they will also have something more. They will have an energy made out of indignation and irreverence, in equal proportions. The indignation will be of a kind more suitable to the 1920's than today; yet it will still be contagious. The irreverence too will have a slightly old-fashioned look when compared with the nihilism of the Beat writers. It will look naughty instead of nihilistic. But that will be part of its pleasure for us. And the best of his poems will have love.

It was love, as a matter of fact, which furnished Cummings with the basis for his most attractive experiment in verse. This was his effort when young — all the more interesting for being doomed to failure — to put into words exactly how it felt to make love. He made the effort with patent delight. In doing it he found an organic reason for scattering phrases and syllables over the page. His attempts to speed up or to slow down type reflect the way time varies with the pace of love. Though his tone is the tone of a generation ago, the appeal remains fresh. On the surface Cummings is tough and sensual. If any sentimentality slips in, it is only of the sort which maintains that the prostitute is the kindest girl of all. Even this happens seldom: most of his prostitutes are battered commercial veterans. But underneath the surface of these poems there is at times almost a mystic celebration of the body, purely pagan and far removed from our puritanism with its sense of sin. "I like my body when it is with your body," says Cummings and obviously he means it.

Of the essays at putting the act of love into words: "O It's Nice To Get Up" is typical. As the poem approaches its peak the words draw closer together and then in the climax are exploded. The resources of touch are ransacked to show the reader how Cummings feels. The verbs are strong if trite; the metaphors are uniformly forced. Yet the poem pulls the reader along — in fact he goes readily — through the very strength of the poet's determination to say the unsayable. The strength is not forbidding but lusty, engaging. The same is true for some of the less explicit lyrics such as "the dirty colours of her kiss have just." And, finally, every now and then Cummings surpasses himself. In his three or four best lyrics tone and content match almost, if not quite, perfectly. In these lyrics, moreover, the act of love is an integral part of the poem but never the whole poem. Here is one of them that will stay in the anthologies:

> my girl's tall with hard long eyes
> as she stands, with her long hard hands keeping
> silence on her dress, good for sleeping
> is her long hard body filled with surprise
> like a white shocking wire, when she smiles
> a hard long smile it sometimes makes
> gaily go clean through me tickling aches,
> and the weak noise of her eyes easily files
> my impatience to an edge — my girl's tall
> and taut, with thin legs just like a vine
> that's spent all of its life on a garden-wall,
> and is going to die. When we grimly go to bed
> with these legs she begins to heave and twine
> about me, and to kiss my face and head.

The celebration is frank and open. There are no frustrations, no neuroses. Love may be commercial or not but it is certainly — for the young Cummings — full of force.

The American Imagination

"THE AMERICAN IMAGINATION" is a bold phrase, and it is a hardy man who tries to define it. The noun is perplexing and the adjective anomalous. There must be an imagination (Coleridge has said so!) but what psychologist would be impressed? The psychologist himself discusses it seldom, and then with caution. The students of the behavioral sciences, sober men in general, write little about it. Beneath their feet they glimpse the depths of Freud and Jung; the prospect, if not dismaying, is thought-provoking. Modern writers about literature and the arts prove almost as wary. Only the fact that they have less information than the behavioral scientist induces them to speculate more. And even that is not much. How little they have to tell us is hard to realize until we contrast the mutterings of today with the tumult of talk in Coleridge's time. Today's philosophers, lastly, have spoken more often than the literary critics, and their approach has been more systematic. Notwithstanding, the result has been much the same.

The idea of an "American" imagination has received still less notice. However, the general belief in national characteristics — in things American or Spanish or French — has always been strong. Though racists and propagandists have often used the belief for their own bad purposes, the idea is innocent enough. It has been found in the past in some very good historical writing and continues to be found today. If it does not appear as a formally stated theory, it is evident as a working premise.

In addition to enduring among historians, the idea is quietly coming back into the thinking of certain important, if at times ponderous, social scientists. As one of them has noted, "Rorschach series from different societies reveal different norms for such series as wholes." The most interesting study of national character published since World War II is *People of Plenty*, by the American historian David Potter, who happens to be far from ponderous. He has not only synthesized the previous writing on the subject but has brilliantly analyzed one element, economic abundance, to show how it has helped to form the American character.

Anyone who has known more than one country can testify that national characteristics exist. Of course all Italians are not mercurial; all Englishmen are not reserved. But differences abound. Eat a meal in a Roman restaurant and then dine out in London: the two experiences are indeed unlike. Life in a *pensione* varies from life in a New England farmhouse. Whether it is environment or heredity, or both, that makes the variation no one knows; it need not be argued here. The point is that, regardless of what creates them, national differences flourish; and it is surely not illogical to argue that those differences also are to be found in the imagination. This means, then, that there is an American imagination as distinct from, say, the Italian imagination or the French or even the English imagination. Once granted that it does exist, what is it like? In particular, what is it like now? Any answer is bound to be suspect; any generalization will invite dissent. Nevertheless, experience can be interpreted, and some suggestions can be made.

The better to see the American imagination, we might

look first at those elements in the American experience which appear closest to it.

The land itself is the most massive fact and the best one to begin with. A map of the United States tells as much, in some ways, as a book about its history. Anyone who has not crossed the ocean should be reminded of the sheer size and variety of the American land. There is nearly enough desert, complete with cactus and sandstorm, to make a country as large as England. There are more than enough mountain ranges to do the same thing. And especially in the Middle West there is enough rich black soil to arouse the envy of all the farmers from Cornwall to Cumberland. Nowadays you can fly quickly over those miles and miles of plain, mountain, and desert, but it still takes a long time to drive through them. All this land has, at one time or another in the short span of American history, been there for the taking. There have always been more acres than persons to live on them.

Take this rich and various terrain and add the many kinds of immigrants who have peopled it. They would be as varied as the land itself: gentlemen and bond-servants, Calvinists and Quakers, burghers and criminals. Yet there would be some common denominators. Among those, obviously, would be the general determination of the immigrants to better their lot by leaving their homeland instead of quietly enduring conditions there, and — though this is impossible to prove — probably a restlessness that made it easier for them to move across the ocean. Add enough hardship, when America was reached, so that activity was stimulated and resourcefulness required. Then add a shortage of manpower and a need to conserve it; and the main ingredients are present for an American vitality which few observers have denied.

Of course the individual thrived. He was needed and his

importance was recognized. It did not take the rulers of Massachusetts Bay very long to ignore such British law as prescribed the maiming of a man. Similarly, capital punishment became far rarer in New England than in Old. There were dozens of other ways as well in which the individual realized his self-respect. Then too, if the newcomer did not feel satisfied with New England, for instance, he could always move farther west. He could go to the frontier, take up free land there, and grow with the country. He could grow as America was growing. Land would normally appreciate, trade would increase, and his own status improve. The rewards for energy were greater here than in any other country in the western world. America was a favored nation; no wonder its vigor was manifest.

This happy climate for American vitality continued until the twentieth century. America had its wars and its depressions but not until 1929 did individual enterprise suffer a severe blow. After that, however, the country had ten years in which to learn that progress was a myth, that business did not inevitably become bigger and better, that hard work would not always bring success. And the country did learn something. Then the Second World War taught a few new lessons; so did the stalemated Korean war; and so did Russian space science. Yet in spite of these checks, the American tradition of ambition and aggressiveness remains. There lies a great problem. Most Americans are still affected by the expectation, which is imbedded in the folk feeling, that progress is not only possible but proper and that they should compete against their fellows and surpass their elders. By now, in actuality, they cannot. The conditions of land and culture that favored their fathers and grandfathers have disappeared. In their place are different ones, often kindly enough but not what America has always expected. Out of this drive for a success which seldom can be achieved has grown a good deal of American pessimism, disillusion, and insecurity. As one American psychiatrist has said of many of his patients, they "are driven by a relentless competitiveness in any given field and are at the same time afraid and wearied by this strenuous life of race and struggle."

Here is one of the great contradictions in the American experience. Its results will often be found in American arts and letters. Side by side with vigor will be morbidity; action will be matched with frustration; death will deny life. This will surely be true at both the conscious and the unconscious levels of the American experience and will be similarly evidenced in both levels of the American imagination. It is to the most important manifestations of this imagination that we come now.

American architecture is a particularly good place to start. In his recent book *Architecture USA,* Ian McCallum maintains that three conditions for great architecture are to be found at their best in the United States. As he phrases it, these are "a prosperous and lively building industry, creative freedom, and a conspicuous expenditure"; but they are also, surely, forms of the American abundance, energy, and variety which we have spoken of. Suppose we look at just one type of building, the single-family dwelling. True, many an American suburb has its rows of brick or wooden boxes, all alike and all built by the same callous promoter. But there is likewise a multitude of houses in different styles. Half a dozen great architects, native or immigrant, have put the impress of their thought on the American home. Wright, Neutra, Paul Rudolph, and Gropius are outstanding. Their houses spread or soar, lie in long planes or stand high. The one characteristic they have in common is that they invite the outside in. The big picture window is so nearly universal that it is easy to deride. But its openness, its willingness to dispense with privacy, puts it at the opposite extreme from the English house with its walls within walls and its front door without a door knob.

Within as well the space is apt to be free-flowing. The living-room and dining-room may be the two legs of an L, instead of separate compartments. The interior walls may be lattices or fences and the space they enclose only partly private. In the bedrooms alone will the English home-owner find the seclusion he has always insisted on. Even when the English architect attempts to plan a "Modern" dwelling his client is apt to interfere, while the local council raises its clenched hand against novelty. One of the clearest illustrations of a difference in cultures is provided by the houses going up in America now as compared with those being erected in England. The same thing is true for business buildings. The variety and splendor of New York's latest skyscrapers amaze the visitor; they are in sharp contrast to the great brick squares being built in the West End of London and around St. Paul's.

The outburst of American abstract art is an almost equally clear result of the current cultural environment. Some of this art is so extreme, so experimental, as to be either lunatic or a stunt. But when the painters who paint with their elbows have been eliminated, there remain a number of American experimenters who have genuinely extended the range of paint on canvas. Jackson Pollock has been the most prominent. Easy to caricature as he dripped his house paint on long pieces of cloth, he still provokes the conservative critics either to outrage or amusement. A serious evaluation of his work, however, such as the noted Whitechapel show of 1958 allowed, is all in his favor. His light, elegant swirls of color, in their repeated designs, have warmth and dignity. They are not a representation nor do they have the expected centripetal pattern, but they are pleasing enough to justify a permanent place in the art collections and in the history of American art. At the moment his canvases are perhaps the most influential of any American's. His mark can be seen on paintings as different as those by Sam Francis and Bradley Tomlin.

In his own way I believe Clyfford Still is as indicative as

Pollock. He represents the frustrations of American life as well as the individualism which is pushed to such an extreme that the artist no longer cares to communicate. "Demands for communication," Still says, "are both presumptuous and irrelevant." Yet his canvases, with their huge, apparently random patches of color, have a good deal to tell. They are works of art in their own right. His *Number 2,* for instance, looks at first simply like splotches of maroon and black on a red background. Yet study will show a satisfying balance in the composition and in its strong colors. There is an American amplitude not merely in the size of the painting but also in the design. The frame does not contain the picture. The colors and pattern lead the eye up and down the wall, and across it on either side. The wall is itself engaged and dominated by the painting. Nearly all earlier painting has been centripetal in its pattern; *Number 2* is powerfully centrifugal (Pollock's paintings are neither). In its way it too is a sign of energy, abundance and creative originality.

Perhaps the most salient evidence of these qualities is that American painting changes while we describe it. The regime of abstract expressionism is being ended by a variety of forces. By Greenwich-Village constructions of scumbled paint and lath; by the romanticized expressionism now also popular in England and evidenced, though in different ways, by the painting of Eileen Agar and Ivor Hitchens; by the new American realism, especially as exemplified in Aaron Bohrod's intricate and silkily-painted "fool-the-eye" pictures. And there is obviously much more to come.

American music is neither as brilliant nor as original as American art. Except in its most famous form: jazz. Descended from the music brought by slaves from Africa, it still stands for the dark side of the American experience. It has known many changes and none more significant than those of this century. In two American cities, New Orleans first and then the Chicago of the 1930's, it found itself and became the music now played throughout much of the world. Its driving rhythms attest to American vitality; its free-wheeling instrumental solos to American individualism. But the key for jazz is minor rather than major. Its wailing strains, its feverishness, its cellar atmosphere are the heritage of denial. The Negro has long known the frustration which the white American today is feeling; jazz is perhaps its main artistic expression.

The merits of serious American music are, on the whole, of the same kind as those of American art but they are not so pronounced. The works of Aaron Copland and Charles Ives have a place in the music of the world though they are performed less often than we might wish. Among the younger composers Samuel Barber is probably the most popular; his "Medea's Meditation and Dance of Vengeance" was played in the season of 1956–57, for instance, by ten out of the thirty-one American symphony orchestras performing then. William Schuman, with his "New England Triptych," came second only to Barber in the same season. Leon Kirchner, for whom recognition has come more tardily than for Barber and Schuman, is now being acclaimed for his neo-classic orchestral and chamber music. These men are notable, serious composers. For sheer virtuosity and range, however, they are surpassed by Leonard Bernstein. He has written the music for films, ballets, musical comedies, and for an opera. He has two exceptional symphonies to his credit, "Jeremiah" and "The Age of Anxiety." The second offers an especially good illustration of his experimentalism, since it is written in a jazz idiom and uses the twelve-tone scale.

Some of the happiest of Bernstein's composing has been done for musical comedy. It is actually this form, with its marriage of melody, book, and movement, which represents the most widely admired American venture into the arts. Bernstein's music for *Candide* matches the moods of the action and indeed often sets them. His versatility is remarkable, though he has been criticized for parodying the music of others and so making *Candide,* in particular, the less original because of it. His too is the music for the remarkable *West Side Story*. Yet, good as that music is, it is overshadowed by the strikingly effective dancing, which constitutes in itself another success of the imagination.

Dance as dance and not merely a series of steps has come into its own on the American stage only in the past twenty-five years. The pioneer in developing it was Agnes de Mille. Her ballets for *Oklahoma!* set a style that is still not outdated and nearly every popular musical comedy now has its big ballet number. *West Side Story* is in a sense an extended ballet. Its New York gangs dance with a vigor and flexibility without the slightest need for prettiness.

The leading creators of musical comedy have been the composer Richard Rodgers and his distinguished librettist Oscar Hammerstein. Their successes started with *Oklahoma!* in 1943, included *South Pacific* and *The King and I,* and ended with *The Sound of Music* in 1959 only because of Hammerstein's untimely death. However, these men were merely the leaders in a brilliant company, others being responsible for *My Fair Lady, The Pajama Game, How to Succeed in Business without Really Trying,* and many more. That the stories on which the comedies are based come from without is often true but the synthesis is clearly original.

The dark side of the American experience reappears in American drama. The plays of the leading dramatist of today, Tennessee Williams, dwell on themes of frustration and despair. Their setting is nearly always the most troubled part of the United States, the South. The most notable of his plays are *The Glass Menagerie, A Streetcar Named Desire,* and *The Night of the Iguana*. Their techniques are remarkable for originality, for invention. Symbols appear often, and successful liberties are taken with the standard dramatic forms and staging. Williams does not go as far as Samuel Beckett or other writers of the anti-drama, but he continues the habit, started by Eugene O'Neill, of widening the ways to present a play. Edward Albee and Jack Gelber are the inheritors of this habit. The techniques of both young men are novel, the messages mordant. In range and effectiveness, however, they must yield to the brilliantly varied New Dramatists of England, including Arnold Wesker, N. F. Simpson, and Harold Pinter. The other outstanding American playwrights are two older men, Arthur Miller and William Inge. They prefer to stay in the tradition of the well-made play. Their originality lies in the development of facets of the American character.

Of all that the American imagination has created, American literature is perhaps the most impressive. Both poetry and prose are striking. If we compare the work of contemporary American poets with that of contemporary English poets, there is a contrast almost as strong as in architecture. With this difference, however: contemporary English architecture is weak; but contemporary English poetry is not weak, it is modest. The English poet of this decade writes in a moderate tone, restrains his feelings, and strives for an almost neo-classical effect. He moves his reader by deficiency rather than excess. Phillip Larkin is to me the best English poet now at work, and his verse is characterized by quiet self-depreciation and pensive clarity. He is effective enough to make many an American poet sound hoarse or shrill.

Notwithstanding, an American vitality is to be seen in the lines of a dozen of the best poets in the United States. In many cases the vitality is tense; often its expression is unclear. But the vigor is there. So is the experimentalism. New forms, new combinations of words and emotions frequently appear in the so-called "little magazines." The resources of the word are pushed as far as intention can push them. The imagery is often thick and clotted; sometimes after a few pages of it one wishes heartily for Larkin or Ted Hughes. The most respected American poets make their own sense, however, and time has already seen it appreciated. The early poems of Karl Shapiro and Robert Lowell, the recent ones of Theodore Roethke and Stanley Kunitz, have an organic form and inner logic. Sometimes they demand a fresh approach by the reader; though it may be given reluctantly, its results are often good.

I believe that the obscurity of much of American verse is significant. It stands not only for the fact that the words cannot bear all the meaning one would like to give them. It also represents the isolation of the individual, the man so far away from society that he no longer cares to talk with his fellows. This is the recoil against American openness and neighborliness. More than one American poet would agree with Clyfford Still that communication was not important. The result is a loss to both sides, and the blame for it must be shared by most Americans because of their indifference to poetry. The English poet is better off. One of the reasons, no doubt, that he speaks clearly is that he feels that readers are waiting to understand. Many an American poet feels that he is writing in a wilderness with himself as his only audience.

But all this has its exceptions. In fact they are increasing and it is possible that the exception will become the rule. More American poets are winning recognition without an appeal to obscurity. Richard Eberhart's Romantic lyrics are roughcast but clear; they are steadily being more esteemed. And the Pulitzer prize winner for poetry in 1960 was W. D. Snodgrass, whose finest poems are absolutely straightforward. The noblest exception to the rule of obscurity is the poetry of Robert Frost. Abounding energy, long-continued, characterizes his work but the energy is not feverish, it is almost classical in its control. The idiom is strictly his own. It is New England speech but raised beyond any geographical bounds. His view of life is Olympian in its wisdom and yet is marked both by sympathy and a sense of sin and evil. The sympathy is there often — in "The Death of the Hired

Man," for example — but sin appears seldom. Yet sin and evil have their place and are the stuff out of which such a baleful little poem as "Design" is made.

Frost has been the greatest American poet to appear in this century. The greatest novelist has been William Faulkner. The works of both men are bound to endure. They both explore the range of American character but their emphases are exactly opposite. For Faulkner, unlike Frost, stresses the morbid, the isolated, the lurid. Yet his work too has an American variety. The range of his novels is considerable. The summertime sadness and clarity of plot in *Sartoris* are far removed from the powerful, intricate fiction of *Absalom, Absalom!* The story of Bayard Sartoris is told in a straight line, while Quentin Compson's discovery of the meaning of the past in *Absalom* is effected through the interweaving of three different points of view and the frequent use of a complicated interior monologue. Tone and temper, too, vary in the novels of Faulkner; nevertheless, the stamp is always his own. His vitality is reflected not only in his quarter-century of sustained writing but in his creation of a whole county — much more than a microcosm — in Mississippi for his characters to live in. Yoknapatawpha County is William Faulkner's just as much as if he had homesteaded there and proved his claim.

Among the remaining novelists of importance, Hemingway is still first in the eyes of most critics. Since his death there have been rumors that his reputation will rise even further when the posthumous "big book" is finally printed, but the chances are that his earliest fiction will continue to be considered his best. After him come several others, all writing books with vitality to them. In most cases the vitality is accompanied by a somberness of subject, for the characteristic American fiction of today is dark. The frustration and insecurity mentioned before are stronger stuff for the novelist than the brighter side of life; and often his own rebellion is reflected in his books. The novelist who has gone farthest in repudiating the traditional, and now unrealistic,

American scale of values is Jack Kerouac. To him progress, hard work, and morality are in their various ways nonsense. He detests the top of American life and prefers to be at the bottom, looking up. His characters live a life of negation, and are positive about it. *On the Road* is his best novel still. It is the essence of this negativity which the twentieth century has developed. But the book also has as one of its major themes the restlessness Tocqueville remarked in Americans a century and a quarter ago. Kerouac's Dean Moriarty is always driving headlong from one side of the country to the other. His search for his "kicks" sends him on to the highways. He pushes his automobiles to a steady 110, never really sure of his destination.

The group of San Francisco writers, of whom Kerouac is by far the most absorbing, have attracted a good deal of attention. Some of it has been undeserved. However, they are entitled, at least, to recognition in any study of the American imagination today.

And that imagination has its deficiencies, without doubt. It is sometimes grotesque, often naïve. But it is never pale, never passive. It has the vigor, the variety, and the creativity to justify anyone's attention.

ACKNOWLEDGMENTS

I WANT to say a word or two about my text. When I have reconsidered a judgment or learned something new since writing these essays, I have usually altered the text. I have not indicated the alterations because I feel that it would be taking my work too seriously for me to chart—historically—the changes in my ideas or the additions to my information. I hope the reader will not be inconvenienced. When I have quoted from other writers, especially the nineteenth-century ones, I have generally modernized the text.

I am indebted to the *Massachusetts Review* and the Viking Press for permission to reprint "The Hidden Thoreau," in which I have written about Thoreau in the light of Freud's discoveries. The only place where these have been applied systematically is in an unpublished dissertation by Raymond Gozzi, "Tropes and Figures: a Psychological Study of David Henry Thoreau," 1957. From Mr. Gozzi's stimulating dissertation I have drawn for both chapter and verse. On the other hand, I do not wish to hide behind him from the criticism of devotees of Thoreau. A good deal of what Mr. Gozzi has to say I myself have long felt and have often discussed in my seminars.

I am indebted to the University of California Press for permission to reprint, in its original form "Foreign Ports and Exotic Places" from *The Anatomy of American Popular Culture*; to the *New England Quarterly* for permission to reprint my essay "Hawthorne's *Fanshawe:* the

Promising of Greatness"; to the *American Quarterly* for "Thoreau the Actor," "Lloyd Douglas: Loud Voice in the Wilderness," and "Columbia's Carnal Bed"; and to the *Walt Whitman Review* for "Whitman at Oxbridge." For permission to reprint my lecture "The Sound of American Literature a Century Ago" I am indebted to the British Academy. In preparing the lecture I drew on, in addition to my own previous studies, Robert E. Spiller's unpublished paper, "From Lecture into Essay: Emerson's Method of Composition," William Charvat's "A Chronological List of Emerson's American Lecture Engagements," *Bulletin of the New York Public Library,* Vol. LXIV (1960), Nos. 9–12, and Walter Harding's "A Check List of Thoreau's Lectures," *Bulletin of the New York Public Library,* Vol. LII (1948), No. 2. "The American Imagination" comes from the *Times Literary Supplement* number on *The American Imagination,* where it was the lead article under the title of "Taking Stock." I am indebted to *PMLA* for permission to use "Cappy Ricks and the Monk in the Garden"; to the Society for the History of the Germans in Maryland for the inclusion here of my obituary of H. L. Mencken in the *Twenty-Ninth Report;* to *College English* for "The Buxom Biographers" and "Erskine Caldwell: a Note for the Negative"; to *Religion in Life* for "Lloyd Douglas and America's Largest Parish"; to *Time & Tide* for "The Poems across the Way"; and to *John O'London's* for "The Changing Face of American Poetry," "The Mixed Romantics," and "The Hidden War in American Poetry" (now called "The New Battle of the Books"); and to *Wisconsin Studies in Contemporary Literature* for my reviews of *Franny and Zooey* and *Ship of Fools.* For permission to reprint "E. E. Cummings and Exploded Verse" from *The Great Experiment in American Literature* I am indebted to the firm of William Heinemann; to Harcourt, Brace and Company for permission to quote, in the Cummings article, from Cummings' play *Him* and to quote the poems, "the Cambridge ladies who live in furnished souls," " 'kitty'," and "my girl's tall with hard long eyes"; and to quote extensively from "Poem, or Beauty Hurts Mr. Vinal." For permission to reprint "Adversity's Favorite Son" I am indebted to the *Observer,* where it appeared as "Bloody but Unbowed."

"Jemima and the Pattern" and "Thoreau's Young Ideas" are new to print. In preparing them for publication and in revising the other pieces I drew as usual on the University of Maryland Library, where the director, Howard Rovelstad, and the loan librarian, Miss Betty Baehr, were especially helpful.